20
Great Ways
to Raise
Great Kids

Toni Schutta, Parent Coach, M.A., L.P.

Disclaimer
The ideas and suggestions in this book are based on personal and professional experiences of the author and interviewees. All examples and/or vignettes presented in the
book are for educational purposes.

The author recognizes that no two family or personal situations are exactly the same.
However well intended, no single recommendation or piece of advice can apply appropriately to every specific individual situation the reader may encounter. The author's
intent is to present a broad range of perspectives, recognizing that some might conflict
with others. It is her hope that the suggestions and recommendations will provide
alternatives for parents as they grapple with the many complex daily choices they
must make.

Similarly, suggestions presented in this book are not intended to be a substitute for
consultation, evaluation, or treatment with a qualified family or mental health professional of your choice. Each family's needs, risks, values, and goals are different, and
there is no substitute for personalized assessment, treatment, or advice.

Since this book is intended for general educational purposes only, and the use of the
information is entirely at the reader's discretion, the author and publisher shall not be
responsible for any adverse reactions ensuing directly or indirectly from the suggestions presented here, and they therefore specifically disclaim any liability purported to
arise from the use of this book.

Table of Contents

1. Solutions to the Top 10 Parenting Challenges from Toddler to Teen   23

2. What Values Are You Teaching Your Kids?   45

3. Unplug Your Kids from Electronic Devices   63

4. Are You Overindulging Your Child?   81

5. Raising a Generous Child in a "Me" Culture   99

6. Win the Chore Wars!   117

7. Kids and Sports: Healthy or Overkill?   135

8. Solutions to Five Scary Trends Parents Must Face   153

9. Help Your Child Develop a Mindset for Success   177

10. Better Sleep Equals Happier Kids   195

11. 18 Secrets for Cutting the Family Budget   215

12. Mealtime Dilemmas Solved   235

13. 10 Tips for "Going Greener" as a Family   255

14. Great Ways to Connect as a Couple   271

15. New Year's Resolutions to Make Your Family Stronger   291

16. Best Back-to-School Tips   309

17. Family Fun Nights: Have a Blast With Your Kids at Home   325

18. Stress-Free Holidays   337

19. Lose the Mommy Guilt for a Happier You   355

20. Are You Accidentally Raising a Wimp?   375

Dedication

This book is dedicated to my mom. I'm eternally grateful that you were chosen to be my mom. You epitomized all the best qualities of a mother. Your never-ending love and support fills my heart, even now, with all that I need to flourish in the world. You were a role model of perfect parenting. May God hold you in the palm of His hand.

Acknowledgments

First and foremost, I'd like to thank Mark Pace for his belief in me and my vision for the "Real Parents. Real Solutions." radio show. Mark, you're such a positive, enthusiastic, and kind person.

Thank you to all my wonderful guests for sharing priceless nuggets of parenting advice on the show and for agreeing to share those nuggets again with readers of this book. Thank you to General Mills for their initial support that helped launch the radio program.

Thanks to Annette for providing flawless transcription service. Cathy Reed, thank you for your patience and invaluable editing skills. Wendy Lewis, thank you for your never-ending support.

I want to thank Kevin, Taylor and Brianna for encouraging me do something that I love: helping parents create happy and peaceful families so children can experience extraordinary love that lasts a lifetime. You are my treasures.

And most of all, thank you to my parents who provided me with endless love and encouragement to follow my dreams. You are present in my heart always.

Introduction

One summer morning I was standing in my kitchen making a cup of chai tea latte when my cell phone rang. The caller introduced himself as Mark Pace, a producer from VoiceAmerica.com. Mark said that he and his staff had been researching parent coaches and that they were "impressed" with me. He then asked me if I'd be interested in hosting a parenting talk show.

I went weak in the knees, stared incredulously at the phone, and thought, "I must be dreaming!" For me, this was a perfect marriage of two of my passions. My first career was in journalism, and I had produced, and at one point hosted, a radio show. Psychology became my second love and I've been helping families to be happier for the last 19 years.

I gave Mark an enthusiastic "Yes!"

In the fall, "Real Parents. Real Solutions." was launched as an online radio show devoted to helping parents find solutions that work. I had the freedom to develop the show in whatever way I thought would work best, and I decided to invite experts that I most admired in the parenting field to be guests on my show. I also invited parents that I admired to share their wisdom. No one turned down my invitation.

As a parent, I learned so much. As a parent coach, I felt fulfilled, knowing that I was providing parents with practical solutions. As a journalist, I knew I wanted to share this valuable information with a broader audience.

My radio show aired for six wonderful months before the expenses grew too burdensome. As I resigned from the show, I knew I wanted to create a book containing these interviews.

I've selected 20 of the best interviews to share with you and help you raise a child who is loving, confident, secure, responsible, generous, and kind. Some of the topics also cover self-care for you. It's not a crime to think about taking care of your own needs; in fact, it's essential that you do. Nor is it selfish to take time with your spouse; it's critical to the survival of your marriage and the stability of your family to do so. To raise a child who isn't self-centered, you need to find a balance between your child's needs and your own.

I believe the wisdom collected in this book is invaluable. Experts like Carol Dweck, Ellyn Satter, Mary Sheedy Kurcinka, Elizabeth Crary, Jean Illsley Clarke, and Michele Borba have each spent decades dedicating themselves to research in their chosen fields. Here, in this book, they share their best parenting advice with you. Devoted parents like Janet Montgomery, Stephanie Severson, Jeanne Burlowski, and Beth Weiss also share practical tips that have been successful for them in raising great kids. Here in this one book, you'll be able to glean parenting wisdom from 37 individuals.

In my work, I'm known as The Parent Coach Who Gets Results. My mission always has been, and always will be, to help others have a happy, peaceful family where children feel extraordinary love and support that will last a lifetime.

In this book, my hope is that you'll find suggestions and solutions that will work for your family. I also invite you to visit my website *www.get-parentinghelpnow.com* and become part of my parenting community so we can share resources on an ongoing basis.

I am delighted to be donating all profits from this book to the Family Enhancement Center. This non-profit organization works to prevent child abuse and to help families that have been affected by abuse to begin to heal. I had the honor of working there as a psychologist, and I can tell you that their mission of educating and supporting parents *before* abuse happens is invaluable in assuring that children have a stable, loving family so they can flourish.

Chapter Summaries

1. Solutions to the Top 10 Parenting Challenges from Toddler to Teen

This chapter will provide you with answers to the Top 10 parenting challenges from one of the premier parenting experts, Michele Borba, author of *The Big Book of Parenting Solutions,* and NBC Today Show parenting contributor. You'll receive answers to parenting challenges such as: how to get your child to listen; firming up your discipline; reducing sibling rivalry; helping an angry child; reducing back talk and whining; making bedtime easier; getting homework and chores done; and reducing bullying and lying.

2. What Values Are You Teaching Your Kids?

We get so busy with the daily tasks of parenting that we may not take a step back and look at the big picture. What values do you want your children to have so they can be likeable, compassionate, productive adults? Are you making a concerted effort to teach and reinforce those values or just assuming that your children are receiving those messages from you? Richard and Linda Eyre have made it their mission to help parents teach values – through their best-selling book *Teaching Your Children Values,* instructional materials, media appearances and world-wide speaking engagements. As parents of nine children, the Eyres have taught these values to their own children, and their value-based instructional materials have been shared throughout the world.

In this chapter, Richard shares the 12 values they believe are critical to create a strong family and a child you'll be proud of, and he provides ideas for incorporating these values into your daily family life.

3. Unplug Your Kids from Electronic Devices

TV shows, video games, computer use, cell phones, texting ... kids are so plugged into electronic devices that it seems they barely have time for you anymore! Can the use of all these devices harm your kids, and if so, how? How can you rein in their usage and unplug the gadgets so you can connect in more meaningful ways with your kids? Mike Mann, an award-winning speaker who worked for the National Institute on Media and the Family shares his extensive knowledge to help you be "media wise."

4. Are You Overindulging Your Child?

There are lots of ways that parents are overindulging their kids these days ... buying them too much stuff, not disciplining their kids consistently, and over-nurturing them. Jean Illsley Clarke's research shows that this can damage your kids in ways that you never dreamed of. She'll share concrete steps you can take to turn these problems around so you can raise likeable, responsible, respectful children. Clarke and her co-authors wrote the book *How Much is Enough?* to provide parents with a road map for avoiding overindulgence – which can lead to adult children being depressed, obese and in debt. Clarke will share the highlights of their findings, help you figure out if you're overindulging your child, and provide strategies for parenting differently if you feel you are being overindulgent.

5. Raising a Generous Child in a "Me" Culture

If you'd like to fight the tidal wave of "me" messages your child receives and shift to "we" messages more often, read below as four experts and parents share ideas that can help change your child's attitude from, "What's in it for me?" to "How can I help?"

Corinne Gregory, creator of SocialSmarts, will talk about creating an "attitude of gratitude" that will open the door for increased generosity. Janet Montgomery, mother of four, will share real-life tips on how she incorporates giving in her children's daily lives. Michelle Hollomon, a certified professional coach, will share practical, everyday strategies that make it easy to model giving while teaching your kids the "why" of giving rather than just the "should" of giving. Alison Smith and Debbie Zinman, founders of ECHOage, will help you incorporate giving into your child's next birthday party. ECHOage teaches children about giving to those who are less fortunate and is a whole new way to celebrate a child's birthday.

6. Win the Chore Wars!

Whether your child does chores or not is one of the most important contributors to your child's success as a young adult. Elizabeth Crary, author of *Pick Up Your Socks,* shares tips on how to get your child to do chores, how to make it fun, age-appropriate chores, and whether or not you should pay your child for chores. Crary is the author of 32 parenting books and has more than 35 years' experience working with children. And parent Stephanie Severson provides a secret tip for encouraging her three kids to do chores.

7. Kids and Sports: Healthy or Overkill?

You already know the positive outcomes that kids can gain from playing sports, but sports participation may actually be harming kids more than you know. As a culture, have we crossed a line where fun, exercise and team spirit are no longer the goals, and where year-round sports and traveling teams are causing children physical injuries, burnout, and emotional harm?

Bob Bigelow, former NBA player and co-author of *Just Let the Kids Play: How to Stop Other Adults from Ruining Your Child's Fun and Success in Youth Sports*, shares the facts and also the solutions for making sports fun again for your kids while still enjoying the benefits that sports participation can bring.

8. Solutions to Five Scary Trends Parents Must Face

This chapter discusses five scary trends that you'll want to learn about so you can make sure your child is staying safe and growing strong. We're parenting differently than our parents, and while we may be spending more time with our kids, there are some mistakes we're inadvertently making that cause an alarming number of kids to experience stress, anxiety, depression and narcissistic tendencies. Read this chapter by parenting expert and educational psychologist Michele Borba so you know the red flags. Borba reveals the five trends we need to look at, the reasons why it's important to do so, and the concrete steps we can take if these trends are affecting our family.

9. Help Your Child Develop a Mindset for Success

You want your child to be successful, and you may be spending a lot of money and time on the right school and extracurricular activities in the hope that your child will be successful. But the answer ultimately lies within your child.

Helping your child develop the proper "mindset" is one of the most important things you can do to help your child achieve more success in the world, according to Carol Dweck, a researcher at Stanford, who for the last 40 years, has studied what helps children succeed or fail. In this chapter, she will share her findings and the steps you can take to help cultivate a "growth mindset" in your child. Dweck is author of the book *Mindset: The New Psychology of Success.*

Kristin Boileau, a mother of three and an elementary school counselor, also provides her insights. Kristin believes that your child's social and emotional development is critically important to your child's academic success and she will share tips on helping your child succeed in school.

10. Better Sleep Equals Happier Kids

Most kids (and adults) don't get enough sleep, which can leave them cranky, uncooperative and at a disadvantage in the classroom. Insufficient sleep affects behavior, and it could be that your acting-out child just needs a few more zzzs. If you'd like to reduce bedtime hassles, get your child to sleep longer, and improve your child's mood and performance, don't miss this chapter.

Mary Sheedy Kurcinka, author of *Sleepless in America: Is Your Child Misbehaving ... or Missing Sleep?* (and author of *Raising Your Spirited Child*), offers sage advice on how to work with the three factors of time, tension and temperament to ensure your child (and you!) get a good night's sleep. Following Kurcinka's strategies may help you reduce temper tantrums, morning wars, and homework hassles, and also help you raise a happier child.

11. 18 Secrets for Cutting the Family Budget

Liss Burnell, founder of *www.budget101.com*, the premier website for helping families save money, shares 18 secrets for helping you cut expenses – including your grocery bills, entertainment budget, and home décor and other household spending. With her creative, easy-to-implement tips, you can save money on food, craft items, holiday gifts, cleaning products and more.

12. Mealtime Dilemmas Solved

Many families struggle to make meals enjoyable and to raise a healthy eater. When your child is a picky eater, has food jags, is rude, doesn't eat at all, or eats all the wrong foods, it's stressful. Ellyn Satter, who is *the* leading authority on nutrition and the feeding of infants and children of all ages, will share her 40 years of wisdom working with families. Practical, warm and empowering, Satter will provide advice regarding what your job is when feeding your family and what a child's job is, give tips on how to break out of the short-order cook business, and teach you how to relax around food and create family-friendly meals that will satisfy all of you.

13. 10 Tips for "Going Greener" as a Family

Going green is not only good for the earth; it's good for your health. Certain products contain toxins that are dangerous to you and your kids. Learn the body care ingredients you'll want to avoid, which fruits and veggies you'll want to buy organic, which plastics are contaminating your kids, how to clean your house safely, and other great tips that will help your family stay healthy. Micaela Preston, author of *Practically Green: Your Guide to Ecofriendly Decision-Making*, shares tips from her book.

14. Great Ways to Connect as a Couple

Do you still have dates with your spouse or partner? Do you have meaningful conversations that remind you why you once fell in love? If you're like most parents, you're focusing loads of time and effort on your kids and on work, and your conversations probably revolve around schedules and the to-do list rather than anything that will bring you closer.

If you'd like some creative ways to reconnect with your lover, this chapter is for you. Author Kevin Anderson, who wrote *The 7 Spiritual Practices of Marriage* and has conducted "date nights" in Ohio for hundreds of couples, provides insights on communicating at a deeper level. Dan Devey, owner of *www.coolestdates.com*, spices up the chapter with romantic date ideas sure to light the love flames. And parent Ann Searles shares ways that she and her husband have stayed connected in nearly 20 years of marriage.

15. New Year's Resolutions to Make Your Family Stronger

Many people make New Year's resolutions to exercise and lose weight, but few parents make resolutions to improve the most important relationship of all – family. It's time to take stock and see if you're spending as much time with your children as you think. In today's busy world it's easy to let family time, family meals, couple time and special time with your child fall off the radar screen. Yet, time spent with family is the number one protective factor in keeping your child happy and out of trouble.

Barbara Carlson, co-founder of the "Putting Family First – Making Time for Family" initiatives, and Anne Naumann, a mother of two and a teacher, share strategies for making your family stronger throughout the year. Barbara will also share tips from her book *Putting Family First: Successful Strategies for Reclaiming Family Life in a Hurry-Up World*.

16. Best Back-to-School Tips

As a parent, you want your child to be successful in school, and with a little planning on your part, your child can have the best school year yet. Lynda Enright, a registered dietician, provides tips on how to pack the most nutrients into breakfast, lunch and snacks to give your child the necessary energy to concentrate in school. Audrey Thomas, a certified professional organizer, provides tips on how to organize for success, including building rapport with teachers to help your child in the classroom.

17. Family Fun Nights: Have a Blast with Your Kids at Home

Looking for some fun low-cost activities to beat the winter doldrums? Debra Immergut, senior editor at FamilyFun magazine, will share easy ideas for beating boredom when the winter weather keeps your family indoors. Turn off the video games and cartoon channels — instead, try some kitchen science projects, play a get-active game, or make a stop-motion movie. Immergut makes it simple to have some good, inexpensive family fun.

18. Stress-Free Holidays

Holidays are supposed to be fun, right? Then why do we get so stressed out? And what can we do about it? Three professionals will help you lower your stress so you can enjoy the holidays more. Stress management expert Elizabeth Scott, life coach Beth Tabak, and professional organizer Kathy Franzen will help you simplify, sort through your priorities, and reexamine your expectations; give you suggestions for dealing with "the relatives;" and provide organizational tools to help you prepare for Thanksgiving and the December holidays.

19. Lose the Mommy Guilt for a Happier You

If you're like most moms, you feel guilty every day. You feel guilty because you don't spend enough time with your kids, or because you yell, or because your house is messy, or because you don't spend enough time with your spouse, or because you work outside the home. You name it and you feel guilty about it!

But help is at hand. You can lose the mommy guilt and find ways to be happier and have more fun with your kids by using strategies that Aviva Pflock and Devra Renner share in their book *Mommy Guilt: Learn to Worry Less, Focus on What Matters Most, and Raise Happier Kids.* You can learn the seven principles of the Mommy Guilt-free Philosophy and practical tips that will help you keep your guilt in check at every stage of your child's development.

20. Are You Accidentally Raising a Wimp?

You want the best for your children. You find good schools, sign your kids up for the right classes, keep them safe, and manage a hundred details to make sure that they're successful. Yet, how is it that parents who mean only the best for their kids wind up bringing out the worst in them?

The problem, according to Hara Estroff Marano, author of *A Nation of Wimps,* is that you may be doing too much for your children, which makes them more fragile. In your effort to be a "good" parent, you may be stressing achievement at the cost of independence – and also short-circuiting essential brain development. This chapter will help you figure out if you're a nurturing or controlling parent, whether perfectionism is harming your children, and whether your safety concerns are justified or inhibiting your children's development. Find out if you're over-parenting and setting your children up for failure, and discover how a new definition of success can help all your family be happier.

Solutions to the Top 10 Parenting Challenges from Toddler to Teen

Meet the Expert:

Michele Borba, Ed.D., is an educational psychologist, former teacher, and mom. She is recognized for offering research-driven advice culled from a career of working with over one million parents, educators and children. A frequent Today show contributor and recipient of the National Educator Award, Michele is the author of 22 books, including her latest book *The Big Book of Parenting Solutions: 101 Answers to Your Everyday Challenges and Wildest Worries*. Other books include: *Building Moral Intelligence* and *No More Misbehavin'*. Michele is an advisory board member for Parents magazine. She also appears on Dr. Phil, The View, CNN, American Morning, and The Early Show and has been featured in numerous publications including Family Circle, Parenting, and Child.

******

Toni: One of the biggest mistakes that parents make is not being consistent with discipline: being a discipline wimp, being too strict, or vacillating between the two on a given day.

There are many ways to be inconsistent. One day Johnny gets a timeout for slugging his brother and the next day a parent lets it slide. Or parents in the home disagree on discipline and apply it differently. Or divorced parents may have different rules.

You list seven mistakes that parents commonly make regarding discipline and you have suggested solutions. So, let's dive in.

Michele: First of all, we are all guilty of some of these discipline mistakes, so don't feel bad about it. The key in life is to tune up what you think will help you be a better parent. Use these seven tips on discipline so you don't send your child a mixed message and you can get the results you want.

The number one mistake is when parents think that hitting, kicking, biting or fighting is a phase that will go away by itself. Bad behaviors usually need an intervention and the intervention is called, "you mom or you dad." The longer you wait, the harder it is to turn the behavior around because those bad behaviors become habits.

The second mistake is being a poor model ourselves. Kids come with video camera recorders inside their head. They're watching you at every moment. You don't think you're influential until a relative arrives and you see your behavior coming out of one of your kids. So, tune up your own behavior, particularly with regard to any problems your kid might be having.

For instance, maybe it's lack of control. Watch yourself on how you handle the bank calling you and telling you that you're overdrawn. Are you cool and collected? Kids need good models to copy, and that means you.

The third mistake is not targeting a bad behavior. What does that mean? For instance, you may say he's "misbehaving," but what's he doing wrong? Is he talking back? Is he whining? If you're saying he's "disorganized," how is he disorganized? The more specific you can be, the more successful you'll be at turning the behavior around.

The fourth mistake is: don't target so darn many behaviors. I always tell parents, "Don't get overwhelmed; target no more than two behaviors, even if your kid is doing 50,000 things that drive you crazy."

The fifth mistake is not having a plan to stop it. You can say, "I want him to stop doing that," or "He's got to start behaving," but what do you want him to do instead? Have a substitute behavior ready.

The sixth mistake is: don't feel like you have to do this alone. Your child may see a daycare worker or a babysitter during the week. Pass on your new behavior plan to at least one other caregiver and say, "Here's what we're working on. Anytime he does this behavior, here's what I want you to do…"

What happens is your child begins to realize that everybody's on the same page and you're serious about turning this behavior around.

Toni: One of the things that I advise parents to do is to make family rules and consequences.

I worked for 10 years as a psychologist, and when I'd ask kids, "What are some of your family's rules?" 99 percent of the kids were stumped. The kids weren't able to articulate behaviors that were expected of them.

To develop family rules, parents need to sit down and ask themselves, "What rules are important so that everyone in our family feels safe, secure and loved while they're in our home?" Put together a draft of those rules and then ask the kids the same question. Also ask them what consequences should occur when someone breaks the rules.

And guess what? If your kids go to daycare or go to school, they have rules there too, about how to treat other people. If you can mimic the rules and consequences that are already being used at daycare or school, it's a win-win for everyone.

If you have little tykes, you just develop two or three rules. You probably want to have a rule that says, "Do something the first time that Mom and Dad ask you." Other rules would be to only use kind words or no hitting. Parents find this exercise so helpful.

Michele: Exactly. You made some points that are so on the mark. One of them is that kids learn from repetition.

Parents often say, "But, I gave him that great lecture last night. Why isn't he doing what I told him to do?"

The more he does the wrong thing, the more you remind him; so pretty soon the rule becomes internalized – your goal as a parent is to help your kid act right *without* you. That takes a lot of time and energy; but the more you repeat the rule, the sooner he'll remember it and he won't need any more reminders.

A simple way to figure out if your child has those rules down is to ask your child today, "What are the rules in our house?" If your child can't instantly tell you, it means you haven't reminded him enough.

Of course, the rules are going to be different for three-year-olds as opposed to 16-year-olds, but change them as your child needs them.

Toni: I love your suggestion of hyper-focusing on one rule for a while. Frankly, that can build your confidence as a parent. Parents won't feel overwhelmed; they can feel some success and then move on to the next rule. And your child will start to feel success too.

Sometimes I hear deplorable comments like, "I'm a bad parent." There are only a few bad parents; most parents do pretty well on a given day.

When parents keep flip-flopping on the rules, though, it's hard for kids to be successful. Honestly, we're damaging their self-esteem, although we don't mean to. But if the rules are clear and we're following through, kids are going to feel more successful, and we're going to be less frustrated and yelling less.

Michele: Oh, you're so right.

The seventh mistake is forgetting to make sure your child knows that your family rules may be different than another family's rules.

So, when your child goes to somebody else's house, she can ask, "What are the rules in your house?"

When my son had his fourth birthday party, his friend came running into the house screaming, "Where's the mommy? I've got to find the mommy." I thought somebody had died outside.

I said, "I'm the mommy. What do you need?" He said, "My mom said I've got to know your rules. What are your rules because I don't want to get in trouble?" How precious that the mother had reminded him to find out the mommy's rules.

Toni: I love it. For parents who would like to improve their discipline, I have a "Get Your Child to Listen the First Time" parenting program that parents can learn more about here: *www.getparentinghelpnow.com/pro-grams*. And, of course, Michele has her big book on parenting solutions.

Let's shift to back talk and whining. What can a parent do about that?

Michele: When it comes to back talk, first realize that your child is probably going to try it. Every kid does. They are influenced by very raunchy, racy media. Older kids also use it because that's what gets the laugh.

So first, go back to "Rules 101." In this house we are respectful; we only talk with kind words or respectful words. Make sure *you* are respectful to your child, and then step two is quietly and calmly reminding your child if he talks back: "That isn't the way we talk in this house."

If you have a three-year-old, use the "freeze on the floor" rule, which means you say, "That isn't the way we talk. Your feet don't move until you can replay it back the nice way." Repeat the nice way so they understand that the other way is not going to be tolerated.

As your kid gets older, expect the rolling eyes once in a while, but the most important thing is not to engage with a child who's disrespectful to you. You deserve respect and that's the hallmark for harmony in your home.

If you call them on it every time, you can have a respectful child; but make sure you squelch that whine or back talk at the beginning.

Toni: I love labeling it. I'll say, "That's back talk and it's disrespectful. I'll give you one chance to turn it around."

Michele: I like the repeat rule; you don't really need to say anything. You can just put your finger up and they'll know that they blew it.

Have the child do it again the right way, because the whine, if you're not careful, goes to back talk; the back talk goes to disrespect; and the disrespect goes to defiance.

No child started out being defiant. They started when the parent didn't catch each step along the way. Or they may pick it up somewhere else. Make sure the child knows, particularly at age three and four, what a "nice voice" sounds like.

So just rewind it, play it back, and demand respect if you hear whining or back talk.

Toni: The next topic is the number one parenting complaint: "How do I get my child to listen the first time? I'm sick and tired of repeating myself." What solutions do you have, Michele?

Michele: When I surveyed parents, this was the number one problem at every age. The first step to getting your kids to listen is to model good listening yourself.

Tell your child to always look at the color of the talker's eyes. It immediately makes your child look up and look at you, which is always the best way to give a direction to a child. Also, if a child does this, she'll look more confident and assertive.

So, before you speak, get them to look at you. Some kids need a transition, so give them a reminder, "Mom has something important to say to you in 10 seconds."

The second step is: once you get your child's attention, limit your words. Use the 10-second rule. If you can't say it in less than 10 seconds, you're saying too much.

Once you give directions that are short and simple, ask your child to rewind them or repeat them back.

For some kids, it's tough for them to retain information; but if you use this simple rule, you're going to really help that kid in the classroom, because most content is taught through lecture.

Another quick little rule: some children, particularly those with attention deficit, have a tough time retaining too much information. So, do quick tests to find out how many bits of information your child can retain at one time. Is it one statement or more?

A final rule that's really effective is: lower your voice, don't raise it. If we give a direction in a whisper, kids are startled and they pay attention, because they're not used to us using a calmer, quieter voice.

Toni: I had a mom in a parenting class I taught who increased her compliance by 80 percent with her defiant three-year-old. The mom went in the same room as the child, put her hand on the girl's shoulder, looked her in the eyes and spoke in a quiet voice.

Often, parents yell from another room or another level of the house, and this is typically ineffective.

Let's talk about bedtime hassles now. I worked with a mom whose husband was serving in Iraq, which was very stressful for all of them. She had three kids and she worked too. And it took her two hours each night to get the kids to bed!

This poor woman had no time on her own, and no time to complete all the single parent chores she was doing by herself because her husband was serving in the military. She called me in tears and said, "You've got to help me."

Of course I did, and we reduced the bedtime routine to 30 minutes. She gained back 90 minutes a night to herself! But it's not uncommon for bedtime to drag out. So what tips can you provide for shortening bedtime?

Michele: The research says: If you want to cut down bedtime hassles and get your child to sleep, get into an everyday routine and stick to it.

Kids need about 20 to 30 minutes to wind down, depending on the child.

I would strongly suggest turning off the TV, the computer and the video games at least half an hour before bedtime. All the research says those flickering lights are actually ruining your kids' REM sleep, making it tougher for your child to calm down and get a restful night's sleep.

Then develop a ritual of routine. First teeth, then pajamas, then we read a story. For little ones, you can make a chart with pictures, using a digital camera. It will help your child be more organized.

The final thing is the bedtime story, which is absolutely golden. It gets your child into the simple ritual of calming himself down, which is exactly what your child needs so he gets a more restful night's sleep.

For the tween or teen, take the cell phone away from your child at bedtime. The majority of research is saying that those kids are actually sleep deprived. They keep using their cell phone and have text messages coming in when you think they're asleep.

Toni: Exactly. In her book, *Sleepless in America*, Mary Sheedy Kurcinka estimates that a high percentage of misbehavior comes from kids of all ages not getting enough sleep. (For those who want more information on improving sleep, reference Chapter 10 in this book: "Better Sleep Equals Happier Kids.")

Anger is another issue that all parents have to contend with. Your child may say, "I hate you" or have a complete meltdown. What are some tips to get parents started with anger management?

Michele: I think the number one thing is to be calm yourself so your child can mirror you.

If you have an angry child or a child engaged in power struggles, and you go up a notch, your child will feed off that. So anytime you see your child's anger escalating, the first step is to calm down and take a deep breath yourself so your child can mirror you.

Number two is to watch your child very carefully and get to know your child's anger signs. You'll begin to see that before your child has a verbal meltdown, he almost always does the same thing physiologically. Some kids will hold their hands in fists. Some kids will move their feet back and forth; other kids will start twirling their hair or mumbling under their breath.

They'll do the same thing every time. Stress comes before anger or fear. Anger is the next level up, so you need to figure out the signs so you can respond immediately before it escalates. If you want proof, go home and ask your kid what your anger signs are, and they'll tell you. "Right before you get mad, Mommy, you always do that weird thing with your eyes."

Number three is to respond and tell them what to do instead. When you see little kids starting to escalate, you can distract them, maybe by giving them a back rub, or do emotion coaching by saying, "Looks like you're starting to get angry."

For a two-year-old you can say, "You seem to be really mad. Are you feeling really mad?" Exaggerate it and say it immediately. When you use emotion coaching, it actually helps kids, because they don't have the words to be able to express how they feel.

Get the kid to acknowledge that anger is normal. I get angry, you get angry, the Queen of England gets angry; but it's how you choose to show your anger that will get you in trouble or keep you out of trouble.

For an older child, write the word anger, A-N-G-E-R, on a piece of paper and say, "Look at it. And now I'm going to put the letter 'D' in front of it. 'Anger' is one letter short of the word 'danger.' Watch how you choose to show your anger."

The final step to anger is to teach kids a new habit. How do you get rid of the anger or show it more appropriately? I teach "one plus three plus 10."

"One" is to inhale when you start to feel yourself getting angry. Tell yourself inside your head to "chill out" or "slow down."

"Three" is to take three slow deep breaths. Getting oxygen into your brain is the fastest way to chill.

"10" is to count slowly to 10.

It may take you six months, or it may take you three years, to teach the whole formula to anger control, but if you keep modeling it over and over again, your child will have a new habit that will last a lifetime.

Toni: It's so critical to teach anger management to your kids and to model it yourself. I have a parenting program called "8 Weeks to a Happy, Peaceful Family: Dramatically Reduce Yelling, Arguing, and Fighting in Your Family" to help parents make positive changes that will benefit their family. It's on my website at: *www.getparentinghelpnow.com/programs.*

When teaching a child about anger management, I like to sit down during a calm time (not in the heat of the moment!) and ask the child, "What do you think might help you calm down when you start to get mad?"

Is it blowing bubbles? Squishing clay? Coloring?

Then I ask the child to pick a word that might help him or her to calm down. Lots of kids pick "chill."

Deep breathing is also essential to the process.

So when your child starts to get angry, you're going to have to be the coach and remind them to take deep breaths, say "chill," and go squish some clay. They will never remember it on their own unless you coach them through it hundreds of times. I really don't think I'm exaggerating on the number of times.

Michele: No. You're not exaggerating, and I think it's a big mistake if we think, "Okay, I taught him once."

The other thing is to make an "anger box" in your home. It's nothing more than a shoe box, but your child can help put things in the box that will help him, right in the moment, to calm down. It could be a koosh ball, clay, or photographs of a place where he feels calm or peaceful, like a tree fort or grandma's house.

For older kids, it's an iPod filled with music, or a movie that's calming and soothing. You can always suggest, "It looks like you need to chill; let's go to the anger box." Be pro-active and do it together.

I love bubble blowers or picture books for little kids. Put those together in a box and it becomes a habit that your child can repeat over and over again to find a healthy way to deal with anger.

Toni: Exactly. I like to help the child find a "comfy corner" to chill out too. Is it a bean bag chair in the den, or a sofa to go lie on? Then you can keep the "calm down box" there.

You have to teach your kids healthy anger management. It's so valuable. Most people probably get angry every day, so your child will be way ahead of others if she can express anger without hurting anyone physically or emotionally.

Now let's talk about bullying. I read that 50 percent of kids experience anxiety and sadness as a result of being bullied. It's a huge issue in our schools and neighborhoods.

Michele: I could spend my entire life on this one. I actually wrote a bill that strives to help prevent school violence and shooting. We discovered that violence was correlated to bullying at a very early age.

I spoke with some of the top researchers in the world on the subject of bullying, and they said they can look at a video and within 30 seconds spot the kid most likely to be victimized on the school playground.

Parents, the first thing is: from a very early age on up, help your children learn how to defend themselves. Stop rescuing them.

I teach the "c-a-l-m" method.

"C" means anytime you are bullied or teased, stay as *cool* as you possibly can because the bully is looking for a reaction.

You're going to have to help your child learn how to not look upset or cry or whine or pout, because it's scary stuff. Remember, the first steps to bullying are usually verbal. If you don't stop it at the verbal level, it escalates to a more severe level.

"A" is learn to "assert" yourself. I want you to teach your child comeback lines to bullying. You figure out the kind of bullying your child has experienced or the kind of comments that other kids are making to your child and you rehearse funny comeback lines. Kids in fifth grade told me the best comeback lines use humor.

A bully might say, "You know you're so stupid." Your child could say, "Well, thanks for noticing." or "It's been a problem my whole life."

This may sound ridiculous, but I've done this with hundreds of kids and the quick retort works. You've got to practice it, though.

"L" is to look the kid in the eye when you do the retort. Teach your child at a very early age to always look at the color of the talker's eyes. If you look down, it takes away your power. You've got to use strong body language.

"M" is to make your voice sound like you mean it. Be firm: "Listen to me. Cut it out."

What will work with the bully? Practice "c-a-l-m" to start with, and you'll find dozens of other responses in *The Big Book of Parenting Solutions*.

Toni: Great answer. Thank you, Michele. You summarized that so well.

Next we'll talk about sibling rivalry. It's as old as time itself, so what can we do?

Michele: First of all, it's normal. You think they're going to love each other. Well, they're human beings. They're not always going to love each other; they're going to have problems getting along. Your goal is to help them respect each other. Respect is the whole goal.

Another tip is to teach your kids conflict management strategies. I combed thousands of pieces of research for *The Big Book of Parenting Solutions* and the one thing that kept popping out regarding sibling rivalry is that families who have less rivalry and lower levels of friction use conflict resolution strategies.

Don't expect your children to be able to solve the problem. Sit them on the couch and teach them how to work it through together.

Use an oven timer, one of the greatest sanity savers you can own as a parent. Set it so each child gets three minutes to talk. Or use a sand dial.

Teach grandma's rule: one child cuts the cake and the other kid gets the first piece.

The final thing is: as a parent, don't step in too often to solve the kids' problem unless you actually have evidence of what the problem was. It can really create rivalry.

Toni: I agree 100 percent. Also check out a fun book called *Mom, Jason's Breathing on Me!* by Anthony Wolf.

Michele: I love that book.

Toni: Wolf advises parents to say, "The two of you stop it now" in response to sibling arguing. Parents will always say to me, "I don't know who started it." And I say, "Honestly, I don't care who started it and you shouldn't either." The proper way to proceed is, "How do we solve this?"

Michele: Exactly. All the research says "solve it" but don't assume your *kids* know how to solve it.

Toni: Yes. So teach them problem solving tips. Here's a link to a problem solving method that families can use: *www.getparentinghelpnow.com/myfreebookresources.*

Now let's shift to peer pressure. At what age do you think peer pressure starts?

Michele: Unfortunately, eight is the new 13. Everything is starting at younger and younger ages. Particularly kids who are shyer, more timid, or more sensitive are getting pushed too fast to kowtow to what another child is saying.

Boys and Girls Club of America did a survey with over 46,000 kids, asking them what their hottest problems were. They said peer pressure is by far one of the biggest problems. They also said that parents' advice to "just say no" doesn't work.

You need to tell the child what to say and then rehearse it, so it comes back to your child in the heat of the moment.

Shoplifting is huge in fifth grade, by the way. So, one of the things that we do is rehearse a comeback line and then use the rewind method.

Tell your child to tell the friend "no" and give a reason, and tell them to not just say it once; they should say it over and then even a third time, because research tells us the more you say the reason, the more it makes you sound confident.

Teach your child strong body language – how to look the kid in the eye and use a strong, firm voice.

And "c-a-l-m" is going to work again for peer pressure: C: stay cool; A: assert yourself; L: look them in the eye; and M: sound like you mean it.

Finally, if you're the parent of a teen, please do the following: Develop a secret code between you and your child. It could be a 111 text message. Your child doesn't have to say anything; it just means he's in a severe situation where he's tried to say no, but he can't get himself out of it – for instance, an unsupervised party. Drop everything, pick up your keys and go pick up your child. Because in some cases your child may be in over his head, and in today's world having a back-up plan is going to help your child be able to counter life.

Toni: Excellent ideas, Michele.

What about homework? Even first graders and kindergartners are getting homework. Many parents and kids are feeling a lot of stress around homework.

Michele: It's sad, isn't it? First of all, the studies say homework should be 10 minutes per grade level and advancing. So, at kindergarten it's 10 minutes, at first grade it's 20 minutes. It just keeps advancing.

Scores of research clearly points out that homework below the sixth grade level really does not increase academic achievement for your child. However, homework *does* enhance responsibility and study skills.

So, first of all, wean yourself off the responsibility of being the doer. You are the guider only; that's your rule.

Number two, make sure your child is organized, and that means helping him help himself. Have your child get together all the things he needs in a homework box so he doesn't have an excuse: "I can't find my pen. I can't find the dictionary."

The third thing is to always do the most difficult thing or the most anxious thing first. Why? Because it gets it out of the way and your child will be able to focus and concentrate on the other stuff.

Do it in chunks. Do a little bit at a time, especially for a child that has a short attention span.

Your goal is to get away from always sitting next to your child. So, start weaning yourself. Do the first problem together to make sure that he can do it by himself; then check when he gets to the end.

For some children who get overwhelmed, fold the paper in half and do just one side at a time. Encourage the child and then have him do the next side.

The best piece of research that's come out in the last 10 years is: if you want to increase your child's persistence, don't praise your child by saying, "You're so smart." Columbia University says it actually derails your child and lowers motivation. Instead, praise your child for working so hard; say, "I like how you're hanging in there. Great effort."

What you actually do is stretch your child's persistence, regardless of IQ. In the end, persistence is the most successful criterion in a classroom.

Toni: Absolutely. Carol Dweck, the author of that research study, is featured in the chapter of my book that's titled, "Help Your Child Develop a Mindset for Success."

I'll just add that it also helps to create a ritual for homework. On Monday, your child starts homework at 4:00. Tuesday, she starts after soccer practice, etc. Developing homework rituals will create a habit and you'll have less resistance.

Now let's talk about telling lies. Every child will do this – so parents, don't be alarmed. Michele, how should a parent handle fibs?

Michele: The research tells us that our kids learn to lie and fib from *us*. Kids start telling lies around age two and three.

Why do they fib or lie? The first reason is: they don't want to disappoint us. So, be very careful, because it will become a habit.

What you don't want to do is call your child a liar. Focus on the reason behind the lie and focus on what you saw or heard. Stick to the facts.

You want to demand the truth but not be too strict. You want the child to feel safe coming to talk to you so he can admit what he did wrong, and together you can make it right. It's a fine line.

Toni: I wrote a newsletter article about lying. I learned that the average adult tells four lies a day, or over 1400 lies a year. So I totally agree with you that we have to change our ways and start being more honest. Here's a link to the article on how to handle lies: *www.getparentinghelpnow.com/myfreebookresources.*

Michele: Let's look at an everyday situation. You tell your girlfriend, "Your hair looks beautiful," and 10 seconds later you turn to your child and say, "Oh my God, where did she get that haircut?" There's a fine line between tact and a fib.

Your child really needs to understand the difference because honesty is so important.

By the way, research also says that reading character-building stories such as George Washington's confession of chopping down the cherry tree actually does help your child learn honesty. Get out those books and start reading to help instill honesty as a virtue in your child.

Toni: Next, let's talk about chores. The research tells us that we need to have our kids do chores. Yet, so many parents are not doing it. How can parents get started?

Michele: I'm just going to applaud you, because every bit of research says that chores are critical. They will boost your child's responsibility and teach him everyday skills so he can leave home prepared. That's what parenting is all about.

So first ask your child what chores he would like to do. Or pick chores that are age-appropriate.

Number two: have family meetings once a week where you sit down and review what the chores are. Put the chores down on a chart. Charts really do help kids. I had three boys and we rotated chores each week. We created a list that looked like a pie chart with easy and harder chores. Each child had one each day, and then at the end of each week they rotated so nobody got stuck with the same thing.

And don't assume that your child knows how to do the chore; show your child what you expect by having him watch you do it. Then guide him by doing it together. "Okay, I showed you how; now let's do it together – you show me that you can do it."

Number three: step back, watch, and make sure your child can do the chore all by himself. Once you're sure, never redo it. Know that your child can do it.

Toni: On my website, I also have a free listing of age-appropriate chores that parents can use: *www.getparentinghelpnow.com/myfreebookresources*.

Even kids two or three years old can help by washing lettuce with you, ripping the lettuce, picking up toys, or putting napkins on the table.

Not to be depressing, but Elizabeth Crary says that, due to cognitive development, most kids will still need reminders to do chores until age 11. So you need to remind kids for a long, long time. This is where chore charts can really help because everything is written down and you can just point to the chart. (For more information, see Chapter 6, "Win the Chore Wars.")

Our last topic is shy kids and what a parent should do…

Michele: One out of five children is shy. So, let's look at some quick pointers, and there are dozens more ideas in *The Big Book of Parenting Solutions.*

Number one: Don't ever label your child as "shy." Your child is born with a biological temperament and is probably destined to be shy, but studies at Stanford say that if you label the child, it's more likely to become a problem.

Number two: Studies from Yale tell parents not to rescue their child or do too much for him. The study looked at moms with shy kids and then checked in 20 years later. The study says your parenting response at early ages is critical in developing the child's confidence. If the parents encouraged their kids to try and didn't push, those kids were far more likely to become comfortable later.

Number three: Give your child warm-up time. Shyer kids are watchers. So let them watch a little more from the sideline. If you do encourage them to participate, have them approach one child, not a whole group of kids. Even though their heart will still beat faster, they will be less threatened.

Finally, always rehearse with them the first thing to do when they get to the new situation. "When you get to the party, the first thing you can do is give the mommy or the birthday boy the present."

Knowing the first thing to do actually reduces the child's level of anxiety because the first thing is always the hardest thing.

Toni: Michele, you're fabulous.

Contact Information:

Michele Borba

Website: *www.micheleborba.com*. To find out more about Dr. Borba and her speaking topics and media appearances, read her blog on late-breaking parenting news and contact her for an appearance.

Resources:

Michele has written 22 books. Here are her latest parenting books, all published by Jossey-Bass.

The Big Book of Parenting Solutions: 101 Answers to Your Everyday Challenges and Wildest Worries

Nobody Likes Me, Everybody Hates Me!: The Top 25 Friendship Problems and How to Solve Them

No More Misbehavin': 38 Difficult Behaviors and How to Stop Them

Don't Give Me That Attitude: 24 Rude, Selfish, Insensitive Things Kids Do and How to Stop Them

12 Simple Secrets Real Moms Know: Getting Back to Basics and Raising Happy Kids

Building Moral Intelligence: The Seven Essential Virtues That Teach Kids to Do the Right Thing

What Values Are You Teaching Your Kids?

Meet the Expert:

Richard Eyre: As writers, lecturers, and grassroots and media catalysts, Linda and Richard Eyre are among the most popular speakers in the world on family and parenting. Their mission statement is: Fortify families by popularizing parenting, validating values, and bolstering balance. One of the Eyres' bestselling co-authored books, *Teaching Your Children Values*, became the first parenting book in 50 years (since Dr. Spock) to reach #1 on the New York Times bestseller list. Their new books are *The Entitlement Trap: How to Rescue Your Child with a New Family System of Choosing, Earning, and Ownership* and *5 Spiritual Solutions to Everyday Parenting Problems*. The Eyres lecture and present seminars worldwide on parenting, life balance and values-based time management. They have done several around-the-world speaking tours and frequently address church and community groups on a pro bono basis. They also advocate for strong families and balanced life styles on major network shows. They founded and run the international parents' cooperative organization *www.valuesparenting.com* with a membership of more than 100,000 parents throughout the world. Richard and Linda have nine children.

******

Toni: I thought it would be really great to look at the values that we're teaching our kids. Let's pretend for a minute that our kids are listening, exclusively, to the values that are in the media and in our culture. What do you think they'd learn by listening to those messages?

Richard: That's a frightening question, isn't it? They'd get a lot of messages about instant gratification.

We were on the Phil Donohue Show when our book was a bestseller and we did a national press tour. The Donahue Show always wanted controversy, so he had another guest who essentially was making the absurd point that you should give kids the freedom to develop their own values. He said that parents shouldn't try to cram their values into their children. He asked, "What makes you so presumptuous that you, as a parent, can decide what values your children should have?"

It was so absurd that it was hard to argue, but my first instinct was to say to him, "You know that's a wonderful theory. It's like putting a child in a boat in the river above Niagara Falls and saying, 'I hope you figure it out before you get to the precipice.'"

It's so frightening to think about leaving the teaching of values to our society: the peer group, the media, the Internet, the rap music, and the movies. Their teaching is even worse than teaching negative values. They're teaching amorality. They're teaching the absence of values, which is more sinister. I would rather have my child exposed to negative values than to an attitude that says: "It doesn't matter. There are no values. You can do whatever you want." And that, frankly, is what's out there in that vacuous world that engulfs our children.

So let's take the offensive and develop a systematic way to impart values to our children that will create a happy life.

Toni: I think many people live by their values and children absorb those values by watching their parents, but I think that parents are less likely to speak of values in a systematic way. Is that what you found when you traveled around the world lecturing?

Richard: Well, let's be really blunt. There are two problems, Toni. One is that parents often don't live the values they're trying to teach, and it often happens in very subtle ways. A parent may think she's pretty honest, but then the phone rings and the child answers. The mom says, "Tell them I'm not home." We do these things that undermine the values that we're trying to teach.

The second problem is the one that you mentioned. Even when a parent is living a value and assuming that the example he or she is setting will be enough; frankly, it isn't enough. That was the impetus that helped us to write the book. We were seeing so many parents saying, "Well, I think my child knows discipline," and in fact, the child had no idea what the word meant.

Think about a value. A value is simple on one level but complex on another level. It has various applications. Sometimes it's important and sometimes it's critical. A parent who ignores all those nuances and just assumes that a child will learn a value makes a grave mistake.

Kids are remarkably absorbent. You can teach a child how to read when he is three years old, to do square roots when he is six years old, and so on. But what is the single most important teaching or series of lessons that I can give my children? What is the thing that will leave them a legacy of happiness?

The minute you ask that question, 90 percent of parents realize that the answer is values.

When we open our lectures to questions, Toni, it's predictable that the first question will be, "How do I protect my child?"

What they mean is a variety of things. How do I protect them from pornography? How do I protect them from predators? How do I protect them from peer groups? And the real answer is: you teach them values. It is the only vital, reliably long-term protection we can ever give our children. So why not be systematic and organized and structured in terms of how you teach values to your child? Why leave anything to chance? Parents have the opportunity to take control of the situation and to literally teach children values. So why not do it?

Toni: To use the boat analogy: would you send your kids out to sea in a boat without a rudder and you haven't taught them how to sail the boat? Their chance of success would be grim. But if you teach them how to sail the boat and provide values as the rudder, they're going to have the skills they need to be resilient, even in troubled waters. If you teach them problem-solving, they'll have the confidence they need to figure out, "How can I get out of this mess?" I agree with you that values are probably one of the few reliable tools you can give your kids.

Richard: It's never a guarantee, but it's the closest you can come to a guarantee.

Let's make the analogy even stronger. Ultimately, what you give them is an outboard engine. You give them something that is so strong that they can actually go upstream. The stream contains the media, peer pressure, and the Internet, and they're all flowing in the wrong direction toward Niagara Falls. The values you teach provide them with an outboard engine to steer that boat against the current. To do that, they need a pretty strong tool.

Toni: I love that analogy. I'm a visual person and I'm going to keep that in my mind.

What are the 12 values that you and Linda chose?

Richard: Let me tell you why we picked 12 values; and frankly Toni, I think this is the reason the book was a bestseller. I *know* it's the reason. Oprah liked it so much. She said parents need this book because there's only one value for each month, which makes it simple.

She hit the idea hard that parents are busy. They don't have time every day to think about all the values to espouse. But if you just work hard on one value during the whole month, you're going to see some results by the end of the month.

We decided on the number of values before we decided on the values. We thought, "This is going to be tough to figure out 12 universal values."

We did some serious polling and asked a lot of parents. As luck would have it, parents have exactly the same values. A good definition of a conservative is a flaming liberal with a teenage daughter. In other words, when it comes to our kids, we're all extremely conservative.

Toni: So what are your 12 values?

Richard: The first one is honesty. Some people might say integrity or truthfulness.

The second one is loyalty and dependability. The third one is respect. The fourth one is love. The fifth one is unselfishness and sensitivity. The sixth one is kindness and friendliness. Number seven is courage. Number eight is peace ability; that's one that requires a little explanation later. Number nine is self-reliance and potential. Number 10 is self-discipline and moderation. Number 11 is fidelity and chastity. And number 12 is justice and mercy.

Toni: Your goal was to find universal values. As you traveled around the world, did you find that those values resonated in other countries too?

Richard: Absolutely. In fact, the only place we had any controversy at all was in the United States.

Toni: Oh no. Why?

Richard: We've been in Muslim countries. We've been in Hindu countries. We've been in Buddhist countries. And they're all in absolute agreement with each of these values.

Occasionally in the U.S. someone would say, "I don't know about fidelity and chastity. I really want my kid to go out and experiment a bit." When someone would say that, they'd essentially get shouted down by all the other parents around them.

Toni: So you really did a great job when you picked the values.

How should we prepare our kids before we start teaching the 12 monthly values?

Richard: That's a good question, Toni. The first thing families need to do is to get organized. The best organizational tool we have ever found is a very simple one. Have a weekly meeting. I'm a Harvard business school graduate, and I can't imagine running a company without the regular Monday morning meeting where you organize what you're going to do for the week. So we suggest families have a weekly meeting.

Most families find it works best on a Sunday because it's the first day of the week and their kids are out of school. Have a simple family meeting which kids can actually conduct; children between eight and 12 seem to really like it. They call the meeting to order and look at the schedule for the week.

You can also determine the value for the month and determine how to work on it. A lot of families develop a simple system of awards. For example, if you're working on honesty, you may have an Honesty Under Pressure Award. Every family member can share a time when they had a challenge, or were tempted to be a little dishonest, or to exaggerate, or to tell a little white lie, and then share what they did about it. The person with the best story gets the award for the week.

A lot of families make a banner to put up in the house: "The Smith Family Value of the Month is Respect."

You raise awareness at the meeting, and then throughout the week almost everything that happens is a teaching moment.

You may be watching a TV show and find a perfect example of how easy it is to be dishonest when you're with your friend. Something may happen at school and the kid will say, "Mom, I was so tempted to cheat because I could see Billy's paper, and then I remembered that we're working on the value of honesty and I didn't do it."

When you have a weekly meeting and a banner on the wall, kids really get into it.

On our website, *www.valuesparenting.com*, there are some inexpensive CDs that tell the story of each value in kids' language with music and action.

When you have small children, even up to 10 years old, they may not be clear about what the value means. So the first step is to be sure they really understand the definition of the value you'll be working on that month. Then you can begin to illustrate with examples.

Toni: I'm a parent coach, and I also tell parents about the virtues of family meetings. In my own home, I have to admit we do them sporadically.

Richard: I travel a lot, and Linda is like the CEO of our family. She said, "You'll be at the family meeting. Arrange your travel so you leave earlier Monday morning but not on Sunday. If you have to be gone, you'll teleconference in."

I had a lot of family meetings on the phone, but the kids knew I was there. They knew that there was no excuse for not being there.

You have to serve food at the family meeting, and you have to keep them short, and you have to make them exciting.

If someone were to say to me, "What's the single best family tradition you can establish?" I think it would be a Sunday weekly meeting. You can have the kids give you feedback to clear the air and you can get everything done.

Toni: I like the idea of rotating the leadership responsibilities. It's a great experience for kids to lead a meeting and decide on the agenda. I have an article on developing family meetings for parents who would like more information at:

www.getparentinghelpnow.com/myfreebookresources

Let's dig into honesty, Richard. I think that's one value that every parent can agree on. I saw some research stating that the average adult tells four lies a day, and that adds up to about 1,460 lies a year. But then we tell our kids that honesty is one of the virtues that we want them to have. So we have to clean up our act.

You and Linda have nine kids. What would you do when a child told a lie?

Richard: Let me back up a little. With each value there are two questions you can ask. One is: What do you do when your child violates the value?

20 Great Ways to Raise Great Kids

53

But that's a defense move. The first thing you should think about is an offensive system, or a proactive system. What can I do to prevent the lie from happening?

Too often we think of parenting defensively. What will I do if my kids have a problem? What will I do when he violates the value? Most parenting books are written that way.

If Johnny does this, then you do that. If you have this problem, try this solution. I think what parents need is an offense. In a sense, that's what this value program is.

The book and the website are divided up by the age of the kids. For honesty, for example, you could use a "true or not true game" for a preschooler. It is just a simple game where you say, "The sky is blue." Your kid says, "True." "Chickens give eggs." "True." "Cows give milk." "True." "Your hat is purple." "Not true."

All you're doing with preschoolers is getting them to distinguish between true and false. Then you can say, "Why is it better to tell the truth?"

One of my favorite methods for an elementary-aged child involves a little 3 x 5 card. It is called "the consequence game." On one side of the card it says, "The man at the store gives you too much change. You keep it and you buy a candy bar and so the short-term consequence is you get a candy bar." But then you turn the card over and the long-term consequence is that every time you go back to the store you feel the man is looking at you and you don't feel happy about yourself.

On the other card it says, "You give the money back to the man and you don't get to buy a candy bar." You turn the card over and the long-term consequence is that the owner compliments you every time you come in the store. "There's that boy that's honest." For an eight or 10-year-old, he really starts to get it.

With a teenager, you get in a discussion as a peer. You say, "Look honey, you're 15 and I'm your parent, and frankly, I have a problem sometimes with honesty. I'm going to work on it this month. Will you work on it with me? Will you just watch me and I will watch you? By the way, what are the kinds of dishonesty?"

These are offensive, proactive things that you can do. When a child does tell a lie, you're not suddenly saying, "What am I going to do to punish you?" You can say, "Remember what we learned about honesty? What do you think about what you just did?" In other words, you've given the child a framework in which to evaluate his own mistake.

Toni: Great advice. I love that you and Linda created many games for kids. It really invites their participation and makes the child think about different situations that they might be in. Whereas a lecture, for example, would turn kids off.

Respect is another hot button for parents. When we were growing up, it was a given that you would respect your elders. But in today's world, respect does not come automatically. I think we really need to earn it as parents, and some parents feel that they don't get respect.

Where do you think parents have gone wrong in terms of earning respect from their kids?

Richard: I think we've gone wrong in two ways. One: we don't respect our kids enough. Listen to how most parents talk to their kids and there's no respect. As a result, the parents get no respect back. So the first thing we have to change is ourselves, in terms of how we speak to our children.

Respect is the worst value in the United States. It's much better in other parts of the world, especially Asia. You just don't find disrespect from children, and the reason is that it's expected. Parents don't let their kids get away with it.

When families work on the value of respect, they should set up a family meeting and decide that if anyone speaks disrespectfully in the family, there will be a little time-out. Time-out means that the child starts over.

We like the time-out signal. When you hear disrespect, you give that old T-sign with your hand, like a technical foul in basketball. So maybe the mom says, "Son, take out the garbage," and the kid says, "I can't. I'm busy." … or some other disrespectful answer. You do the signal, then the parent asks more respectfully, "Son, will you please do your job and take out the garbage?" and then the son knows he is required to say, "Yes, mother."

Then the child knows that you're going to start over 50 times until he gets it right. In other words, once the child gets it in his head that this is not tolerated, the child will get it right the first time. The bottom line is that most disrespect is just a bad habit. It's not a dark part of little kids who are trying to be evil. It's just a bad habit and he picks it up from the peer group and from the media. It's one of the easiest problems to correct, once you discuss it in a meeting and start a system where you start over every time it happens.

Toni: I like labeling it too. I just say, "That's disrespectful. Let's try it again." If it's the tone of voice that's disrespectful, then I'll say, "Please change your tone. It's disrespectful."

Sometimes they're not conscious of it. So we have to remind them until they get it right.

Richard: By the end of the month they usually get it right.

Toni: Any other practical tips on respect, Richard?

Richard: One of my favorite games for respect is to have family members list the people who you might be prone to show disrespect for. It becomes interesting. Kids are amazingly smart. They always list "my parents" and "my teachers," and they'll say something like: "But how about nature? Maybe we're disrespecting nature when we litter." Or "How about old people? What if we don't help them when we see them?"

In other words, you broaden a child's view, so he starts to think, "Wow. I'm an expert on respect. Now I can go out and be an example, because unlike most kids my age, I really understand what respect is."

Toni: I think the media is a perfect opportunity for teaching this value too. If you sit down and watch a sitcom with your family and you see disrespect, you don't have to lecture but you can ask, "How do you think that kid treated his parents?"

Richard: You bring up a good point. Before you start watching the show, you can say, "Our value this month is respect. Let's see if we notice anything disrespectful."

We know one family who has a TIVO system. They can stop the show whenever they hear something disrespectful and talk about what just went on.

Any sitcom you watch will have examples of every single one of the values being violated. And each one can be a perfect teaching moment.

Toni: We were watching The Middle. It's advertised as a family show. They used seven swear words in a 30-minute sitcom. I was aghast, but we had a good conversation about it.

Let's tackle another value, Richard. I speak in a lot of schools, and teachers tell me that many children are not taking responsibility for their actions. They're so quick to blame others. Then when the teacher talks to the parents, chances are that the parent is going to side with the child and not support the teacher. Parents become defensive.

If we don't hold kids accountable for their actions when they're young, what's the outcome?

Richard: They become people who can't behave responsibly in society.

Here are two practical things that parents can do. One is what we call "the repenting bench." It's a tool parents can use. It's like a time-out, only it's for two kids, and it can be used any time there's a conflict, argument or fight in the family.

Instead of the parent saying, "Who started it? Who needs to be punished?" or acting like the judge and the jury – which is just a hopeless situation for a parent – you send the two kids to the repenting bench.

The only way the kid gets off the bench is to think it through and think what he did wrong. It will do him no good to say what the other kid did wrong; he will never get off the bench. But once he can reason it out, he can raise his hand and say, "Mom, what I did was wrong. I provoked him (or I hit him or I took away his toy)."

Then he gets up and all he has to do is say, "I'm sorry" to the other child, give him a hug, and off he goes. As elementary as that sounds, it's an enormous lesson of responsibility. Kids as young as three really get this, because what you're really teaching is that it always takes two to tango. You are always partly to blame.

What was it you did and how do you repent for it? How do you get forgiveness? How do you resolve it so you can go on? You give your kids ownership of their own relationships, of their own arguments. Now they understand what responsibility is.

The other tip is going to be a little controversial.

I think that giving kids an allowance diminishes responsibility. Most parents say, "I give my kids money so they learn to handle it. They learn to spend wisely. This is how I teach responsibility."

The problem is that kids don't perceive the allowance money as their own money. They don't perceive ownership. They perceive it as a goal. They perceive it as something given by their mom. They buy a shirt with it. They buy a toy with it; they throw the toy on the floor. They didn't own the money; they don't own the toy. The parent is simply setting up a family bank.

A payday should replace an allowance. Use a peg board or a star chart to keep track of the chores they do and determine how much money they earn on payday. Then they have ownership, and they begin to learn delayed gratification. They begin to learn responsibility and they begin to take care of themselves.

Toni: Great points. And here's a question parents will ask: How do I get started?

Richard: Parents can go to our website: *www.valuesparenting.com*. Right in the middle of the page you will see a place that says "free." You get a CD on honesty that will just blow you away because it's so geared to kids and they will get that concept in their mind.

Try that, and if you love it, you can get one every month with a different value.

The CDs give the parent a talking point. The worst thing you can do with kids is lecture them or just talk about a theory. You want something concrete, and that free CD will give it to you.

Toni: Your book has lots of concrete examples too. It's almost like a cookbook where you can pick and choose what ingredients you want … it's very practical. I was impressed by that as well.

I speak in a lot of corporations, and people tell me horror stories about the quality of younger employees. Some parents are even coming to the interview with their adult kids or calling the manager when the manager reprimands the adult child. Some parents go way over the top.

I know you also have a book called *Self-Reliance*. Can you provide some tips on how parents can teach their children independence without crossing boundaries?

Richard: A parent's natural instinct is to give their children everything they didn't have. Parents do their kids a huge disservice when they do this.

Let's talk about the elimination of allowance and the elimination of free hand-outs all the time. Kids are actually respected and honored by a parent who pays a certain amount of money for chores.

Let's say you tell the child to clean the hallway. Every day the child does that, he marks it on the chart, and at the end of the week the number of marks he has determines how much money he gets.

How about if we make it possible for you to earn a lot more money than you're getting for your allowance? But there's a catch. From now on, when you want to buy something, you use your own money.

Then you give the child a checkbook, to keep track of his money in the family bank. If he wants money, he writes a check and keeps track of the balance. Even kids seven years old can add and subtract.

Kids feel respected, and then the miracle happens. They start paying attention to how much things cost. They start putting money away. And a lot of families pay interest for money in the family bank.

Some families have them pay part of their tuition when they go to college. There are endless things you can do.

Getting back to your point, when an employer has a person that comes to work for them who knows how to handle money, suddenly that person's a gem for that employer.

I think parents have to think of their home as *the real world* and make it work that way. Otherwise, you send an 18-year-old into the college world and they don't have a clue. Your 18-year-old will get pre-approved credit cards in the mail when they go to college. Then there's a real opportunity for responsibility.

So why not teach them before they leave your home – how to earn, how to save, how to value money, how to make wise purchases out of a budget. These are the things that will make them successful in life.

Toni. Let's talk about teaching children to be less self-centered and more generous.

Richard: Here's how we do it. We suggest that parents separate the giving from the getting on Christmas. We suggest that the 24th of December is reserved for kids to give their gifts to each other and to the parents. There's no Santa Claus, no getting presents. It's all about giving each child honor for the gift he gives. All the focus is on the child who is giving, not on the one who is receiving. It's amazing how well they respond to that.

Normally, parents let Christmas become: What are you going to get? What do you want? What is Santa going to bring you? That's the entire focus, and all it does is deepen their sense of selfishness and self-centeredness.

So that's a holiday suggestion for parents.

Toni: Throughout the year, a parent can help their child to learn empathy and "emotional intelligence" so the child can identify their own feelings but also identify the feelings of others.

Richard: A great way to do that is to sit down with your child and pick up any magazine. Start thumbing through the pages and see if your child is good at reading faces. How does this person feel? A lot of the time a child will say, "I don't know." Well, look at his face. How does he feel?

Kids are remarkable, once they are given the opportunity. "He looks sad," or "He looks mad."

Ask, "Why would he be mad?" Then they look and try to figure it out just from looking at the picture. Then you begin teaching them more complex emotions, like confusion or frustration. For kids it's like a game.

Empathy is a learned skill. It's not just something you naturally have, so parents need to teach it. I love the "magazine faces" game.

Toni: Parents can share their feelings too, modeling healthy expression of feelings. When there's more than one child in the home, siblings can learn how their actions have impacted the other sibling by inviting those conversations.

Thank you for the great conversation, Richard.

Contact Information:

Richard Eyre

Email: *www.theeyres.com/contact_us.php*

Website: *www.valuesparenting.com*

Unplug Your Kids from Electronic Devices

Meet the Expert:

Michael Mann is an award-winning storyteller, author, parenting columnist and speaker.

Michael was a spokesperson for The National Institute on Media and the Family for many years. His extensive storytelling and public speaking experience ensures an engaging environment for adults and children. Michael does workshops, keynotes and presentations on a variety of MediaWise programs and is the founder of the Center for Imagination.

Michael presents to more than 15,000 children and adults each year.

He has appeared on Channel 9's Good Morning Minnesota, KARE 11 TV, and Twin Cities Public Television; and he's been the subject of feature articles in the St. Paul Pioneer Press and Minneapolis Star Tribune.

Michael is a winner of the Parents' Choice Award, the Storytelling World Award and the National Parenting Publications Gold Award.

Meet the Parent:

Mark Gauer is a father of two. He and his wife work full time and their children are involved in multiple activities.

✳✳✳✳✳✳

Toni: We're going to talk about unplugging your kids from electronic gadgets – for good. I bet that 96 percent of parents could benefit from this information, myself included.

Wait until you hear this! Kids between the ages of eight and 18 spend more than 44 hours a week, or six and a half hours per day, in front of an electronic device. Isn't that just appalling? It's more than any other activity besides sleep.

Trust me, this does more harm than good, so I've invited Mike Mann, a spokesperson for The National Institute on Media and the Family, to help us pry our kids away from these devices and get engaged in other activities – like connecting with us, which would be fabulous!

We're going to learn how to be "media wise."

Of course there are many benefits to living in an electronic era. The problem is that electronic gadgets are overused by kids and probably by parents too. There are compelling reasons why parents need to pry kids away from these gadgets.

David Walsh, the founder of The National Institute on Media and the Family, talks about a media culture that's been created by TV and advertising. He calls it a "yes" culture in which media present life as "easy, fast, fun" and always offer more and more stuff. How is this affecting our kids?

Mike: Let me first share a story. When I was a kid, I grew up in south Minneapolis and there were 12 of us boys, all age nine through 11, and we kind of cruised the neighborhood. We thought we were in charge, but, of course, parents were really in charge. At that time, there was a particular toy that we all wanted to have and I tried to convince my mother that life wouldn't be complete unless I had it. She kept saying "no" and my brother and I pleaded with her, but we still didn't get it. Then, one of the neighbor kids got it.

We thought, "How come we can't have it? Dougy is so spoiled."

Well, as it turned out, 11 out of us 12 boys did not get it, but in today's culture I would say that it would be the opposite. Eleven out of the 12 boys would get the "it" toy. Parents feel that they need to provide the "it" toy for their child.

Why was it easier for my parents to say "no"? And why is it more difficult today? It's not because they were better parents back then. It's because today's culture really doesn't support parents. The "more, easy, fast, fun" message in the media is no longer supportive of good parenting.

Toni: This has negative ramifications for kids because they don't learn the self-control that they need to get along in school and other environments. Once they leave home, they don't know how to say "no" to themselves; and they're more likely to end up obese or in financial debt because parents haven't had the discipline to say "no" over the past 18 years. Would you say that was correct?

Mike: Parents should say "no," but that's not the end goal. The end goal, as you suggested there, is that our children learn to say "no" themselves.

Toni: Exactly. They learn self-control when parents model it for them. How many ads do kids see in a year? What is the latest figure?

Mike: It's one million messages per year.

Toni: That's astounding, and each ad is teaching them to get more stuff, and to get it fast and easy.

Mike: Yes. They see ads everywhere: in magazines, in newspapers, on billboards, on the radio, and on their cell phone.

Toni: The negative ramifications of this are also seeping into the class-room. Teachers are reporting more discipline issues in the classroom. The fast pacing of TV is also causing problems because teachers can't keep up with that in the classroom, can they?

Mike: No. A child learns from a very early age to expect entertainment, to expect to be entertained, and that everything should be fun, and it should all be easy – nothing challenging, nothing difficult – and then a teacher has to teach in that environment.

It begins very early. Roughly 28 percent of America's children under the age of two have a TV in their bedroom, and this in spite of the American Association of Pediatrics saying children under the age of two should not see *any* electronic screens at all. Children learn immediately that they should be entertained.

So when they get into the classroom, and there's the classroom teacher, and the teacher can't make the letters dance across the top of the white-board, children come home from school and when parents ask the ques-tion, "How was school today?" they say, "School was boring."

Toni: I hear that almost every day. I think media also creates a culture of disrespect, and teachers experience that in the classroom.

Mike: Right, and teachers across America are telling us they're spend-ing more and more time on classroom discipline, and less and less time on teaching content. Dr. Walsh calls it "an epidemic of DDD: discipline deficit disorder." The symptoms are a culture of disrespect, impatience, a need for instant gratification, unrealistic expectations, and a sense of entitlement, self-centeredness, and ramped consumerism. America's kids spend 500 percent more than their parents did a generation ago.

Toni: Parents, I hope some of these problems are hitting you in the gut. I'm practically trembling.

We know that excessive TV usage can lead to obesity, and too many kids in America are overweight or obese. Is it primarily from the sedentary activity of sitting and watching media, or is it all the sugary food ads they see?

Mike: The fast food ads all influence how we eat. The latest governmental study shows that 32 percent, or nearly one out of three kids, are now overweight or obese. This is a huge epidemic. The good news is that it has leveled off in the last year or so, but it's so extremely high that we just can't afford to continue that way.

Toni: The research also shows that boys and girls are growing up with a warped view of what they're supposed to look like due to pictures in ads that have been altered to show perfect people. Right?

Mike: Exactly. The average woman in America is 5'4" and she weighs 140 pounds and wears a size 14, which is a healthy size. The average Hollywood actress is 5'11" and she weighs 117 pounds and wears a size six.

Toni: Oh, my goodness! I haven't weighed that since 12th grade! So clearly this has an effect on how we all view our body image.

We'd be remiss if we didn't mention the effect of media violence on kids. Your research shows that kids will have witnessed over 200,000 violent acts by the time they're 18, from watching TV – and that doesn't count video games.

For one thing, it numbs kids to violence. How else does it play out in our daily lives?

Mike: The important thing to know about video games is that when kids – and most often it's teenage boys – are immersed in violent video games, it doesn't mean that they're going to pick up a gun and shoot somebody, or that they're going to shoot up their school or something like that. But what it does mean, and the research shows this clearly, is that they will see their world as less safe.

When they are challenged in some way, or find themselves in a challenging situation, they will feel unsafe, and they will fall back on the solutions they have habitually learned in the playing of video games. We need to understand that video games are excellent teachers, and we need to recognize that video games use best teaching practices to teach, and so what we need to do as parents is pay attention to the *content* of the video games.

I showed a video game, not the most violent one, at a state-wide PTA conference. I showed portions of Grand Theft Auto, and the PTA parents came up to me afterwards, and they were outraged. Their outrage had to do with the fact that they owned that video game; they had the video game in their house; and they didn't realize that type of content was in the game.

Toni: So, those screening ratings that your institute has helped promote really are important. And then there's the idea of watching these programs with your kids – hey, show me how this game works – and then you really get the insider's view on what it is that's in front of their eyeballs.

Mike: Yes, too often violent media teaches violence as opposed to teaching *about* violence, and that's an important distinction. And just a quick example: the movie *Saving Private Ryan* is an extremely violent movie, but it *teaches* about violence, and while I would not recommend that movie for children at all, it does teach about violence and the consequences of violence. And there are many other examples that teach about violence as opposed to just being violent for the sake of violence, which is too often the case.

Toni: Yes. Now one last problem we're going to talk about is the idea that kids are losing sleep because of media use, and part of that occurs when a child has a TV in the bedroom. But what effect does that have when the kids are in the classroom, Mike?

Mike: Well, the research shows that the average sixth grader with one hour less of sleep has the brain function of a fourth grader; and the research also shows that our school-age children across America are averaging one hour less of sleep than children a generation ago. With children, an A student, on average, gets 15 more minutes of sleep every night than a B student; and a B students get 15 more minutes than a C student.

Toni: No kidding? Parents, if sleep is an issue in your house, please check out Chapter 10 in my book for my interview with Mary Sheedy Kurcinka, the author of *Sleepless in America,* or pick up her book.

So, excessive media use contributes to childhood obesity, a culture of disrespect, a "yes" generation, a loss of sleep, and a numbing to violence. I hope all those reasons have moved some of you. I know I've been motivated to make some changes.

Now let's start talking about solutions. TV is still the biggest magnet for kids; so Mike, please give us some tips for wrestling them away from the TV.

Mike: The easiest and most effective single thing you can do is to take the television and Internet connection out of the child's bedroom. Children with TVs in their bedroom watch twice as much TV and they don't do as well in school. Children with an Internet connection in their bedroom spend twice as much time on the Internet and they go places where their parents wouldn't want them to go.

Bring the TV and Internet to a place in the house where there's more public access so you can monitor what's going on. That's number one.

Toni: Okay, what else?

Mike: Avoid using TV as a babysitter, and know what your kids are watching. When it's in a public place that you have access to, it's easy to pay attention to what they're watching. Set some guidelines about when and what children watch. You want to participate in that and then practice "appointment TV." Decide in advance what's good to watch and watch it as a family.

Another thing is to talk to your children about what you're seeing on the screen, because try as you might to keep your children shielded from all of the bad things that might show up on the screen, they're going to be there. If you're there at the TV, you can talk about it. Discuss how you feel about what you're seeing on the screen so they hear the authoritative voice of their parent saying, "This is how I feel about what I see." That's extremely important. Parents underestimate the power of their words.

Toni: I think we're going to use a coupon system to limit TV use. The kids are going to get something in the palm of their hand, like Monopoly dollars, that will each be worth 30 minutes of media use overall – not just TV, but media use. They can look at a TV guide at the beginning of the day and decide what to watch, or decide what they want to play on the Wii.

Mike: Well done! With our kids, they had to do some things to earn screen time. One of the things they had to do was spend time outdoors.

Toni: I love that.

Mike: Research clearly shows that there are certain things a child needs to experience to develop a healthy brain. And when they're spending

40 hours plus with electronic screens, it's important to understand what they're giving up for that.

Toni: I wrote a newsletter article about that called, "Surprising Secrets to a Successful Summer" that's available at *www.getparentinghelpnow.com/myfreebookresources.* The brain is deprived of growth if kids are not given free time and time with nature. Certain brain connections are not made, and those pathways *need* to be made, so our kids can be great problem solvers and be creative and inventive.

So parents, even though you may think, "This is just down time," think again; because there's actual brain growth occurring when your kids play outside or commune with nature.

Now, I know kids will go through a withdrawal period. If you say, "I'm cutting you off from X hours of media use," the kids are going to be whining; they won't know what to do. Mike, how do we get through this tough withdrawal period?

Mike: Well, finding things to do when they're bored is the way kids learn to be on their own and to find out what interests them and what *isn't* boring. So, one of the things that we can do to help them with that transition is to look for ways to build up their sense of resourcefulness by creating a list of boredom-buster activities. Then when they walk up and say, "Mom, Dad, I'm bored," you can remind them of that list and they can choose from it.

If I ever dared to tell my mom that I was bored, I would be given her chore list and end up doing things like weeding the garden. I learned very quickly that my boredom was my own responsibility.

The important thing is to understand that if we make a dramatic change in our children's life, they won't have the tools to deal with that boredom. So how can we help them with that transition?

Toni: Let's talk about video games, Mike. Apparently the average kid plays video games about 49 minutes a day. Are we talking about Wii and handheld and computer video games?

Mike: Yes. In fact, that's all starting to work its way together. The media industry calls it "convergence." So we won't be able to define television use and separate it out from computer use and video game use because it's all going to work together.

Toni: So how can we put some parameters around electronic gaming?

Mike: We want to establish the rules ahead of time; that's one of the clear steps to avoiding a power struggle later. Then parents want to pay attention to the *rating* of the video game industry – thanks to the National Institute on Media and the Family for encouraging the industry to improve their rating system over the years by adding more detail on the content.

It's important for parents to read about the content and understand exactly what's in the game. Then ask yourself: "Is that the experience you want your child to have?" Then, as I suggested earlier, the video game console needs to be in a public place where you can monitor what's happening on the screen.

Consoles now allow the players to connect on the Internet and use the Internet as a type of computer so they can play the games online as well.

Toni: I just got a shiver when you said that – because of online predators. Do they have any idea who they're playing with online?

Mike: Not exactly, no. In some of the bigger, more popular video games, you're playing with people all around the world. So as a parent you need to understand that with that type of Internet connection, you've opened up a window on the world.

One of the other issues that's coming up with video game use is video game addiction.

For a small percentage of regular gamers, this is a serious, serious problem.

Toni: If your child is in that category, you should definitely seek professional help.

Mike: Exactly.

Toni: Let's talk about cell phone use, which is the number one concern that parents of adolescents have.

Mike: It's a big one. The important thing to do is to choose a cell phone plan with reasonable limits, and then make sure your child has consequences, both financial and otherwise, if the limits are exceeded. Establish that ahead of time, and review the cell phone bill with your child. It's an opportunity to communicate and to sit down and talk about how it's going. Is this the way we had planned it to go, or is it taking a form that was unexpected?

Another thing is to make sure adolescents understand that there's no texting or talking while driving, no matter what.

Then, keep cell phone use in balance. Try creating cell phone free zones in the house or perhaps even dropping cell phones in a basket before dinnertime and at bedtime – which can be an issue.

Then talk with your kids about cell phone manners. We were out for dinner the other night and there was another family sitting at the dinner table in this wonderful restaurant. They were all having a good time and then Dad's cell phone rang. Dad answered the phone and was talking for quite a while. The message that he sent was that this call was more important than his family time.

Toni: Yes, so we have to be good role models.

Mike: Exactly. Also, make sure that you have meaningful consequences when violations of the family rules happen and then follow through.

******

Toni: We have a caller named *Mark* from New York. Mark, thanks for calling in.

Mark: My pleasure. Actually, this is an excellent topic. I have one comment when it comes to parenting. I think parents have a tendency to put down the child, always saying "no," and I think that shuts kids off from the link between the parent and the child; whereas giving them positive reinforcement and respect instead helps kids really listen to what their parents are saying and channel that properly. What do you think?

Mike: I think that you make a really good point.

Media use creates opportunities for us to communicate to our children and to communicate our values. It's about how well we monitor the use of media, not about keeping our children away from media. It comes down to how well we establish and communicate our values, because in the end, when our children become adults, we want them to have values like honesty and integrity.

Toni: I agree with Mark that positive discipline options such as praise and rewards, spending time together, and using positive communication like empathy, all keep the doors to communication open. That means that when one of these potential dangers does occur – like cyber bullying, which about 50 percent of kids are now experiencing – your child will be more likely to tell you about it, because you have built a base of respect and positive communication.

Mark: Absolutely, and I believe there's a fine line between developing respect and becoming a pal with your child, which is not healthy.

Mike: Mark, that's a very good point. Parents of my generation and the baby boomers decided we wanted to be our children's friend. Yet, when we asked adolescents across the country, "What do you want from your parents?" they said the number one thing they want is parents; they can find enough friends.

Mark: Thank you.

Toni: Thank you very much for your call.

******

Toni: Now let's talk about computer use and some of the hazards.

Mike: With computer use, parents need to understand that the critical thing is the Internet and they need to monitor it. It's a window on the world, and if you want to know where your child goes when they go out the door, you also need to know where they go on the Internet.

Toni: Yes. And now I'm pleased to welcome **Mark Gauer**. Mark and his wife work full time and they have two children who are involved in multiple kid activities.

Mark, I know you have a couple of success stories that you'd like to share with us on limiting media use. You've developed a family rule about homework and chores, so can you share that with us, please?

Mark: One of the things that work best for us is to write down reminders for the kids every day about what they should do.

Most days, they need to do their homework, dishes and laundry before watching TV. We have them earn TV time by doing a few chores first, and then ideally they also practice their piano before they turn on the TV.

Toni: So TV is a privilege. You give them a checklist and then they earn the privilege of tuning into a media device.

Tell us what you do with media use when you go on vacation with your kids.

Mark: If it's a long trip, then it's okay to have a DVD recorder and watch a movie to keep the kids from getting too antsy, but we set rules in advance that they can only watch it at nighttime. Because if we're going on a trip and we're going across landscape they might never see again, I want them to look outside.

Toni: This goes back to the pre-planning that Mike was talking about earlier by setting parameters that reflect your values. "Hey kids. We're on vacation. I don't want you looking at a screen. I want you to look at America."

Mark, I know you have a question about cell phone use, so jump in with that.

Mark: We heard a speaker at our church mention that parents should be careful about taking cell phones away from kids. I'm a little paranoid now because he mentioned that cell phones, and especially texting, are a valuable connection to peers, and he suggested not using that as a disciplinary device.

I'm especially concerned about having a cell phone in the bedroom at night because I'm really afraid that he's going to lose sleep by staying up late and texting with friends; but my wife and I have different ideas on how to handle that.

Mike: It's important for both parents to be on the same page, so have a discussion about what you can agree on, because your kids will pick up on it immediately if there's a disagreement.

Yes, it's true that a cell phone is one of the primary tools for teens to communicate, but it's still a privilege and there has to be house rules. A child can be connected and still live within the parameters of the house rules.

When it interrupts things like sleep, then there's a problem. I think you can easily define that sleep is not negotiable, even if your teen doesn't agree.

It's an adolescent's job to push against the rules, and it's a parent's job to establish and enforce the rules, so don't expect a lot of "Yeah, Mom and Dad, you're right."

When our children turned 25, they called back home to say thanks for hanging in there, not giving up on us, and sticking to the rules. That's about the age when you can expect them to call back and say, "Mom and Dad, you were right."

Toni: This comes down to us conveying our values. Sleep is important. Limiting violent media is important. Staying safe on the Internet is important.

When you and your wife limit media use, what do you and the kids do instead?

Mark: The kids are involved in activities but we also want to get better at having family reading time.

Toni: Check out Chapter 17 of my book: Family Fun Nights. There are lots of great ideas.

We talked earlier about modeling positive media use. Are you and your wife working on that, Mark?

Mark: Not as much as we should be.

With the kids, we encourage them to watch educational TV. What I worry about is using the TV as a vegetative state, like when you come home and if you're tired from work you lie down in front of the TV. I want to try and get rid of that and instead model the behavior that if I'm tired I go straight to bed.

Toni: Mike, is there anything final that you'd like to mention?

Mike: Well, the holidays are approaching, and if you want to know what to get your children, Dr. Walsh says spend twice as much time *with* them, and half as much money *on* them, and your children will be healthier for it.

Toni: That's so true. Bill Doherty says the number one protective factor to prevent teen pregnancy and alcohol and drug abuse is time spent with parents.

Thanks Mike and Mark for all the great information!

Contact Information:

Mike Mann

Phone: 612-724-7074

Email Address: *mike@storymann.com*

Website: *www.storymann.com*

Are You Overindulging Your Child?

Meet the Expert:

Jean Illsley Clarke is a mother, grandmother, parent educator, and the author of numerous parenting books. Her latest book is *How Much Is Enough? Everything You Need to Know to Steer Clear of Overindulgence and Raise Likeable, Responsible and Respectful Children*. She and two colleagues have conducted 10 research studies on the impact of childhood overindulgence on adult life skills, attitudes and parenting beliefs. She presents workshops nationally and internationally, and her *How Much Is Enough?* book has been translated into nine languages. Clarke holds a master's degree in Human Development and has an honorary doctorate of Letters and another in Human Services. She is committed to helping families and believes that children's needs are best met by adults whose own needs are met. Her next book, due to be published in December 2013, is entitled *How Much is Too Much?*

Meet the Parent Guest:

Jeanne Burlowski is an academic consultant specializing in college and medical school success. She's also the mother of two children who made a commitment to raising responsible children.

******

Toni: We're here today to answer the question: Are you overindulging your child? And if you are, how can you make some changes, because it's really harmful to your child. Jean, please define "overindulgence" for us.

Jean: Well, in the book *How Much Is Enough?*, there's a very long definition that was developed by adults who had been overindulged as children; but as I boil it down, it means giving children so much of anything that looks good that it keeps them from learning their developmental tasks and it has a negative effect on their adult lives. The message of overindulgence is: You're not competent.

We've been told for years you can't love a child too much. However, a lot of people in our research told us, "They loved me too much." I think that's about giving in, though, rather than real love.

Overindulging is giving children too much because we're tired, or because all the other kids have it, or because we want to keep them happy. Without meaning to, we keep them from learning their developmental tasks. Our research showed us that the consequences for adults who were overindulged as children aren't pretty.

Toni: It's okay for parents to splurge occasionally for a birthday party or present, but overindulgence is a pattern of parents doing this consistently with their kids. Correct?

Jean: I would guess that all of our listeners overindulge now and then because we live in an overindulging time.

When I recognize that I'm overindulging a child, I go back to the child and say, "I made a mistake." It's not going to hurt if Grandma overindulges sometimes or the ex-spouse does, or the neighbor does, as long as we name it and say, "There it is again. That was over the top." Kids are going to have to learn to cope with it. It's when, as you suggest, we make it a steady practice that it's really hard on the kids.

Toni: I love your idea of owning up to mistakes with the kids. I think many parents find that hard to do, but it's incredibly important to role model that.

Jean: Oh sure, but once you do it you'll find that it's not hard.

Toni: It can be freeing to admit, "I'm not perfect. Oops, I made a left turn when I should have made a right turn."

I want to help parents figure out if they are overindulging their kids. So you have something called "the test of four." Is that the best way for parents to figure this out?

Jean: It's the best way we've discovered; and many, many, many parents have told us that it's helpful. My husband and I use it with our grown-up kids and with our five granddaughters.

It goes like this: There are four questions and the first question is: Does this, would this, could this get in the way of the child's development? And if we're going to know that, we have to know something about development. The best book if your child is under six is called *Is This a Phase?* It's by Helen Neville from Parenting Press.

Helen combines a child's temperament with their development, because not all children have their temper tantrums at two-and-a-half. Some of the really laid-back kids wait until they're four-and-a-half. All kids are different and we have to do what works with the individual kid.

You can also check with the Gesell Institute for books about kids six and older and the developmental tasks that are appropriate.

The second question is: Would giving this, or doing this, use too much of the family resources?

When we hear "family resources" we think right away of money, but it's also time, energy, and focus. Is it meeting the wants of the child, but not the needs? Is it giving so much to this child that the other children are being neglected? And it also includes mom's psychic energy – can you handle it?

"Child, you can't join one more sport because I'm in the car every minute of the day that I can be, and we're not going to add that."

The third question is: Whose needs are being met? And Toni, I just hate that question because it always turns out to be *mine;* I'm tired or I'm busy or I just plain don't know how to do this.

Let me give you an example. When my first little grandchild, Addie, was one, I cleared the whole day for her and I was going to be the best grandma that had ever been invented.

I kept saying, "What would you like to do next, Addie?" and pretty soon she started to get grumpy and by the end of the day I wanted to step on her! I thought, "This isn't how it's supposed to be!"

Then my daughter came along and did everything that I had been doing and I could see it.

Jennifer asked Addie who she wanted to ride with, and who she'd like to sit with at dinner. When Addie didn't get her way, she had a tantrum.

So I got the message. No one had ever asked me those questions when I was young.

The next time Addie came, I got out post-it notes and I said, "This is what we're going to do. And when that's done, you have to help Grandma clean out her jewelry drawer. And then you can choose the order of the other things we want to do." Toni, it was a totally different day because children need adults who are in charge.

Toni: Excellent. Tell us the fourth question.

Jean: Is there possible harm to someone else, or the community, or the environment, or the globe? It's not just about us.

If you look at these four questions and any one of them raises a red flag, then you step back and say, "I need to look at that."

Toni: One of the things that I love about your book is the comments that you shared from the study participants.

Here's what a few people said about being overindulged as a child.

"My parents did things for me that I could or should have done for myself."

"My parents did not expect me to do chores."

"I was allowed to have all the clothes I wanted."

"I was allowed lots of privileges."

"My parents gave me lots of toys, lots of freedom; they let me lead or dominate the family."

"I didn't have skills that the other kids did at their age."

"My parents gave me too much attention."

Those are powerful statements from adults looking back on how they were raised. Let's talk next about the three types of overindulgence that you and your colleagues uncovered in your research.

The first type is "too much." It includes having too many things, over-scheduling your child, and giving too much of your attention and time to your child. So what harm is there in doing this? What pain does an adult child who experienced this report?

Jean: The biggest pain that people told us about was, "I don't know how much is enough."

In the in-depth interviews that I did, one woman said, "I hope that before I go to my grave, I have one afternoon of knowing how much is enough of something."

Toni: Isn't that sad?

Jean: The second thing is that these children grow up with disrespect for things and other people.

They continue to believe that they're the center of the universe. Kids are supposed to start pulling away from that idea when they're two, but for those who are overindulged, it's still all about me. And why are they overindulged? That's easy – marketing. The marketing messages go right by adults, because they're different from the way we were marketed to.

So it's helpful to teach the difference between a "need" and a "want." For each child, decide how to give them everything they *need,* and then decide what proportion to give them of what they *want.*

Toni: So should we sit down as a family and discuss whether electricity, food, cable TV and other things are a "need" or a "want?"

Jean: That would be cool to do with kids age six to 12. Before that, children are learning more by absorption. They hear you at the dinner table saying, "I saw a new sweater and I really want it, but I have enough sweaters. My sweaters from last year are fine."

Or they're grabbing a toy and you say, "I know that you want that, but we need to go to the grocery store and buy milk."

Toni: Another idea would be to stick to the items on your list when you go to the store in order to avoid impulse buys.

Jean: Sure. You can show the list to the child and say, "It's not on the list." Or, before you go into the store, say, "Today, you can choose one thing that's not on the list."

That starts to teach them the difference between a need and a want.

Toni: We need to teach kids the tricks that advertisers use to get us to spend money too.

Jean: Yes, and the advertisers are so good at it. When kids are six, seven, or eight years old and the reasoning part of their brain kicks in, we can start teaching them about marketing.

When you see an ad that's aimed at your child, talk with your child, "They want you to think that you won't be okay without this doll or truck. How do you think they're trying to make you feel that way?"

Teach them about imbedded ads. When you're watching TV with them, and you see a particular product in the show, point out what they're trying to sell.

We should be constantly teaching children to raise their awareness. I gave my seven-year-old granddaughter a new nighty. She opened the package, lifted it up, looked at the label and said, "I like this brand."

When I was seven, I wore a cotton flannel nighty and never looked at the label.

We need to be reading books about advertising to children. Just go to your favorite bookstore or a website and pick one that looks interesting.

Toni: Let's talk about over-scheduling and why this is harmful.

Jean: Well, one reason is it takes too much of the family's resources.

Second, kids aren't left alone to develop their own methods of entertaining themselves.

Third, it decreases creativity because their activities are always determined by adults.

Toni: We can also examine our own stress level orchestrating these events, look at how stressed our child is, and add up how much time and money is being spent on the activities. If one of those tilts the scale toward the heavy end, then we should cut one activity or pick another one that isn't so consuming.

Jean: Yes, and we should notice if we ever hear kids say, "I'm bored," because if they never say that, they don't have enough down time.

Toni: I have a friend with six kids and if her kids say, "I'm bored," she tells them that she'll give them a chore to do, and guess what? They always find something to do!

We're going to talk next about "over-nurturing." There's a great quote from your book that I want to share: "If you water a plant too much, it dies. Even if you water it too much out of love, it still dies."

I think the image of a withering, dying plant is a great visual to keep in mind for parents when we talk about over-nurturing. Please define it for us.

Jean: The antidote to it is saying "no." Parents should know that "parent power" is greater than "pester power."

Here are some examples:

"Honey, I'll do it for you. You're looking tired, and anyway you don't do that as well as I do, and I'm in a hurry, so I'll do it for you." The message is: "Don't be competent."

With over-nurturing, when parents do something for the child that they can do for themselves, they should ask, "Am I doing this for my child or for me?" Parents may have done certain things for kids when they were younger and then they get in the habit. The end result of over-nurturing is an overblown sense of entitlement.

There are a hundred billion neurons in the brain when kids are born and only 17 percent of them are connected. This 17 percent wants to grow and make the child more competent.

The brain is forming every day in response to the environment. When we keep children from being competent by not letting them do things on their own, not letting them make mistakes, not letting them go ahead, we're actually going against their brain programming.

When they're little, we need to say, "You can do it." "You can try that." "I'll watch you and then later on maybe you can do it by yourself." Or "Do you want a suggestion or help from me?" But always the response is "You can do it."

I can tell when children have been over-nurtured because they say, "I can't" or "You do it, you do it better" or "I'm tired" or "I have a stomach-ache." And when I hear those things, I think, "Ooh, we've got a child in trouble because children's nature is to jump in." Do you remember when your girls were two and you wanted to scramble eggs and they wanted to help?

Toni: Yes.

Jean: Let kids do things like making scrambled eggs, and let them make mistakes that are safe. We should always be saying, "You can do this. I will show you how."

Toni: The message we want to give is, "You're capable."

Jean: Right.

Toni: You've identified another type of overindulgence called "soft structure." You've said that this is hard for parents to identify. Please provide us with some insights.

Jean: With "soft structure," we have people who grow up with lax boundaries, with uneven competencies, expecting immediate gratification, and this makes it tough to be successful in the workforce.

People in our research who grew up with soft structure really resent this because they came out of it incompetent. What they complained about was that there were no rules and there were no chores.

Toni: Amazing.

Jean: So what is firm structure? It's the parents being in charge. It's the parents knowing which rules are negotiable and which are not and telling the kids. It's having household rules posted way before the children can read, so you can take the two-year-old to the poster and there's a picture on there and it says, "What does our poster say about hitting?" And the child looks and says, "Oh, you're not supposed to hit." We are then putting the problem back with the child; whereas if I put my finger in the child's face and say, "Don't hit," I'm owning the problem.

So we make our boundaries, and then when the child crosses them, we give it back to the child to be responsible for his actions, and we teach non-negotiable rules. You have to do that because you live in this community, or you're a member of this family. Non-negotiable rules teach children obedience, which we want them to learn, because when they're 16 and they drive, we want them to drive on the right hand side of the road.

Also, as soon as the brain is ready, we start negotiating. Before age six we're saying, "Would you like to wear the blue socks or the red socks?"

Toni: We're giving kids choices that are also acceptable to us.

Jean: After age six, we start negotiating with the "who, when, why, where, how, and where."

The child says, "I want to go to Jimmy's house," so that's the "where."

How are you going to get there?

What are you going to do?

Who's going to be there?

Are the parents going to be at home?

What time will you get home?

How will you get home?

The negotiating is always based on the non-negotiable rule. The non-negotiable rule is that you don't play at a house where there's no parent at home.

Toni: Exactly, so keeping your child safe is always the number one priority and the non-negotiable rule.

Jean: Right, and this teaches the child self-responsibility, and how to think and solve problems. So we're always sorting out with children the difference between the negotiable rule and the non-negotiable rule. Then as the children grow, the rules change.

Toni: Jean's book is a great resource for parents. And I have a "Get Your Child to Listen the First Time" parenting program that teaches parents 10 positive discipline options and how to develop effective family rules. The details are on my website at *www.getparentinghelpnow.com/programs.*

Jean, I'm 100 percent behind you when it comes to developing family rules. When parents don't have firm rules and consequences, it's so harmful to kids.

So families need to give chores, and they need to develop family rules and consequences, with some rules that are negotiable and some that are not. What other tips can you give parents?

Jean: Well, don't run a popularity contest with the kids. If your kids are never uncomfortable, you're shorting them; and so many of us have a rule in our head – and I was one of them – that we should keep the children happy and comfortable all the time.

So instead of asking, "How did school go today?" when your kids get home from school, ask, "What did you learn?" and "What did you do today that was kind?"

That puts the onus back on the child.

We're constantly saying, "I'm in charge of the family because I'm the parent and it's my job to lead the family. I'm in charge of some things and you're in charge of some things, but because I'm in charge, I decide what you're in charge of."

Then as the kids grow through the teenage years, we loosen it and loosen it and loosen it, so it's offered with firmness, but not rigidity or criticism. It's just how it is; I'm just doing my job.

Toni: There are some parents who equate the word "discipline" with punishment, and they just hate the word "punish." I like to share with parents that the word "discipline" comes from the word "disciple," which means one who teaches.

So parents can reframe the idea of discipline. They can think of themselves as a teacher and ask, "What do I want my child to learn from this?" and then pick the best discipline tool to teach the child that lesson.

Jean: Punishment is about hurting the child. Discipline is about teaching the child.

Toni: Exactly.

Jean: Huge difference.

Toni: Now let's talk about chores.

Jean: Marty Rossman at the University of Minnesota did a longitudinal research study in which he found that the most successful young adults in their mid-20s were the ones who started chores at age three.

If you haven't started chores, start tomorrow, and that includes me as a grandparent.

When my little granddaughters come, the first post-it note says, "Do something that helps Grandma."

Why? Because it's good for the child. It helps the child know that he or she is a contributing member of the family and the community.

Toni: You bring up a great point. The parents may be too permissive or over-nurture, but the grandparents may be overindulging by buying too much stuff. So you have to look at the whole family system to see how it impacts the child.

It can be very uncomfortable telling your parents or in-laws that they're buying too many gifts, or that they're letting the kids rule the roost when they visit or when they take care of the kids. What do you recommend?

Jean: Always tell them what you want them to do. "This is what we'd like you to give for Hanukkah or Christmas or Kwanza. Will you give two books and one toy, and then if you want to buy more, could you make a contribution to a children's fund?"

You can also give them a copy of my book *How Much Is Enough?* It's not blaming and it's not shaming. Don't say, "This will be good for you;" just say, "I want to see if you think that this book makes sense."

It's the kind of book you can pick up and read for 10 minutes anywhere in the book. It's purposely written that way.

Of course, with a spouse or an ex-spouse it's harder, but in the book there's a highway pointing out that we need to stay in the middle.

So you don't want to overindulge, but you shouldn't go over to the ditch of rigidity either. Keep yourself in the middle so you have negotiable and non-negotiable rules.

"We're doing assertive care. I'm doing this for you because you need it. You don't have to like it, but you need it. We're doing supportive care. How can I help you?" And teach them to recognize when they're being overindulged.

Toni: Jean, you also wanted to talk about life goals.

Jean: Yes. We continue to do studies, and study number six is on life goals.

We found that the more people had been overindulged as children, the more their life goals were wealth, fame and image. They were not interested in personal growth or contributing to society unless that particular contribution benefitted them. People who had not been highly indulged had as life goals meaningful relationships, personal growth and making community contributions.

Toni: Thanks, Jean. The information you shared is critically important.

******

Jeanne Burlowski is going to join us now. Jeanne is an academic consultant specializing in college and medical school success. She's also the mother of two children and she's going to share tips on raising responsible kids.

Jeanne, what is your philosophy about chores, and when did you start doing them with your kids?

Jeanne: My kids started doing chores when they were old enough to pull themselves up on the door of the dryer. My little boy loved to throw things, and so when I was taking the laundry out of the washer and putting it in the dryer I would drop it onto the dryer door and say, "Matthew, hit the back" and he would pick up that wash cloth and pelt it at the back of the dryer and then I would say, "Good job. You're really helping me."

Every time I'd do the wash I'd say, "Come with me; time to do your chore."

He'd pull himself up on the dryer door and stand there wobbling, because he couldn't even walk yet, but he was helping me.

I think that a lot of parents have trouble with chores for two reasons. One: parents wonder, how do I get started? And two, how do I enforce children doing chores without reducing myself to being a screaming meme?

I started when the children were very, very little with the tiniest little thing that they could do.

A little tiny child can't load the dishwasher, but they can put the cups in. Then my daughter graduated to bowls and spoons. If they start when they're little, kids get a tremendous charge out of being given a chore to do.

I concur with Dr. Clarke that it builds in them a sense of confidence in their ability.

People who come to my house are shocked when they hear my children, who are eight and nine, say, "It's my turn to do laundry. I'll go get it from everyone's rooms and load it into the washing machine." They're doing full loads in the washer and dryer now. A guy I knew in college couldn't manage that.

Toni: That's a perfect example of how to teach your kids about chores. You started young, you made it fun, and you broke it down into age-appropriate tasks, which helped them build confidence in their abilities. Thank you for sharing that.

Jeanne, you've created "The Great Depression" in your home. What is that?

Jeanne: Well, this relates to not overindulging our children and not giving them so much that you begin to destroy their love of work and their love of contribution and their chance for future human happiness. I heard from another source that you should try to recreate the Great Depression in your own home. To do that, you limit resources so children are forced to reach into their deep well of creativity, which every child has.

They reach in the well and figure out ways to get their own needs met for entertainment and stimulation. It may be putting on a pair of white socks and sliding up and down on a polished floor, or getting out toys and using them in an unconventional way. So we've given our children very limited resources in our home, and then the message that we give them is: you have such a good brain and I know that you can do something with that.

Toni: This is exactly the message you want them to receive: "You're resourceful, you're smart, you're capable, and I have confidence that you can do this." That's excellent.

How do you limit overconsumption during the holiday period?

Jeanne: Well, two ways. In our home we drastically limit television and we've done that since they were little.

This may be hard for families with older children who've been watching TV consistently, but the American Academy of Pediatrics recommends that children not view screens until they're two years old. That worked well for us. Then we limited TV and our children don't watch TV commercials.

It makes it much easier for me to not overindulge with toys. I don't have to fight a battle about "I want this thing that I saw on TV."

Here's the second thing that we've done since the children were little. Anytime I'd say the words "buy a toy" I'd always follow it with the words "at a garage sale." "If we save a little money here, perhaps we can buy a toy at a garage sale…"

So my children started to look at garage sales as the source of where toys come from, rather than the toy store. I kept them out of Toys R Us and the back of the warehouse store for as long as I possibly could. You know what: if you're shopping for your toys at garage sales, it really limits your choices.

Toni: With the way that kids grow out of toys, or lose interest in them, it makes so much more sense to spend 50 cents or a buck on a toy rather than $15.00.

Jeanne: Absolutely. We also bought each of the children one giant shelf that has nine cubby holes, and nine boxes that go into those cubby holes.

I make it a practice to take toys to the basement when the shelf gets too crowded. Once in the basement, they pretty much disappear from everybody's radar.

Toni: We have a rule: "One toy in; one toy out." So when it's a birthday or a holiday and you get a present, then you also have to donate one item. It helps keep the clutter down in the house, limits some consumption, and encourages empathy for others.

Jeanne: I love what you're saying about encouraging children to give. When we expose our children to people who have very little, whether it's Operation Christmas Child at our church or giving to the food shelf, it shows kids there are people that don't have very much. It helps children develop character by knowing, "I'm giving. I'm helping," and they are more likely to appreciate what they have.

Toni: Jeanne, thank you so much, and thank you to Dr. Clarke. You've both been fabulous guests with lots of great ideas.

Contact Information:

Dr. Jean Illsley Clarke

Mailing Address:16535 9ᵗʰ Ave. N., Mpls., MN 55447

Phone: 763-473-1840

Email: jiconsults@aol.com

Website: *www.overindulgence.info*

Raising a Generous Child in a "Me" Culture

Meet the Experts:

Corinne Gregory is the creator of SocialSmarts®, a nationally-recognized schools-based program that teaches good social skills, positive character and values. She's an education expert, author, speaker and mother of three children.

Janet Montgomery is a mother of four, volunteer, and president of Janet Karvonen Basketball Camps. Encouraging generosity in her children is a high priority.

Michelle Hollomon is a licensed mental health counselor and professional coach with thousands of hours helping people achieve their personal and professional goals. She works with top level executives, individuals and couples, helping them realize significance, meaning and happiness. Michelle is the author of the book, *God Unwrapped: God is Love...but Not the Kind You Are Used to*, published by Harrison House. She is the mother to Sweet and Sassy and wife of Mr. Dashing. Michelle, her family, and their naughty black lab live near Seattle, WA.

Alison Smith and Debbie Zinman are the creators of ECHOage. Loved by busy parents across the U.S. and Canada, ECHOage is an online birthday party-planning website with a unique charitable giving twist. ECHOage gives multi-tasking parents all the tools they need to plan and manage an effortless birthday party and teach their children about giving at the same time. Through online invitations, guests securely contribute funds towards birthday gifts: half goes to the charity of the child's choice and the other half goes toward the child's desired birthday gifts.

******

Toni: Our topic today is raising a generous child in a "me" culture. I thought of this topic because the holidays were coming up, but I invited five guests today to talk about how we can raise a generous child through-out the year. Each guest has suggestions on raising a generous child.

Corinne, you believe that parents need to have the right mindset to raise generous children. And you believe that many parents come from the mindset that they don't have enough, rather than being thankful for what they do have. How does the "not enough" mindset of a parent affect children?

Corinne: First of all, given the economic climate, I don't mean to be criti-cal of parents, because it can certainly be difficult not to be pessimistic sometimes. And many people are jobless, so there are a lot of challenges, and it's natural for us to worry and fret about the things we aren't able to have. But you do have to remember that the first thing a child will look to is the modeling that you provide as a parent.

If you're constantly focused on, "I wish I had this," or "If only I had a new car," or if you're envious of what your neighbors or your friends have, that will affect the mindset of your child. They will think more about what's missing in their lives and less about being grateful for the things they have.

Toni: So one tip is not to vocalize envious feelings in front of our kids. Another tip is to ask ourselves if perhaps we need to make changes to our mindset? Yes, we are affected by the current economy, but as parents, hopefully we can still find things to be thankful for.

Corinne: You're absolutely correct. Even if you feel you don't have enough, the more you appreciate what you have, the more you find that good things happen to you.

As I explained to my children the other day, appreciative and generous people tend to like to do things for other people. If you have a mindset of appreciating what you have and showing gratitude, that can translate into your life expanding in positive ways, including helping others.

Toni: So if we have a thought pattern of abundance and express gratitude for our home, food, health, and family, we're going to be more prone to be generous. If we have an attitude of scarcity, we feel we don't have enough, so we tend not to be generous.

Corinne: You're absolutely right, Toni, and that's one of the things we try to point out to parents. You can't raise a generous child if the child is always looking over his or her shoulder thinking, "I don't have enough. How can I possibly spare anything for anybody else?"

And that doesn't necessarily mean stuff; it can be energy, time or resources.

Toni: Exactly.

Sadly, we do live in a "me" culture. Mike Mann, from The National Institute on Media and the Family, was on my show, and he said that kids are exposed to over one million advertisements each year. Of course, the advertisements are all teaching kids that they don't have enough and that they must have the next new gadget to feel good. So there's a tidal wave of media messages targeted at our kids. How can parents counteract the enormous number of messages we're all receiving?

Corinne: It would be nice if we could say something simple like, "Don't expose your children to as much TV." The problem is that with over one million ads, messages are coming at them from all directions – print, radio, TV and the Internet.

So it's very important for parents to point out to their children that they don't always need to have the next big thing; that they don't always need to have more. And parents need to talk to their children about not letting possessions define their identity. It's very, very tempting for kids to think, "How come I can't have the latest gadget like my friend Heather?"

It's not necessary, and quite frankly, we can become owned by our possessions. That's not where we'll truly find happiness.

Toni: Right. I think it's helpful to go through an exercise with kids to differentiate "wants" versus "needs." You can take your family budget and ask, "What are those things that we really need?" Go through your grocery bills, electric bills, health insurance, etc. and see how many things are necessary.

Then, you can define things that are "wants." You may have a healthy debate about this and that's great, but I think that it's a helpful starting point for families.

Then you can ask them, "What do you think will bring you lasting happiness? Is it the latest gadget? Or is it relationships with people you care about? How long will you keep that gadget? Then point out that family members will care about you and give you support throughout your life.

Corinne: Another exercise is to ask, "What will it take to keep you healthy … to keep you happy?" You can then look at the bare minimum: "Could you live without this? Could you live without that? Could you manage to be happy?"

What we discover is that the things that truly make us happy, make us connected, make us whole … have very little to do with stuff.

Toni: Absolutely.

If you feel like you're fighting the "million advertisements" battle alone, it can be helpful to find organizations your kids can join that support the values you want them to have. Girl Scouts and Boy Scouts, for example, are built on service to others. If you're in a faith community, your child can join the teen group or the youth group.

I find that it's really helpful if you're not the only one preaching these values to your kids.

Corinne: The other thing that's very true is: the more you focus on other people and the less you focus on yourself, the more you discover what's truly important. There's nothing that tends to bring out generosity more than the simple act of giving. The more you give, the more generous you feel, because you also get the reward of making other people happy.

Toni: I couldn't agree more. In your curriculum, you teach kids how to develop an "attitude of gratitude." Tell us how to teach our child the attitude of gratitude.

Corinne: As we said in the beginning, it's very, very important to model it. You must be a "do as I do" not a "do as I say" kind of parent; be a role model.

One of the things that we really like to focus on is: how much do you really have? We walk people through an exercise that asks, "What things can you be grateful for today?"

Even if you've had a rotten day, is there one thing that you're thankful for? Did you have a warm meal? Do you have a roof over your head? Are you thankful that you have friends? Are you thankful about how well you did on a test? It's an opportunity to think about what you're grateful for.

As you pointed out, it's also extremely valuable to do things for other people. Join a helping organization. Work in a soup kitchen. Have your child pick out a gift or toy for a child in need as part of a giving tree or toy collection.

Those are concrete ways that you can take part – physically – in developing the attitude of gratitude. Don't just talk about why it's important; go out and do something.

Toni: Exactly. How can we make that relevant throughout the year? There are so many opportunities during the holidays, but we want kids to have this opportunity year-round.

Corinne: The holidays are an obvious starting point, but of course the reality is that people have needs all year long.

So in order to develop a long-term attitude of gratitude, I strongly recommend that you find something you can continue year-round. Instead of adopting a military family just for the holidays, why not adopt them for an entire year?

Most of the time, deployments for military are six months or longer. Why not adopt the family for that year? Check in with them periodically. Find out when family members' birthdays are and use that as an opportunity to give throughout the year.

Or, if you're going to work in a soup kitchen during the holidays, maybe pick one day every month for your family to work in that soup kitchen.

Toni: I think it's so important to develop rituals around volunteering, because otherwise it slips off the radar screen. If you're going to volunteer the fourth Sunday of each month, then just put it on the calendar.

I'm going to share a couple of things that we do as a family that have helped us build an attitude of gratitude.

Every night at dinner one person is the "special person." They eat off a special plate and other family members thank the person for something that otherwise would have gone unnoticed. The next night it's another person's turn until you rotate through all the family members. And every night you start the meal with an expression of gratitude.

I started a new ritual with my teenage daughter at bedtime. I have a small rosary with 11 beads on it. We place our fingers on each bead and say something that we're grateful for that day. She loves it so much that she keeps going round and round the rosary.

Corinne: Another thing we teach in our curriculum, although it may seem obvious, is to thank people whenever you're leaving somewhere and saying goodbye.

What are you thanking them for? Maybe it's for their hospitality, or for whatever you did together, or it could be a teacher who helped you. Don't take it for granted; be grateful.

Toni: Exactly.

******

Next I'd like to introduce you to Janet Montgomery. Janet does a fabulous job of volunteering and is teaching her kids the value of generosity.

Janet, you believe that generosity is learned. Did you have a mentor?

Janet: I've learned a lot about financial generosity from my husband whom I've been married to for more than 17 years. Of course, as well as the financial part of giving, there is the generosity of time and of using your gifts to benefit others. My parents modeled those values by helping others in the small community where I grew up in western Minnesota.

My father owned a furniture store and he would often bring a mattress out to someone's house if he knew they didn't have a bed, or deliver something to help them meet their basic needs. I remember being on some of those deliveries with him.

And I saw my mom cooking in the kitchen and bringing food to people who had experienced a death in the family, and also serving food at church. So I saw that kind of giving firsthand as a child, but I really didn't learn about financial generosity until I married my husband.

Toni: As a family, you've helped support several families throughout the years. Please share an example of what you've done and how you've involved your kids in helping others.

Janet: Well, we've befriended several different families, but one family in particular needed to do some community service in order to get the closing costs of a HUD housing loan paid for. Our family volunteered and contributed hours toward the hundreds of hours they needed. We cleaned windows at church and pulled weeds. My son, who's 13, just mentioned that experience the other day.

We also bought the same family Christmas presents. We shopped for the eight children and bought several presents for each of them, thinking about their age and interests, and then wrapped the gifts and delivered them on Christmas Eve.

When the children were smaller, we even brought over a whole Christmas tree and put the lights on it. When we left, we really did feel like Santa Claus bringing Christmas with all of its splendor right into their home.

It felt so good, and I can't tell you how much that meant to our children. They still talk about it.

Toni: The key point is to involve your kids, and I love the way you involved them every step of the way with the shopping, wrapping, and delivering of the gifts.

I think it's ideal when kids can actually meet the individuals or families they're serving and see the joy that they're bringing to others. When they meet the people, they realize, "Gee, they're regular people like us."

Janet: That's so true. That family started out 20 years ago as people that we gave Christmas gifts to, and then it turned into an all-year event, just like you and Corinne were talking about.

We helped their mother – who came from Thailand and had poor English skills – to get into a driving school, and we found someone that could speak her language so she could learn how to drive.

We also helped her daughter with her college application process, and I'm proud to say her daughter is the first family member to graduate from college.

Their family recently attended my husband's birthday party. We asked each guest to write a letter to my husband in lieu of gifts. We made a book and it's not fancy or anything, but it has brought Al so much joy to see the letters from all of those families saying, "You're the best friends we have" or "You've changed my life." That's pretty amazing.

Toni: I bet it just brought tears to his eyes.

Janet: Yes, it's been awesome.

Toni: Volunteering is such a win-win for everyone who's involved.

You mentioned that Al's been a mentor in making financial donations. You two have a philosophy of "giving off the top." Tell us what you mean by that.

Janet: Well, we're thoughtful people. We manage our lives with Christ at the center, and we want our values as Christians and our other values of love and kindness to permeate all aspects of our life. We don't just want our faith to be something that only occurs on Sundays.

So when it comes to giving, we feel that we need to be thoughtful about it. We need to plan it because it's very important to us. We also talk to our children about it.

Instead of saying, "What's left over this year to give to charities?" we decide at the beginning of the year an amount that we'll donate. We didn't start out donating a lot, but we decided what the amount was going to be for our family and we gave it away.

The next year we'd decide if we could live with that again, or should we make it more? Most of the years we've been able to increase our giving; but again, when we give our gifts to organizations or the church, we give it at the beginning of the year so the organizations have those dollars in January instead of December. If you wait until the end of the year, you're probably going to have less to give, because you've probably thought of yourself a little more along the way.

When we sit down to decide what our charities are going to be, we ask for our children's input as well. We have a lot of fun making those decisions together.

Thank you so much to Janet and Corrine for your thoughtful suggestions. Michelle Holloman will join us now.

✶✶✶✶✶✶

Michelle, you believe that parents should teach the "why" of giving and not just the "should" of giving. What would you say to a child to bring this point home?

Michelle: It's easy to teach kids why we should be giving, but it's another thing to model it for them. I think you can talk about giving gifts in a way that's positive instead of saying we "have to" go buy someone a gift.

For instance, we were doing some holiday shopping and I said, "I'm so appreciative of your dad because this year he's gone through a lot of changes with work and he's given so much to our family. I can't wait to buy him his gift this Christmas."

Your attitude can make a difference.

Another way of modeling the "why" of giving is to introduce your children either to an organization that's helping other people or to the people that you're helping. Face-to-face contact makes such a big difference in helping them understand why giving is important.

Yesterday was a great example. We had 10 Girl Scouts in our kitchen making pancake mix for the YWCA. With all the flour flying everywhere, we already had a white Christmas!

When we dropped the bags of pancake mix off at the Y, we were given a tour. We got to meet the children in the child care facility, and it put a face on what the girls were doing and why they were doing it. It really gave them a sense of ownership. They created the gift, and then they delivered it and they had the opportunity to meet the recipients.

Toni: I think that's an ideal situation when they can go through all the steps and meet the people who are receiving the gift.

I'm a Girl Scout leader too. My oldest daughter's troop earned their bronze award and I can tell you that it's not always easy to find places where kids can volunteer. If you can find a place that accepts kids, it's great to make it a regular event. It's so important.

I want to share a quote at this point because it seems appropriate. This is from www.oprah.com. I just loved it.

It's by Rabbi Shmuley Boteach and it reads, "Being a good person means doing good things. It doesn't mean just having a good heart. A good heart is worthless if you don't have good hands. The heart is supposed to inspire generous action."

Michelle: I like that it requires good hands. Parents have to model a culture of generosity in the home and then the kids can experience it first-hand. When they experience their parents being generous to one another and to the world around them, it really is more "caught" than "taught." Then the kids start to internalize that generosity is a value that their family has. For them, it becomes a normal way of life to think about being generous with other people.

Toni: Exactly. Janet was just saying that her parents were role models for her. Now Janet and her husband are establishing that value with their children.

Michelle, you also suggest that families set aside a certain percentage for giving and that children set aside a portion of their allowance each week to donate. What recommendations do you have?

Michelle: We have a simple plan. When allowance time comes, we separate it out in dollars. They have three jars. One jar is a "spend jar" for spending money, the second jar is the "giving jar," and the third jar is the "saving jar."

When fundraisers come up, they get to choose how much they're going to give for that organization out of their giving jar.

Toni: We do the same thing. Each girl has three plastic see-through piggy banks that are different colors so they can see the amount of money that they have in each one. Donating money to others is a value that we've established from day one.

Michelle: When kids have a sense of ownership with their own money and then make a donation, it really infuses their self-esteem. They feel like they can affect positive change in significant ways in the world and they start to feel empowered.

Toni: I couldn't agree with you more. I think as parents we should focus more on praising acts of generosity. It's easy to praise your child for a good grade or scoring a goal, but I think we have to change our perspective too. We should praise kids for sharing with their siblings, using manners and being kind to others.

Michelle: I like your example of sharing with siblings. I think it's important for kids to use some of their own money to contribute to buying gifts for their siblings.

Toni: I bet some parents are thinking, "I don't have time to research and set up volunteer activities for our family." We should point out that you can model generosity without leaving home.

When kids outgrow their clothes or their toys, you can have them pack the stuff up and come along with you to Goodwill. A neighbor may need some leaves raked or their driveway shoveled, and helping with those kinds of things demonstrates to kids the importance of helping others.

Michelle: Opportunities present themselves all the time.

Toni: Michelle, thank you. You've been a fabulous guest.

******

Now I'd like to introduce Alison Smith and Debbie Zinman. They're the creators of ECHOage. Alison, tell us what you were observing about kids' birthday parties and how this inspired you and Debbie to create your company.

Alison: As parents of young children who were being invited to many birthday parties, we were observing a great deal. One thing we observed was that parents were very busy scurrying to the toy store in search of the perfect gift, only to arrive at the party to see this gift being placed on a table with many other gifts. And the children were often more interested in one another than they were in the gifts.

At the end of the parties, we also noticed that the children were not necessarily interested in the types of gifts they received.

We also noticed the almost overwhelming amount of waste with all the packaging and wrapping. Debbie and I said, "There's got to be a way to make the birthday party experience more meaningful."

We asked ourselves: "How do we keep the best parts of the birthday party, but just add a new element of meaning to it?" So we created echoage.com. When you have an ECHOage birthday party, it allows your child to get one big beautiful gift instead of perhaps 20 less meaningful gifts, and it allows the child to have a great impact on society because they're also choosing a charity to donate to at the time of their birthday. It's actually a very simple concept.

Toni: I love the idea because we know that birthday parties are way over the top. Debbie, let's pretend my child's birthday is coming up. How does your service work?

Debbie: It's an extremely simple process. All you do is go to the *www.echoage.com* website. You select an invitation and a charity and you email the invitation out to all of your friends.

Parents can do this with their children or they can do it themselves – at midnight if they choose to – and just talk to the child about it later.

The invitation says, "I've decided to make a difference in the world at the time of my birth date and you can help me. Please do not bring a wrapped gift package to my party, but instead make a contribution."

Then all the contributions are pooled together. Half of them go to buy one big gift for the birthday child and the child can choose anything he or she wants. ECHOage sends the funds to the parents to give to the child. Some of the children have bought an iPod or a bike.

The other half goes to the charity that your child has selected. It has a huge impact on children to be able to do something for other children in need at the time of their birthday.

Toni: Tell us about the 20 charities that you've pre-selected.

Debbie: We've selected charities that directly improve the lives of children. Each charity does something that children can understand, such as providing food, or sending children with cancer to camp, or planting trees in school playgrounds, or helping children who suffer from autism. It's always a tangible thing so the child can understand the impact that they're having on society.

Toni: What type of feedback have you received from parents who've used your service?

Alison: It's amazing. We get letters every day from mothers and children saying things like, "Thank you for solving the birthday party problem. We've wanted to honor our child on this special day, but we've been struggling with the current ritual. So now we've found a way to solve that problem and make the experience even more meaningful."

It's certainly more convenient for everyone, but it also opens the dialogue of giving with your children in a simple, fun and exciting way.

It puts the child in the driver's seat when it comes to choosing a big, beautiful gift that they really want for themselves. And the child also chooses the charity to donate to through ECHOage, so they have ownership of that experience too.

Toni: How does the child know that the charity has received the donation?

Debbie: The child receives a thank you note, from the charity, that explains how other children's lives have been improved. It makes the giving process tangible and meaningful for the child.

Toni: Thank you so much Debbie Zinman and Alison Smith for telling us about ECHOage, and thank you Corinne Gregory, Michelle Hollomon and Janet Montgomery for your great ideas on how to raise a generous child in a "me" culture.

Contact Information:

Corinne Gregory

Email: *corinneg@socialsmarts.com*

Website: *www.corinnegregory.com*

Michelle Hollomon

Mailing Address: 8201 164th Ave NE, Suite 200, Redmond, WA 98052-7604

Phone: 425-242-0541

Email: *michelle@counselingtheeastside.com*

Website: *www.GodUnwrappedbook.com, www.hollomoncoaching.com*

Alison Smith and Debbie Zinman

Mailing Address: 23 Lesmill Road, Suite 304, Toronto, Ontario M3B 3P6

Email: alison@echoage.com

Website: *www.echoage.com*

Win the Chore Wars!

Meet the Expert:

Elizabeth Crary is a parent educator and author. Crary is the author of 32 books and many articles for parents and children. Among her books are *Without Spanking or Spoiling, Pick Up Your Socks, Love & Limits, Dealing with Disappointment, Am I Doing Too Much for My Child?,* and *STAR Parenting Tales and Tools: Respectful Guidance Strategies to Increase Parenting Effectiveness & Enjoyment.* All her books are published by Parenting Press. You can see them and other helpful books at *www.ParentingPress.com*

Crary has more than 25 years of experience working with parents, and 35 years working with children. She teaches parent education for North Seattle Community College and also independently; and she developed the STAR parenting program for child guidance. You can find out about it at *www.STARparent.com*

Crary is a frequently requested speaker for parenting and professional groups across the United States, Canada and Japan. She has appeared on numerous media shows, including the Oprah Winfrey Show and Dateline NBC.

She is also the parent of two grown children and four grandchildren, all of whom she enjoys spending time with.

Meet the Parent Guest:

Stephanie Severson is a mother of three children who has also worked as a teacher.

Toni: I want to start off today by sharing information from a research study that made an impact on my parenting and how I approach chores with my children. There was a longitudinal study that followed kids from the time they were babies all the way up until they were 25 years of age. The study question was: What is the most reliable predictor of a child's success as a young adult?

The study defined "successful" as finishing college, being responsible, having healthy relationships, not being drug and alcohol addicted, and on the path to a successful adult life. A researcher at the University of Minnesota, Marty Rossmann, concluded from the data that the most important factor was whether or not your child had chores while growing up.

So whether a child had chores was a better predictor of success than IQ, family income or a two-parent household.

That study motivated me to look at the big picture of *why* I wanted my kids to "pick up their socks," beyond just having a cleaner house.

So Elizabeth, do you agree on the importance of giving kids chores?

Elizabeth: Absolutely.

There is research by Jean Illsley Clarke and the co-authors of the book *How Much is Enough?* that is also important. They found that one of the problems for children, unfortunately, is that parents do things for children that they should do themselves, like chores.

Then when the children are adults, they pay a penalty because they don't know how to do a chore, and they also have a sense of entitlement. They don't have a good work ethic and they haven't learned how to take things and follow through with them. So it does seem to make a huge difference on several levels.

Toni: You've done research, too, that shows it's important for parents to figure out why it's important for their child to do chores.

Elizabeth: There are a number of different reasons. Some parents want their children to do chores simply to build life skills and that makes sense. Some parents have the belief that children should contribute to the family. Others want their children to have good self-esteem; and learning to be responsible will do that. Some parents want to reduce their workload.

By looking at the parent's motivation, the parent can determine if they're accomplishing the goal.

For instance, a parent will say, "I want my child to have good self-esteem," but then when the child doesn't make the bed right, they criticize the child and it doesn't build self-esteem.

A friend of mine wanted her children to have life skills, but she had become dependent on her son to clean the bathroom since he did such a good job of cleaning it. She realized that she would need to rotate chores among the kids so that all the kids learned a variety of skills, not just one.

Toni: Honestly, as a parent, I want my kids to have life skills. I certainly want them to contribute because they're part of our family. I definitely agree that it helps increase self-esteem. And I want some help. So I want it ALL!

I also agree that it's important to rotate chores because it's more interesting for them and it teaches them more life skills.

Another important point you make in your book *Pick Up Your Socks* is the difference between obedience – when your child does it because "I'm the parent and I said so" – and the child taking responsibility for chores. Tell us a little bit about that.

Elizabeth: This is a really intriguing concept because very often parents will say, "I want my child to be responsible about their room" when, in fact, they may mean "obedient."

So, obedience may be the motivation and the follow-through comes from the outside. The child does it because you told them to and they have to.

If the child takes responsibility, the motivation comes from the inside. They can't actually be responsible unless they have a choice in the matter. So if you tell the child that they have to do it, that they have to have it done now, and that they have to do it this way, then what you're really asking for is obedience.

 With responsibility, the child has to be able to have input into how they want to do it and what the pieces are.

If they don't have any part in it, then it's not really responsibility; it's obedience. There is a place for obedience, but there's also a place for responsibility, where children are learning how to manage themselves – and that's the key difference.

Toni: It's such a great point, Elizabeth. I think that this really gets to the heart of the matter because we want to raise responsible kids.

We do not want to be nags, reminding them and reminding them. So how do children get that internal motivation that you're talking about that is the essence of responsibility?

Elizabeth: One thing to keep in mind is that it doesn't happen overnight and it usually doesn't happen in weeks or months. It's developed over time.

First of all, appropriate training is important. Help the child learn the skill. Don't just tell the child what to do; help the child learn the skill so they can manage it.

For example, if your child is very distractible, they're not going to be able to clean up the room or remember to finish the dishes until they have strategies to refocus themselves whenever they drift.

So part of that is learning what skills the children need to manage themselves and then asking, how do they motivate themselves? Or, how can they make it fun? There are different kinds of things that one can do.

Toni: When should parents start giving chores?

Elizabeth: Well, the study you quoted says that children having chores at ages three and four seems to make a difference. I think that depends on your understanding of what "chores" mean. With the younger children, it's more like helping with chores and being involved in the chores.

For instance, if the child spills water, give them a sponge and involve them in the clean-up with you. They're learning that they're a part of what's going on.

Toni: Parents can find a list of age-appropriate chores here: *www.getparentinghelpnow.com/myfreebookresources*. When kids are three or four, you don't necessarily call them chores, but they can help wash lettuce or put napkins on the table and help pick up their toys. I agree that three or four is the ideal time to start, but if a parent has a child who's 10 or 11, is it ever too late, Elizabeth?

Elizabeth: It's never too late, but it will take more time and more structure to get things started. It's very hard for a person who has been going through life without having responsibilities to all of a sudden have them. Some children will be very happy while other children will be resistant.

You may need to look at the child's needs to find some sort of a payoff for the child to start learning this new thing.

For example, if the child really wants to go to the park, you can say, "I'd love to take you to the park, but I have to do this and this. If you'll do one of those, then I'll do the other and we can get to the park faster." You shouldn't assume that they know how to do the chore, though.

So, begin to involve them in ways that meet their needs; then once they get some skills, you can say, "Now that you're 10, what chores would you like?" You can put down five or six chores as options and then let them choose what they want to do to help.

In my book *Pick Up Your Socks*, I have a table that has a lot of household jobs. For example, at age four they can help make their bed, but it isn't until nine or 10 that they can do it themselves with some reminding, and more like 11 that they can do it alone. Just because they can do this task when you're present, doesn't mean they can do the task when you're not, so a reminder system helps.

The reminder system needs to have two parts. One is to remind the child to do the job, and the second is to remind them to do the *whole* job, because sometimes children forget about what parts to do. So develop a checklist for doing the job, or a five-fingered check where you assign one task per finger.

When you just *tell* the child how to do a chore, it's not going to be as helpful as when you actually go through it with them – because they learn best by doing.

Toni: I think a good place to start, Elizabeth, is with a family meeting. Get everybody together and say, "We have fun together. We live together. And guess what? We make messes together too. So let's try to find a way that we can have a neat home so that nobody gets hurt. Let's talk about how we can do that as a family."

Do you agree that's a good place to start?

Elizabeth: Yes. And there needs to be benefits for each person if they fulfill the contract, and then consequences for each person if they don't.

Toni: Should parents pay kids for chores or not?

Elizabeth: Not for standard chores. Different people feel differently, but what I feel works better is this: children do chores to contribute to the family and they get an allowance because they're a member of the family, but one is not dependent on the other. If you pay a child for chores, then when they become 12ish and are able to babysit or mow lawns outside the home, they often choose not to do family chores because they don't pay as much.

Toni: Yes, I agree. Next, let's talk about steps for setting up a successful chore system.

Elizabeth: Well, the first thing is to figure out what is reasonable for your child to do. Then, look at your child's temperament and developmental stage.

Once you know what is realistic for your child, you need to make the job clear. Sometimes parents will whistle through the room and say, "I want you to clean up the toys before we have lunch," and the child says "Uh-huh," but no communication really took place.

So, the first step is to get the child's attention, which often means getting on the child's level – eye level – and then being specific about what you want. Elaborate on what you mean by "clean your room." Do you mean put your dirty clothes in the hamper? Put your books on the shelf? Pull up your bedspread?

So try to be very specific about what you want the child to do. Then create a deadline. Don't just say "soon." What does "soon" mean?

With younger children it's helpful to say "before you eat supper" or "before we read a story." I wouldn't say "before you go to bed" because children might purposely forget so they can extend their bedtime. With older children, choose a deadline using the clock.

The second step is to offer some choices so that the child plays a part in the decision.

You might say, "I need your help this afternoon. Do you want to empty the trash or do you want to set the table?" or "Do you want to clean your room alone or would you like my help?" or "Do you want to pick two chores or do you want me to assign two?"

So, somehow involve the child and give them some control over what they're doing.

Then, once the chores have been chosen, you can choose whether the chores need to be done on a daily or weekly basis or whether they can be more flexible.

The third step, if you have a regular system, is to create a reminder system, because the challenge for children is that they are able to understand the task before they are able to carry it through to completion *regularly*.

So, there are three steps. The first step is that they help with the task; the second step is that they do the task with a reminder; and the third step is that they do the task alone.

Toni: I have to admit that when I first read the information in your book about how long it can take before kids become independent in doing chores, it was depressing. I thought, "Oh my goodness, I have to be involved in some of these tasks for years before they're going to do it on their own."

It did help me realize, though, that it's normal, because certain brain functions just aren't in place yet. So it's not about being a nag; it's about helping them to develop these skills. I think we really have to prepare parents for the long haul if they want their kids to do chores and take on increasing responsibility.

Elizabeth: Some people are lucky and their children just naturally enjoy having a particular responsibility. And some children are far more resistant. But it's helpful to know that all children go through different stages, and it's important to note that it will take years, not just weeks and months.

Toni: You also talk about "language for success," and I think that's a really important point to share, especially when the child says, "I forgot."

Elizabeth: Sometimes parents will say, "Okay, but don't forget again." What needs to happen is the parent needs to ask, "When are you going to do it?" and "How can you remember next time?" so the child doesn't use it as a technique to get out of a task.

Toni: A key point is that parents should not complete the task because it's easier to do it themselves rather than to keep reminding the child.

Elizabeth: Right. Don't let the child get away with not doing their chores. If they forget their spelling words at school, then ask them, "How are you going to get them tonight?"

This is partly why chores are good. If you leave it up to your child, then the child has to figure out how to cope with their screw-ups. This does two things. One, it helps them learn that they might as well do it right the first time because it takes less time. Two, it gives them skills on how to recover when they do forget something.

Toni: I totally agree. It helps kids become better problem solvers when you throw the ball back in their court.

Now, let's talk about learning styles. For the sake of ease, we're going to say that there are three learning styles: visual, auditory and kinesthetic-tactile. Tell us how that might apply to chores.

Elizabeth: Well, there are two ways. One is how you present the information. So, if you have a child who is visual, then they need to see you do the chore, and if they can read, lists are a good idea.

If you have a child who is auditory, they need to hear you talk about it. Be very clear about what the steps are. You could also have them start chores when they hear the sound of chimes, for example.

Toni: Exactly. If you have a visual kid you can also use pictures to lay out the steps of a chore or to make their to-do list. For the kinesthetic-tactile kid, you need to show them how to do the chore and let them try it with you.

Elizabeth: If you have a high-energy child, they would be the ones who are vacuuming or raking leaves or something that takes a lot of energy.

Toni: So in summary, we need to help our kids to learn to do chores. First, show them how to do the chores, and then consider their temperament and learning style when assigning chores. Then, remind them and build in accountability. And be patient, since it will take a long time before they can do the chores alone.

Elizabeth: Yes.

Toni: Next, let's shift to practical ideas that parents can use right away.

Elizabeth: Each family has a different style, but family meetings are a wonderful process for working things out together.

One mom I know believed that all family members need to work for the good of the family. So sometime in the hour after dinner they set a timer for anywhere between 10 and 20 minutes. During that 10 or 20 minutes, everyone in the family stopped what they were doing and went and cleaned. It was a really cool thing to do together.

Another thing is establishing some kind of reminder system that the children like, and it's often helpful to have them create it. One idea is to have a board with a picture of each person on it, and then have cup hooks, one for each person. You put up the tasks that they have to do that day and they move the chore tag over when they complete the task, so there's physical involvement in the system.

With some children, old fashioned star charts work fine.

And here's another thing I want to say about rewarding or encouraging behavior. If you want obedience, that's fine. But, if you want responsibility, then reward the responsibility more. For example, if your child gets one sticker on a chart for setting the table when you ask, then they might get two stickers on the chart for setting the table *before* you ask. Try to reward responsibility and independent thinking more highly than compliance.

Toni: I like that a lot.

I also want to touch on doing chores *together*. My girls and I clean our bathrooms together. For one thing, we can chat while we're doing it, and honestly, they stay on task better if I'm in the same room with them. We also inspect each other's work. If I'm cleaning mirrors, someone else is doing counters, and someone else is sweeping the floor or cleaning the toilet. Then, we'll inspect each other's work. They can look at my work and say, "You left a smudge on the mirror here."

Then I'm not the only one "criticizing" them. So cleaning together has several payoffs for us, even though we're all squeezed into this teeny bathroom.

Elizabeth: Well, that's a cool thing to do because it's setting the standard. Children love to find mistakes a parent may have made when doing a job and they can learn from that. And it makes them look closer at not just your work but also their own.

Toni: Are you suggesting that you could purposely leave a pillow on the floor when you make your bed and then have your child come into your room and ask them, "How did I make my bed today?"

Elizabeth: Yes, because then you're teaching them about standards. You can rotate a chore like cleaning the kitchen after supper. On a day that it's your turn, leave something undone. Then the child is learning to look and scan for details, so that's a really helpful skill for kids.

Toni: I think so too.

Elizabeth, you were kind enough to share two resources from your book and they are on the resource page for my book. Parents can go to *www.getparentinghelpnow.com/myfreebookresources* to see a copy of a "contract" and a "bedroom score sheet." I've also included a handout about age-appropriate chores there.

Now tell us what you mean by a "contract."

Elizabeth: When children are a little reluctant, or falling behind, it's helpful to make a written contract about what to do.

For example, if you were trying to help your child be responsible for giving food and water to a pet, you would decide what the parent's responsibility is and what the child's responsibility is.

Many children don't like to be reminded, but if you do a contract, you start by asking what the child needs to do. Then ask the child how you, the parent, can support the child in doing it. It's very interesting because parents sometimes are surprised by what the children say.

Toni: Sometimes parents do have to get some things ready for the child, like buying the pet food, so it's good to acknowledge that and put it in writing.

Now tell us about the "bedroom score sheet."

Elizabeth: The idea is to be clear about what's involved, because very often parents don't make expectations clear. The score sheet is going to differ depending on the age of the child.

For example, with the younger child, it might say "pull up the quilt," but with an older child it might say "make the bed without any wrinkles."

Or when you say "pick up your toys," can the kids just shove them on a shelf helter-skelter? Or do you want them to be lined up on the shelf? It's important to state the standard and then you can change that as the child gets older and has the skills.

Toni: So write down exactly what you mean by "cleaning your room" and have a checklist the child can check off.

And tell me about your idea that you call "the growing book."

Elizabeth: What one family has done is: every year on the child's birthday, the child chooses a new privilege and a new responsibility. I love that because very often children expect to just get privileges. But, this links privileges and responsibility.

Toni: What a great idea!

Let's talk about teenagers next. I think when kids turn 13, a messy gene appears. The parent could do all the right things with chores, and then when the child turns 13, everything comes to a screeching halt because this messy chaotic gene kicks in.

Tell us about the exercise we can do with teens.

Elizabeth: One mom asked her child to list all the benefits that the child got from being in the family and then list all the ways the child contributed to the family. In this case, the child had been complaining about doing chores, and so the mother said, "Okay, you talk about what you contribute and what you receive, and then we'll talk about whether or not that's equitable."

What happened was, the child began to realize how much she received and, as much as she didn't like it, she realized it was reasonable that she contribute a little more.

Toni: I'm sure that would be an eye-opening experience for some teenagers – to see how many more benefits they get from the family than what they give back.

Elizabeth: Yes, it was quite shocking for that person. Then the mother said, "What would happen if I didn't want to do my jobs? Or if I didn't want to take you to the mall?"

Toni: I think it's important to link responsibilities with privileges. If you give the child a choice between two chores, and they say they don't want to do either one, you can say, "Well, I don't feel comfortable bringing you to soccer practice tonight."

******

Stephanie Severson is joining us now. Stephanie's a really great mother of three who I've known for 13 years. She's going to share some fun ideas she's used to make chores more interesting for her kids. Please share what's worked for you, Stephanie.

Stephanie: Well, my two oldest are only 16 months apart, so there were some long, long days at home with the kids. We just tried to make things fun for them. I remember when my oldest daughter was about four and my son was about five and she was really into Cinderella. We would play Cinderella, complete with crabby step-mother. The kids really got into their parts. We would laugh because I was the crabby step-mother who attacked the house with a duster. They just thought it was super fun.

Toni: Did you give them any props like little crowns or torn dresses?

Stephanie: I would put on the apron and have the duster, and my boy would probably wear an apron too. And then sometimes we'd put on music downstairs and have a ball.

Toni: I think music is a fabulous motivator.

Stephanie: Cinderella got to go to the ball, so she'd wear a fancy dress and we'd have the ball at the end.

My husband used to be in the Army, and so there are times when we have Army inspections when the jobs are done. Everyone has to answer "Yes, sir" or "No, sir." It's very much over-the-top play acting, but the kids always laugh.

Toni: Isn't that fun? If kids have watched the Pink Panther movies, they can wear a beret and a white glove and pretend to be Inspector Clouseau, who goes around and inspects the tables that were just dusted or the kitchen counters that were just wiped off. If your kids have a theatrical flair, those type of things work fabulously.

And you have another idea for older kids to share with us…

Stephanie: We have chore charts, and I'm a big fan of changing them every couple of months because kids like it better if they're new. But if Grandma's coming to visit and we have some extra jobs to do, I'll put up a list of the extra jobs that I need done. I'll let the kids bid on how much they're willing to do those jobs for.

I don't pay for other chores. We give the kids an allowance because they're in the family, but they don't get paid to work. However, on those days when there are extra jobs, we'll let the kids bid, and whoever wants to clean the toilet for the cheapest price, I'm willing to pay for it.

Toni: Isn't that fabulous? I love your creativity.

Stephanie: Well, it's taught the kids that they can choose a job that they want and decide what it's worth to them. My middle daughter is quite the cleaner, so she's willing to clean the toilet for 25 cents cheaper than her brother.

Toni: You've created a little eBay or Craigslist in your home!

Stephanie: I think they're getting onto my system now, because they team up and divide it up so they aren't bidding against each other.

Toni: Smart kids. Stephanie, do you have any questions for Elizabeth?

Stephanie: Yes. My oldest is an 11-year-old boy who sometimes seems to become paralyzed by indecision when he's doing chores.

For example, when he's cleaning the entryway, we make it really clear that shoes go here and coats get hung up. But if he finds something that doesn't belong in the entryway, he just doesn't know what to do. How do I help him feel empowered to make decisions about what to do with things?

Elizabeth: That's a really interesting question because some children are very, very rule-oriented. They do exactly what you're telling them, and then something falls out of the ordinary. One of the things that you can do is simply have him make a box for miscellaneous items.

There are different ways that kids can pick up a room. They can start at the door and then head to one wall or another, but give him a process for how to move through the room in such a way that decisions don't involve "what shall I do with this?" Then give him a box for anything that belongs somewhere else or if he can't decide.

Toni: That's a great idea, Elizabeth, because it prevents him from getting stuck.

Elizabeth: We all get stuck on small decisions sometimes, so this would give him a process for coming back later to anything that's difficult. And later he can think it through or ask for help.

Toni: Perfect.

Elizabeth, my kids are good at doing chores, but it's the day-to-day clean-up that's a problem. For instance, if they've just had breakfast and if mom isn't there to say, "Put your plate in the dishwasher," it just sits there. Do you have a quick tip for that?

Elizabeth: My suggestion is to tell the children the problem and let them come up with how they want to be supported. Then they won't be fighting you about it, and they might come up with something quite surprising.

Toni: I like that. Chores are such an important topic for all of us, so thank you Elizabeth and Stephanie. You were fabulous.

Contact Information:

Elizabeth Crary

Mailing Address: 2132 N. 115th St. Seattle, WA 98133

Phone: (206) 367-6425

Email Address: *ecrary@starparent.com*

Website: *www.STARparent.com*

Resources:

Elizabeth Crary is the author of 32 books which are available at

www.ParentingPress.com.

Without Spanking or Spoiling

Pick Up Your Socks

Love & Limits

Dealing with Disappointment

Am I Doing Too Much for My Child?

STAR Parenting Tales and Tools: Respectful Guidance Strategies to Increase Parenting Effectiveness & Enjoyment

Kids and Sports: Healthy or Overkill?

Meet the Expert:

Bob Bigelow is one of the foremost youth sports speakers in the country. He advocates fully meeting the needs of children as the top priority in youth sports programs, and he provides new approaches for positive change in youth sports. Bob is a former NBA first-round draft choice and played four years for the Kansas City Kings, Boston Celtics, and San Diego Clippers. He played collegiately at the University of Pennsylvania for Hall of Fame Coach Chuck Daly. Bob has devoted thousands of hours researching and lecturing about organized youth sports and its effects on children – and adults. Since 1993, he has conducted over 2500 talks and clinics worldwide. Bob's also been selected as one of the "100 Most Influential Sports Educators" by the Institute for International Sport at the University of Rhode Island. With the publication of his book, *Just Let the Kids Play*, adults throughout the country are reflecting on how they can give youth sports fun back to the children.

******

Toni: We're going to be talking about kids and sports, and particularly: Have we gone off the deep end? Is it healthy or is it overkill?

Bob, in your book you talk about some alarming stuff going on, with officials for youth sports being offered default insurance, kids being robbed of their childhood, an increase in injuries, and half of the kids saying, "My coach and my parents are yelling at me about sports and I'm upset about it."

So there are some crazy things going on in youth sports…

Bob: There has been now for several decades, if not generations. I do want to emphasize before we start that there are certainly challenges and problems out there as you just cited; but despite the fact that we could do a lot better in this world of organized youth sports, there are many people doing some very good things.

Toni: Yes, there are lots of benefits. Perhaps the biggest one is trying to fight the huge obesity problem with kids in our country. Getting exercise, having fun, and learning about team spirit and discipline are all great benefits that sports offer, but somewhere along the way we've gone overboard with youth sports.

Every parent is concerned about safety, so tell us what you learned from your research when you consulted with the American Pediatric Association and other heavy hitters about injuries from youth sports. Have they increased?

Bob: I don't know the statistics, but children are starting sports earlier, and oftentimes they play the same sport more and more, so they play it a bigger percentage of their year. By the early teenage years or even preteen years, they may already have "overuse injuries."

The most alarming, and the one that people have known about for decades, is called "Little League elbow." The baseball player throws too much and throws too many curves and throws too many pitches. Little League officials in Pennsylvania and some other youth baseball organizations have been trying to get after this the last five years or so and have made some progress. This is probably the most well-known injury because Little League baseball is one of the oldest brand names in youth sports in this country.

Soccer, hockey, basketball, or any sport played all year long certainly has the chance of putting kids at risk for injuries at a young age. The American Pediatrics group advises that every kid should take at least three or four months off per year from a sport.

Toni: Is that regardless of the child's age, Bob?

Bob: I don't remember the cutoff. My rule of thumb, based on my own experience and talking to a gazillion people, is that a kid shouldn't play *less than two sports* until they're 16 or 17 years old or in their junior year in high school. I like kids to play other sports even throughout high school. One of the fast-disappearing species in this country has been the three-sport high school athlete.

About the time kids are 14 or 15 years old, they think they should drop down to one sport to get a college scholarship, but that's a myth.

Toni: So the takeaway is that kids' bodies were not built for the repetitive motion of one year-round sport while they're growing, because of the toll it takes on their growing body.

Bob: Do you want to know a secret, Toni? Adult bodies aren't built for it either.

Toni: So even if you're a professional athlete, you take some time off.

Bob: Right. They don't play 365 days a year. They can't. It's a given that you have to take active rest, or time away from your sport. So, even the greatest athletes in the world, the ones that are getting paid 10-20-30 million dollars a year, are taking time off.

So why should we expect a 13-year-old to play 12 months a year?

Toni: What a great point. They need a break.

Bob: I tell people this all the time and they say, "How are they going to get better than the other 13-year-olds who are playing 365 days a year?" But that is the common adult interference and the myth that grows up around this stuff.

Toni: I know 13-year-olds who have specialized in one sport and played it year-round, and they're dropping out of the sport after playing hundreds of games because they're burned out.

Are you seeing this across the country?

Bob: Have you ever heard of "the seven-year itch" when it comes to marriage?

Toni: Of course.

Bob: This is the "the seven-year child sports itch." These kids probably started playing around the age of six and guess what? By 13, and by the time the hormones are flying, the good old sport doesn't hold quite as much allure in their lives as it once did.

Toni: Right. Playing sports where you have to travel takes a lot of time and discipline, on top of homework. And for teen girls, socializing takes more prominence.

Bob: Well the code in our country, and the myth, is "more, more, more, younger, younger, younger, better, better, better."

It's big in organized youth sports. The idea is that the more you play the sport and the younger you start, the better you'll be later on. It's called "quantity." But it's also the land of diminishing returns, which is a chemical property.

Toni: Because they burn out and their bodies can't keep up?

Bob: Because at some point the wonderful four-letter word called "play" becomes the dirty four-letter word called "work."

When you're working at playing, that's when the staleness comes: just another day at the hockey rink, just another day at the soccer field, just another day at the basketball court. After five years, seven years, 10 years, all of a sudden the teenage mind says, "Is this all there is? I've already been to every darn rink in Minnesota. How many more rinks do I need to be in?"

Toni: I can just hear the parents saying: "Bob, if they don't start playing when they're four or five or six … they're not going to be able to play varsity sports in high school, and they won't be able to get a college scholarship, because they won't be good enough." What do you think?

Bob: Very simply, the median-size 10-year-old in America is 4 feet 7 inches and weighs about 80 pounds. Do you mean to tell me that because your 4-foot-7-inch, 80-pound kid has now played 3,642 soccer, hockey, or basketball games, we can now predict if that child will get a college scholarship at age 18?

There is no human being in the history of this earth that has been able to look at the athletic ability of a 10-year-old and know what it's going to be at 18 years old. Pre-pubescent athletic ability is meaningless when it comes to predicting post-pubescent athletic ability.

Toni: No kidding? What if the coach tells you that you have a little "superstar?"

Bob: No one's been able to predict this … ever.

Someone's gonna be the superstar. Someone's always gonna be the best out of the group. All you're measuring is the current relative athletic ability of 10-year-olds, and the kids who are the best *aren't* the best, they're the least worst.

Toni: Are there any sports that are more injury-prone than others?

Bob: The two most notorious in this part of the world are football and ice hockey. Concussions are a very big issue on the nation's radar screen.

Basketball tends to be more sprains and contusions. Girls in soccer and basketball get some torn ACLs, knee joints. The real problem there is over-use and body design.

Now there's lacrosse, which is a very fast-growing sport in our country, and it tends to lead to collisions. Whenever you get collisions in sports, you're going to have more serious damage to bodies.

Toni: What are some of the solutions for these physical injuries?

Bob: Well, there's a counter-intuitive argument. You'd think that the more you end up padding the kids, the fewer collisions. But some folks are saying that better helmets lead to more fierce collisions.

Some people are asking, "Do we really need helmets? Would there be fewer collisions or less of an impact without helmets?"

Two of the larger sports around the rest of the world are rugby and Australian-ruled football, where there are a lot of collisions. But they don't wear helmets and they have fewer concussions per capita than the athletes here in sports that do wear helmets, like ice hockey and grid-iron football.

Toni: So, perhaps helmets give a false sense of protection and people think they can be more aggressive?

Bob: Yes. When the NHL went to "mandatory helmets" about 20 years ago, they worried about the collisions getting more violent.

Toni: Can we prevent some injuries by discouraging year-round sports?

Bob: I like multi-sport kids for several different reasons: different muscles, different coaches, different kids you play with, different activities, different styles of sports.

Especially before high school, kids should play as many sports as they can, without driving their family nuts by being too busy.

For kids in elementary school, I recommend keeping any sport to three times a week: a game and two practices. Of course, that goes against the grain of the way sports work in this country.

Toni: Are parents around the country demanding less practice time and game time, or is it quite the opposite?

Bob: There has been a bit of a backlash. Barbara Carlson and Bill Doherty started an organization in the Twin Cities that tries to rein sports in, and one suburb put together a plan.

Richwood, New Jersey, a go-go suburb of New York City, tried to dial back all organized kid activities, even homework, so families could have more time.

There have been several religious leaders trying to preserve Sunday morning from six in the morning until 12 for worship, and therefore restricting sports activities during that time. So, it hasn't been a huge groundswell, Toni, but there has been *some* backlash out there.

Toni: How did we get into the mess of trying to turn kids into mini-adult players and taking the fun out of playing sports?

Bob: In short, in the last 30 to 35 years there have been two major sociological changes:

Number 1: Mothers working outside the home

Number 2: Divorced, single-parent families

Because of those two cultural changes, we want to know what to do with our kids during those non-school hours. Into the void of those after-school hours have crept organized youth activities, particularly sports.

I'm in my 50s and I grew up in a neighborhood where every mom was home all the time. I was just outside playing all the time, but that has now changed drastically.

Toni: I think that our culture has gotten incredibly competitive. It doesn't just apply to sports. There's a push to get your kids into the right preschool, into the right high school, and then into the Ivy League.

Bob: Like playing Mozart music to a baby in the womb.

I asked my parents who are now in their 80s: "Did you guys compete through your kids?" And my dad answered, "It probably had more to do with material possessions, such as bigger houses and bigger cars, back then. Whereas, with baby boomers, the competition seems to be around the activities and accomplishments of their children."

And of course, what has been more perfect than sports? You get to compare and contrast your kid against someone else's kid in this whole world of sports.

Toni: I definitely see that. I was at a New Year's Eve party in St. Paul, Minnesota, and a mom told me her 13-year-old was on an "elite" soccer team and the team competed across the country.

I asked her, "Aren't there good enough soccer teams in the Midwest they could play?" and she said, "No, there aren't. We have to go to California and other places to find players competitive enough to beat our team."

My mouth dropped to the floor.

Bob: I have one real solution to offer. If you go to a party and you run into someone who starts talking about their kids and their accomplishments, say, "See ya later."

Toni: At first I felt a little insecure because my oldest daughter wasn't on any "elite" teams. And then I did a brain realignment. Is my daughter kind? Is she generous? Does she do volunteer work?

I thought about how people never talk about the inner qualities. No one says, "My daughter logged in 12 hours volunteering at Feed My Starving Children last month."

I think we need to readjust our values.

Let's give parents more ideas. Could they put their kids in a recreational league at the community center or place of worship, so they can still play sports but also have fun, and maybe not break as many bones?

Bob: I like that.

I like the soup kitchen approach, though. It's great that kids give back by volunteering, but especially for young potential divas in the athletics hierarchy whose parents think they're the greatest thing since sliced bread. Get them involved in some volunteer work and they might develop a little bit of respect that they don't have now.

Toni: How can we make sports more fun for kids again?

Bob: We can do a couple of things. I would say that 98 percent of the baseball that I played as a kid was pick-up baseball with other kids on the field and no adults around.

To give the fun back to the kids, we need to eliminate the adult's ego. You can set up "supervised pick-up," or as I like to say, "organizing the time and un-organizing the process."

Get the kids on the field or in the gym or in the ice rink, and then let them pick sides and throw out the puck. The only reason the adults need to be there is to make sure the kids don't get hurt, just like a teacher does at school for recess. Leave the kids to their own devices to modify the rules of the game and all that jazz.

That's what I call giving the game back to the children. The adults have a supervisory role, but they don't have any chance to interfere, and that's something I've been advocating for years.

Of course, that's hard for adults to let go of, because they feel they add value by being on top of things. I tell them there's some value to be added, but everything in moderation.

Toni: What red flags will help a parent figure out if they've crossed a line where their ego is too involved in their child's sport?

Bob: When you start talking about your kids' athletic accomplishments one minute into the conversation with a stranger at the New Year's party, you know that you've gotten too involved.

That's an easy one when conversations with strangers often times revolve around your kid's activities and "accomplishments." That's when you have to look in the mirror and say, "My god."

A friend of mine calls it ABP, "achievement by proxy." You're proud of your kids' achievements, however real or imagined they are, but you may be living too closely to them. You may be defining yourself as a parent by your child's accomplishments.

Toni: Sometimes a parent can be a "bad fan" sitting on the sidelines, directing their child, or worse yet, yelling at their child. That's another red flag, right?

Bob: Yes, when you find yourself over-extending your voice during your child's games, that's a red flag. When I coach, I tell the parents, "You've got two choices. Either leave and go read a book in the lobby, or shut up."

Toni: Yelling at the ref would be another no-no.

Bob: I ask people, "Are thousands of dollars riding on this athletic event?" and of course the answer is "no." If the Boston Celtics are playing the New York Knicks in basketball, yes, thousands of dollars are riding on that event. But when you're talking about your child's hockey game or basketball game or soccer game played at age 12, there's no money riding on the event.

Toni: We have to give coaches a lot of credit. It's usually a volunteer position and they're spending so much of their time involved in the sport. So, let's give a huge "hurrah" for all those parents who have volunteered over the years.

There are some coaches, however, who yell at kids and degrade them. What can we do to improve the coaching experience for kids who may end up with emotional injuries?

Bob: My rule of thumb is that 90 percent of all coaches at the youth level in this country are not properly qualified or credentialed.

I always ask coaches: "Are you going to coach the process or are you going to coach the outcome?"

The outcome is the final score. The process involves a kid wanting to play the game and loving it during the course of a season or more.

No matter how good their intentions are, coaches oftentimes coach the final score, which to them is the outcome of their ability to coach. "We won; I must be a good coach. We lost; I must be a bad coach."

If you're coaching the score as a youth coach, you're automatically going down the wrong road. Problems often ensue very quickly.

Toni: So we need better training for coaches?

Bob: We need more training and better training. It's out there, but often I'm not impressed with the training.

In my sport of basketball, I try to eliminate the adult coaching ego. Instead of playing five-on-five full-court basketball, I'll play three-on-three half-court. There are two games going on at once with two different baskets and they still keep score. I want adults to be facilitators and teachers and help the kids grow and develop, rather than getting caught up in the score.

Toni: So the child gets a lot more ball contact in three-on-three?

Bob: Yes, and even beyond that, the adults don't take the game as seriously. Therefore, they'll spend more emotional energy making sure the kids are being helped.

It's no different than what an elementary school math teacher does with 4th graders.

Toni: The elementary school teacher has 20 kids, and she's in charge of making sure that by the end of the year they all progress into 5th grade math. She has to give all the students time and attention.

Bob: Yes. They all need nurturing and help, but in different ways. You won't just let one kid get left behind, which brings us to another point. Typically, kids are grouped together by age on a team, yet kids mature at all sorts of different levels.

Toni: Do you think it's best to group them by age, even if they're at different abilities?

Bob: Yes, even though physically, cognitively, socially and emotionally there can be two, three, four, or five years difference, especially as you get to pre-teens and teenagers. Socially and emotionally, your 13-year-old will generally be on the same page with other 13-year-olds, whether they're six feet tall or four feet tall.

When kids are better players than their peer group and get moved up a couple of age groups, you run into challenges. Let's say a nine-year-old is playing with 11- and 12-year-olds. They may be physically talented enough to compete against an 11- and 12-year-old, but they're still a nine-year-old socially and emotionally.

Toni: Let's say a parent wants to see some changes. Do they work within the system that's there? How can they scale back and make it more fun for the kids?

Bob: It's a multi-layered question.

First, look at your own family. If you have three kids and they're involved in a number of activities, you have to decide how much running around you want to do. It's going to be an internal discussion, generally between parents first and then with the kids.

Then you decide on your parameters. How much per year? How much per season? How much per week do we do?

How does that match up with what your community youth sports club, traveling club or elite club is doing?

Then you have to ask yourself, "Do we really fit into this?" and "Are we strong enough from an ego standpoint not to keep up with the 'Joneses'?"

Toni: That's a big challenge. I had to examine my values at the New Year's Eve party when the mom told me about her daughter's "elite" team.

Bob: I hate using that term for kids' teams.

You don't want to raise a generation of divas, but too often we do. I feel bad for those kids, because they don't know any better. "My parents think I'm the greatest thing since sliced bread and so do my coaches." So what is the child supposed to think? They're 12 years old and they don't have any perspective on this.

Toni: I just had a flash in my head of Tiger Woods, and we saw how that perception ended up in his demise.

Was there anything else you wanted to say about different maturity levels?

Bob: I just want adults to know that there's a potential of six years maturational and developmental differences for kids who are the same age.

So you can have a 13-year-old boy who looks 16 and a 13-year-old boy who looks 10. Even though they're the same age, they are six years apart developmentally. The kid who looks 16 is probably going to be better in athletics at age 13 than the kid who looks 10, because the kid who looks 10 is a later bloomer and isn't going to get any sort of athletic ability for another few years.

This is why I'm constantly cautioning people to be very careful about making athletic evaluations of these young kids, because it could all change, very quickly or maybe not so quickly, in the next two, four, six, eight or 10 years.

Toni: If you're the kid who's lagging six years behind the "star" of the team, you're probably getting the perception that you're not a good player, right? Is that kid more likely to drop out because he's thinking, "Oh, I'm not that good anyway," when he's comparing himself to the superstar early developer?

Bob: Fantastic insight. Oftentimes the coach who wants to win games won't even recognize this and would actually be happy the kid quit so there's more playing time for his or her supposed better players.

This is one of the biggest challenges that I have, and the biggest indictment I make in the organized sports system in the United States. It legislates against later-blooming kids. Millions of kids are later bloomers, but we'll never know what might have happened to their athletic talent, because by the time they get to that point, they've been marginalized and they've eliminated themselves from the system.

Toni: That makes me sad.

Bob: It is sad. It's something that shouldn't happen, but unfortunately because of the "more, more, younger, younger, better, better" syndrome, this goes on all the time.

Toni: What do you say to your kid if they say, "I'm not any good. I just want to quit."

Bob: It depends on the age and I've had this argument with people.

In the early elementary school years, if your child doesn't like the sport, let them stop. It may be the coach, it may be the other kids, or it may just be because he or she doesn't want to play soccer, and that's fine.

Parents will say, "If they quit this, they'll quit everything else in their lives." And I tell them, "They're seven years old. Gimme a break."

By grades four, five or six, if your child commits to a season, then the child should stay.

Toni Schutta

The whole razzmatazz of running around a soccer field can be pretty daunting for a six- or seven-year-old. There are lots of kids, there's a ball, people are running around, and it's just too much. So I've often suggested to parents: if your kid doesn't seem to be getting in on team sports, maybe you should try an individual sport. There are certainly plenty on the American plate, like martial arts, tennis or golf.

Toni: Our neighbors have done such a good job with their teenager. She plays basketball for a church league, and she loves bowling so she bowls with a club at school. She loves both sports and has never been stressed out playing them.

Bob: Bowling is one of those great hybrid sports, because it's an individual sport but it's also a team sport. You're on a bowling team, but you're also bowling against yourself, just like golf, track and field, and swimming.

Too many people get caught up in the big four of soccer, basketball, softball, and baseball. And lacrosse will make it the big five in the next five or 10 years.

Toni: How can a parent be a good fan and be supportive of their kids in sports?

Bob: I always tell parents to ask their children at various junctures, "Do you enjoy the sport you're playing? What do you like about it? Where do you think you can improve?" Ask Socratic questions to draw them out about why they like or dislike the sport.

Then ask them every couple of months, "Why do you still like playing this sport? You've been playing since age five and now you're 11; what do you think you can do to improve? Of all the coaches you've had, who's been the best? Who do you think taught you the most and why?" Engage the child in these kinds of conversations.

See if there's another sport your child would like to try, so you give your child more opportunities.

Toni: I'm so proud of my 13-year-old. Last year she tried three new sports and one of them was diving. So there she was standing up on a diving board at a pool, with people packed in the stands, doing her pretty poor dives because she's just learning, and I thought, "Wow! That takes a lot of courage."

Bob: She's learning.

Toni: Yes and learning is the key rather than the performance. Am I improving each time? Is it fun?

Lots of great information for us to think about today, Bob. Thank you!

Contact Information:

Bob Bigelow

Mailing Address: 52 Jefferson Road, Winchester, MA 01890

Phone: 781-729-6134

Email: *bob-bigelow@comcast.net*

Website: *www.bob-bigelow.com*

Resources:

Book: *Just Let the Kids Play* (HCI Books)

Solutions to Five Scary Trends Parents Must Face

Meet the Expert:

Michele Borba, Ed.D., is an educational psychologist, former teacher and mom. She is recognized for offering research-driven advice culled from a career of working with over one million parents, educators and children. A frequent Today show contributor and recipient of the National Educator Award, Michele is the author of 22 books including her newest book *The Big Book of Parenting Solutions: 101 Answers to Your Everyday Challenges and Wildest Worries*. Other books include: *Building Moral Intelligence* and *No More Misbehavin'*. Michele is an advisory board member for Parents magazine. She also appears on Dr. Phil, The View, CNN, American Morning, and The Early Show and has been featured in numerous publications including Family Circle, Parenting, and Child.

******

Toni: You've really come up with an encyclopedia for parents. In the introduction you have a headline that says, "From June Cleaver to Desperate Housewives: how did we get into this mess?" I think it captures the shift in our culture perfectly.

You state that 60 percent of parents don't feel that they're measuring up. In fact, they're saying their parenting is far worse than that of their own mom and dad's. Why are people so critical of their parenting?

Michele: It threw me too when I saw that statistic, because first of all, the research shows that moms are doing far better than their own mothers in terms of spending more time with their kids, even though mothers don't perceive they're doing as good a job.

They're doing less housework than June Cleaver did and they're finding ways to weave in more time with the kids. So why the discrepancy?

I think one of the big reasons is that we've redefined parenting. Instead of who we are with our child, it's all about what we do, and whoever does the most or has the longest to-do list wins.

We're competitive as parents. We're greatly concerned about our own kids (out of love), but we're always watching what everybody else is doing, instead of doing what really good parenting is, and that is tailoring our parenting to our own child.

Toni: Parents still need to focus on attachment, closeness and bonding with their child rather than the busyness.

Michele: Yes. The busyness is a huge phase. I always tell parents, "Pretend you're at a family reunion 40 years from now and your child is describing your current relationship. Would you want your child to say, 'Boy, she sure drove a mean carpool'?"

Every kid says they want their parents to listen, to be present, and to spend time together as a family.

One simple solution is to always look at the color of your talker's eyes. Make that a rule in your family. If you teach your child that, he actually learns eye contact. His body language is more confident if he holds his head up. It actually makes him look less timid, and believe it or not, research shows he will then be less likely to be targeted by a bully.

But there's also another point. Kids say that if we look at them it actually tells them we're giving them the power of our presence. So, always look at the color of the talker's eyes.

Toni: That's brilliant because 90 percent of the time parents are multi-tasking when they're "listening to their kids." I don't think the child really feels heard when we're in the middle of making dinner and we're saying, "Yeah, yeah, yeah," but we're not really listening with our hearts.

Michele: Exactly. And the kid picks that up really quickly. We are geniuses at multi-tasking – let's give ourselves some credit there. But when we interview kids, they say unless we're looking at them, we aren't giving them our presence.

Now, here's another thing. Sons sometimes have a problem going face-to-face, so don't give up talking with your son if you see he's a little intimidated. Instead, sit side-by-side and it'll boost your son's listening skills. In the meantime, you can gently help him to look eye-to-eye; and if a child is really threatened, tell him to look at the bridge of your nose, right at the top of your nose.

I can't tell you how important that skill is. First, it'll get your kid a job when he goes out into the real world, because Wall Street says that they're looking for eye contact.

Second, it'll help your child use strong body language. Whether its peer pressure or bullying, the first step is that the child has to be able to use strong body language and say "no" to a peer with a strong voice.

Toni: What a great practical tip, Michele.

So, parents are spending more time with their kids, which is great; and fathers especially, when compared to fathers in the 50s and 60s, are spending more time with their kids. Yet the truth is, we're making some mistakes too. In your book you talk about *seven deadly parenting styles*. Tell us about two or three of those parenting styles.

Michele: The first one is **helicopter parenting**. That's the one where we protect our kids from every little bruise. We rush in to give them their homework, and it doesn't stop when they leave home. MBA programs continue to see mothers involved in their kids' Harvard MBA classes, and Wall Street sees the same thing. We're also finding that many kids are having a tough time coping with life because they've been dependent on their parents.

Number two is **secondary parenting**. Many of our children of this generation, which we can actually call "generation text," are so plugged in to their cell phones and video boxes and other gadgets, that if we're not careful, we allow the media to become a stronger influence in our kids' lives than their parents.

Another parenting style is called **buddy parenting**. That's where parents try to be too much of their child's friend as opposed to their parent. Being a friend can be a goal by the time your child is age 25 or 26; but when your child is school-age or a toddler, they need a parent who is willing to say "no." All of the research says that when a parent says "no," that kid is less likely to get into drugs or teen pregnancy, and that child will have higher self-esteem and lower rates of depression.

Toni: So, we need to be able to let our kids fail.

Michele: Yes, you let them fail gracefully, in increments that they can handle. You can start at a very early age. Don't be so worried about your child always losing at Candy Land. The key in life, when you're young, is to be able to learn how to lose and win gracefully. Both of them are arts.

When kids do fail, there are certain responses you can give. There's a whole section in *The Big Book of Parenting Solutions* on the best ways to say, "Hey, you failed." Instead, talk about mistakes and ask, "What did you learn? What will you do differently next time? When I made that mistake here's what I did…"

Kids with high self-esteem actually come up with a nickname for a mistake, like a "glitch" or a "boo-boo." The key is to allow them to figure out what to do instead the next time.

Toni: We really need to get over our own perfectionism – the idea of being a "super mom" or "super dad" and the idea of creating this "super kid," because that perfectionism is damaging to kids, isn't it?

Michele: Yes. What we're seeing is a rise in perfectionism amongst our children, particularly among girls, and at younger and younger ages, and that's a scary scenario.

What's the problem with that? A rise in depression, a rise in eating disorders – and by the way, starting at age six now. Depression is now being diagnosed in three-year-olds.

Yes, there's some genetics involved, but we also know, according to Penn State studies, that parenting does matter. Expectations play a key role. We've got to make sure that our expectations are keyed to our child, and that from a very early age we don't put too much weight on our child's shoulders. We don't want our child thinking, "I'm so concerned about failing my parent." This is one of the big reasons why so many kids are developing a perfectionist standard and it's a core issue in *The Big Book of Parenting Solutions*.

Toni: I think that the most alarming statistic from your book is that 50 percent of college freshmen feel so depressed that it's difficult for them to function. This can at least partly be a result of genetics, as you mentioned, but helicopter parenting, secondary parenting and buddy parenting also contribute to our kids crumbling when they have that big responsibility of college.

Michele: One of the most scathing reports I did on the Today Show was around the holiday season when the kids were coming back from freshman year. The first semester in college is the highest point of depression, and also suicide, in a kid's life.

Which is the kid that is not going to get depressed or commit suicide? What will make the difference? It's how they're parented from three to 13, which is why the whole *Big Book of Parenting Solutions* is geared to those ages. Helping your kid learn to cope with and handle life is one of the biggest goals of a parent, and teaching them new habits or a new skill to help with change. If you're stressed, here's how to reduce your stress. If you feel pessimistic, here's how to change your thinking patterns. For each issue there is a way to switch it, with simple parenting solutions that will make a major difference in your child's life, forever.

Toni: What we should do, then, is to provide kids with the knowledge of how to problem-solve rather than always providing the answers for them.

Michele: Yes. Decision making is one of the issues in my book. Starting at age two or three, believe it or not, kids can problem-solve, or at least identify their emotion, which is the first step to solving problems.

So, the first step is to say, "Wow. You look sad." Identify the emotion. "You look frustrated. Are you frustrated?" Name the emotion for the child.

Second, ask: "What's bugging you? What's the issue? What's the problem?" That's the next step to problem-solving.

The third step is: don't give them the answer. Instead say, "Let's storm your brain for ideas. What's one thing you could do differently?" In fact, for little critters, you take their hand and it becomes a "pocket problem solver."

Your thumb is "What's bugging you? What's the problem?"

Your pointer, middle man and ring man are three things you could have done differently. The pinky finger is the one best idea from all the things that you just thought about that you can do the next time.

When they're two and three, obviously, you're going to help them through the process.

But when they're ages four through nine, that's when they learn decision making. They can learn that there's no problem so great that it can't be solved in their brain – but we're going to help them draw it out and figure it out. The big mistake is that if you always give them the answer, they'll never have the opportunity to learn the skill.

Toni: Exactly. I've definitely seen four-year-old kids who can be great problem solvers. The type of solutions kids come up with when given the opportunity is amazing.

Parents need to open that door instead of always thinking that we're the ones with all the answers. I love your five-finger method. That's going to help me remember too!

Michele: Exactly. Here's another one. When your child gets older, you can use S-T-A-N-D. I used to teach special education so everything was an acronym. Here are the five steps to solving a problem if you're a tween.

"S" is "Stop and stay cool." It's the first step to solving a problem because you can't solve a problem when you're out of control.

When you see your little three-year old getting really, really upset, say, "Use your walking feet and walk away, then take a deep breath and come back."

For older kids you tell them to take a deep breath. Now they can solve the problem.

"T" is "Tell the problem, say what's bugging you. But no put downs are allowed." If you can't say it, you can write it, but tell me what happened.

"A" is "Ask what the alternatives are." Then brainstorm. Use your fingers again. What are one, two, or three things you could have done instead?

"N" is "Narrow the choice from the ideas on your list." Get rid of anything on your list that you don't feel comfortable doing or that isn't safe.

"D" is "Decide on one solution and do it." That's your goal.

So, what you've actually done is taught conflict resolution, and you keep adding steps to it until your child leaves home.

Stop and calm down, tell the problem, identify all the alternatives, that's *brainstorming;* narrow the choices, that's *decision making;* decide on one and do it, that's the *goal setting.*

Toni: Problems occur every single day so I truly think one of the best skills you can teach your kids is to be a good problem solver.

Michele: I agree. You'll not only be helping reduce sibling problems in the house, but you won't always be the nagger or the rescuer. And we know that children who are better problem solvers are less likely to be depressed; they have higher self-esteem; and they're more optimistic in their thinking patterns.

Toni: We have a caller … welcome, Beth. What's your question?

Beth: I have two boys: a seven-year-old and a five-year-old. My seven-year-old is definitely going through a pattern of roughness; he's very jealous of his younger brother and can be downright mean and disrespectful.

I struggle with the right discipline action – how to handle the situation at the time. I've been doing time-outs, or no TV for the night, or not being allowed to participate in an activity. I've started a sticker chart to really refocus on good attention and not bad attention. I'd like some guidance.

Michele: Great question.

First of all, it's normal and this is the age it actually peaks. So, at some point it will start to decline.

Here's what you may want to consider doing, instead of the time-out or extinguishing the TV, because that's not working.

Your child, around the age of seven, needs to learn empathy toward the younger sibling. The best way to build empathy is actually doing something for the other person.

So, first of all, tell him it's not permissible to be mean. Number two: sit down with him when he's calm and not being disciplined and ask, "What are some things you can do for your younger brother if you've been mean to him?" Come up with lists. It could be doing a chore for him. It could be making his bed for him. You want the child to give back.

The whole goal is to rebuild empathy after he's been mean. You always ask, "How would you feel if that happened to you? What does the person need in order to feel better?" If they get away with it, it keeps extinguishing empathy and it becomes a habit.

Beth: Great. Thank you so much.

Toni: At our house we have a family rule that we only use kind words. If a mean word is spoken, I stop the kids dead in their tracks and say, "Was that a kind word?" They realize it wasn't, hang their head, and say, "No."

Then I use a logical consequence and ask them, "What is a kind word that you could say to your sister right now because you've hurt her feelings?" They can also make amends in another way that they choose, if that's their preference.

Michele: I love that. The other rule is called the H&H: Was that helpful or hurtful? In this house, we're only helpful. It's also a turnaround rule for any deed that's unkind. You must turn it around and make amends. What are you going to do to be kind?

Beth: Thank you.

Toni: Thanks for your call.

Okay, now I'd like to get to those **Five Scary Trends**.

Scary trend number 1 is peer pressure, the fact that kids are getting even earlier peer pressure regarding sex, drugs, cigarettes, alcohol, and stealing. Pick one or two of these that kids are most confronted with and give us tools to help them say "no" to those risky behaviors.

Michele: First, a parent has to figure out what is the hotspot problem. For fifth grade, it's actually shoplifting. A peer tells them to do it and one out of two kids are being pushed into it. The first drink by the way, is now around fourth grade. Where is it? In your own home when you're not there and a peer is pushing the other kid. Sex, the first sexual encounter, is in your home on a weekend when you're not there.

So teaching your child how to say "no" is really important. First, review the rules so that your child really knows your values and your house rules.

Number two is to review strong eye contact and strong body language. As I mentioned, practice using eye contact at age three, because I don't care what you say to your peer, if you say "no" and your head is down, it doesn't work.

So practice strong, confident body language, and rehearse it.

Number three is practice a firm voice. And by the way, each one of these strategies may take *20 days* to learn.

Number four. The research says that in the here and now kids get sucked in by peer pressure and they give in to the temptation.

So, you actually practice comeback lines for each of the issues. For instance, a peer wants to get you to smoke. Let's come up with an answer you can use. What do you think you want to say? You can come up with an excuse like, "My parents would kill me." Or "My grandpa died from cancer and I don't want to. No thank you."

Also rehearse it with your child a number of times, like a broken record; because research says the more you say it, the more it actually kicks in. The child gets a boost in confidence, actually begins to believe it, and becomes more and more assertive.

Toni: So, rehearse as much as you can with your child so it becomes an automatic memory when they're actually in a tempting situation with a peer.

Michele: Right. Let's look at how critical this is. In a survey of 46,000 teens in the Boys and Girls Club of America, teens said that their number one hot button issue on a day-to-day level was peer pressure, but they also said that just saying "no" doesn't work in the moment.

Comeback lines are important, but the key is to rehearse them *over and over again* until your child finally feels comfortable using them without you.

One other critical point is to have a cell phone code, so that if worse comes to worse, and your kid is in a situation that he just can't get out of, he can just push 111 real quick on his cell phone, and that means, "Stop everything. Go pick up your kid because he's now in a situation where that comeback line doesn't work and he needs help."

Toni: Great information. **Scary trend number two is stress,** the fact that kids of this generation are more stressed than other generations. What are the symptoms?

Michele: The symptoms are different for little kids as opposed to bigger kids. For little kids, start looking at changes in sleep habits, eating habits or homework habits. Nightmares start to come into the picture, clinginess returns, or your child says, "I don't want to go to school."

Homework can be a key one because the inability to focus or concentrate when you're stressed is a big one.

Tweens, those kids age eight to around 12, may have sweaty palms, headaches, or reoccurring colds. Sometimes we think it's illness when in reality it's the immune system breaking down. Watch your child. Each child has their own stress sign, so figure out what the stress sign is for your child.

Toni: I had a nurse and a pediatrician on my show and they said that headaches and stomachaches are the top complaints that children have. And they said the vast majority of those stomachaches and headaches are related to mental health issues like stress, anxiety, feeling angry, feeling sad, etc. It's a pervasive problem that many parents aren't aware of.

Michele: Eighty-five percent of teens tell me they're stressed, but their parents are not aware of it. So, the first step is to know the signs of stress for your child.

The second step is to reduce the stress if you can. Sometimes you can reduce stress; sometimes you can't. For some kids, scary news programs are a trigger, so reduce the CNN news shows. If you notice that your kid is over-scheduled or feeling overwhelmed or has no down time, then cut an activity to help reduce the stress.

If you notice that he's overwhelmed because math class is killing him, make an appointment with the teacher and figure out if the math is too high a level.

Step three is to develop new habits for dealing with change. Teach your child a way to cope with the stress.

For some kids, yoga is really helpful. Many high schools are actually doing yoga classes as one of the required PE classes because it helps kids minimize stress.

Elevator breathing can be used by a school-age child. When a child starts to feel stress or tension, they can pretend they're on the 26th floor of a big building. They take a deep slow breath, push the button for the ground floor, and as the buttons light up, their stress is going to slowly fade away.

Toni: Great tips to share with kids, Michele. So now we have **scary trend number three, which is self-centeredness**. In your book, you say that we have turned kids into narcissists. Kids have always been self-centered. Are today's kids any worse than other generations?

Michele: Good question. First, expect your toddler or preschooler to be egocentric. He's supposed to be. He's trying to make sense of the world. Your goal is to stretch him from "me" to "we." But here's what we know about narcissism. University of San Diego studies have been tracking narcissism in incoming freshman for the last 25 years. The research shows that, per every five years, narcissistic behavior patterns are going up with college freshman.

Instead of the kids going from "me" to "we" as they age, the kids get locked in the "me" and everything revolves around them.

At the same time, Penn State studies tell us that depression is going up and self-esteem is going down. So you're not doing your kids any favor if you allow them to always focus on themselves.

Toni: How can we identify if our child is too "narcissistic?"

Michele: I'm not concerned about the little critter, but around school-age the number one sign is: "Does everything focus around me?"

Number two is: How well can your child handle the glorious word "no?" If he can't handle "no," then that's actually a sign of narcissism because he doesn't have the boundaries.

Three is "give me." He always wants more.

Four: Is he never really satisfied?

And five: Is he really thinking about the other kids, or is he more concerned about how everything will play out around himself?

Toni: If we think we have a problem with our child, how can we turn it around?

Michele: First, flip through *The Big Book of Parenting Solutions*, look at the signs, and see if you have one of those critters. If you do, pat yourself on the back because you've admitted it.

Number two: Start switching your response. Very often our kids have become self-centered because we do everything for them, but if you start to realize your child is always focusing on "me" instead of "we," then start saying "no" and mean it.

The average child whines nine times and we give in. They know which buttons to push. Know your own boundaries and say, "enough is enough." For your non-negotiables, say "no" and mean it the first time.

Number three: Start finding opportunities for your child to give to others. The simplest way to do this is to start modeling that yourself. Kids are copycats. They come with video camcorders; they are watching your behavior. Maybe you bake cookies for the lady next door because she's really down and you deliver them to her.

As a family, start expecting kindness in your child. There's a glorious rule that's called "the two praise rule." From the time your child is age three, you can start using it, and it only takes you 10 seconds. Every time you walk out of the house you're going to say or do two kind things for somebody. Then at the dinner table, let's find out what you said and how it worked.

My girlfriend did that. She has the three kindest daughters you could possibly imagine and it took her 10 seconds a day. She did it for 20 years, reinforcing it over and over again. She stretched their "me" to "we."

Toni: I love that idea. I'm going to start doing that!

Michele: The goal of *The Big Book of Parenting Solutions* was to compile dozens of the simplest things parents can do, but you only choose one thing. It worked for my friend because she stuck to it 10 seconds a day for 20 years.

Toni: Exactly. Don't take on too much. Prioritize your goals as a parent; pick a strategy and stick to it until you feel success. Then move on to the next goal.

Okay. **Scary trend number four is depression.** You state that one in 12 teens is depressed. That's an astounding number.

Michele: It's so astounding that it gives me goose bumps. The greatest increase of depression is among tween-age girls. Two years ago it was a 114 percent increase in one year. It is at such a high level for both girls and boys that the government is now suggesting that medical practitioners should routinely screen every child for depression.

Toni: Please define the difference between sadness and "depression" so everyone is on the same page. What's the line between the two?

Michele: The line is that everybody is going to be sad. You and I may be sad, and it's fine to be sad, but you can zap your way out of it. I use the *TOO index*. First you figure out your child's natural, normal behavior and then use the TOO index against that child's normal.

Here's when to worry about depression. Number one: Is the sadness lasting TOO long? If it's every day for at least two weeks, that's an immediate red flag; pick up the phone.

Number two: It's impacting TOO many other areas in the child's life. She can be sad, but her girlfriend comes over and she jumps up and goes, "Let's go hang out." She can be sad, but it doesn't mean she's going to pull away from all those other things she loves like her soccer team. So that's good; it shows that her sadness isn't impacting her whole life.

Number three is that you begin to see that the sadness is TOO intense.

The sadness could be affecting the child on the inside, or it could be starting on the outside – for example, if the child is lashing out and becoming angry or irritable.

Any one of those three things can be a sign that something's going on – maybe it's not depression; maybe it's bullying, maybe it's stress, maybe the school isn't working out for your child – but it's always a sign that something's going on and you need to look into it further and get help.

Toni: Earlier we talked about kids feeling like they're not measuring up to their parents' expectations, and about perfectionism and over-scheduling and excess pressure on kids. Are these factors contributing to the rise in depression?

Michele: The American Academy of Pediatrics would say "yes" and I agree with them 150 percent.

It appears that some children have a certain amount of genetic or biological predisposition to depression. So, they're more likely to be depressed than others right off the top, but experiences also matter. So, if you already have that predisposition, and then you're loaded with stress, or loaded with expectations, or there's a traumatic experience in your life, you're more likely to get depressed.

We also know that we're not intervening soon enough. The University of Washington is clear on this one. If you can catch the first episode of depression and get the right treatment early on, your child is far less likely to have a second episode or a third episode, which is so common with depression. It's not just hormones kicking in or something your kid is going to walk his way out of.

Toni: Exactly. So Michele, let's talk about solutions if parents sense their child might be depressed.

Michele: Number one is to get some other perspective. If you sense it, talk to a couple of other people who really care about your child deeply and say, "Are you seeing the same thing?"

Number two is: I wouldn't wait. I would immediately pick up the phone and talk to a pediatrician, and if your pediatrician is saying, "No. I don't see it," then go to somebody else. I think the two words I hear most from parents are, "if only."

So the bottom line about depression, if you really see it as depression, is that you're not going to solve it by saying, "Let's talk about happy thoughts." You need to get some really good counseling.

Toni: So start with your pediatrician, but really try to find a counselor or therapist who's trained to help kids turn depression around.

Michele: Yes. The best place to go to is a university that has a medical center involved, because they've got great psychiatrists there. Ideally, go to a child or adolescent psychiatrist. They are trained, and child depression or adolescent depression is far different than adult depression. That person needs to know how to address your child at that age.

Toni: I totally agree. Sadly, there's a shortage of mental health providers for children, so parents are probably going to find a waiting list, aren't they?

Michele: Yes, and that means that you're going to have to be the advocate. You're going to have to be the one that sits on that phone and just hits speed dial over and over again until you do get the help you need. Unfortunately, in the mental health industry you will wait, but the longer you wait the more severe the depression can get.

Toni: Maybe you can ask to be put on a waiting list or on a cancellation list.

Michele: Yes.

Toni: Let's talk about **scary trend number five, which is materialism**. Does this boil down to parents giving kids too much stuff and not requiring that they work hard to get it?

Michele: Yes it does. The other fascinating thing is that, regardless of the fact that there's a recession, we're still continuing to see a rise in kids' materialism, which means they're putting even more emphasis on what I have as opposed to who I am.

The other scary thing is that two out of three mothers admit that their three-year-olds are already calling things by a brand name. As opposed to I want a hamburger, I want a McDonald's. Not I want tennis shoes, but I want Adidas. You can see it's starting at a very, very young age.

Of course we're concerned about our child's financial literacy, but the biggest reason why you want to turn this trend around is that you're not doing your child any favor. The materialistic child clearly is less appreciative of what he has. The more gratitude a child has, the more likely he is to feel that happy quotient, and the less likely he is to feel depressed. And actually, the less materialistic the child, the higher his self-esteem; that's what the research tells us.

The next time your kid wants something, all you have to do is say "no." When the kid has a fit, say, "Honey, I'm worried about your self-esteem. This is going to make you happier." They'll roll their eyes, but really we need to pay attention to what the research is saying.

The University of Minnesota has some of the best research I've seen on how to turn materialism around. They took tweens (the age before you get to be a teen – and that's when materialism peaks) to a camp.

They figured out all kinds of ways to reduce materialism. They discovered that the single, fastest way to turn it around was to start complimenting the child for internal traits that had been earned, like "You're so kind" or "You're so respectful." The more that the praise was earned, and the more the focus was internal, the more the materialism of the child went down and the more the self-esteem went up.

Toni: I interviewed a psychologist for an article about body image, and she said that dads, in particular, play a really important role for girls when it comes to complimenting their daughters.

She suggested that parents never tell their daughter, "You look so beautiful today." Instead, compliment her on her internal traits. Our words are so powerful, and we have to be conscious of what words we say every day to counteract all of those materialistic messages they're receiving. Even three-year-olds have seen over a million commercials already.

Michele: Media literacy is another important topic. Push the remote when the commercial comes on, because the research from the University of Minnesota is also clear on this. The more commercial TV that the child watches, the more materialistic the child will be.

As the kid gets older, push the remote and say, "What are they selling?" "What do they really want?" "What's the real end-product from that particular company?" When kids start to see that the companies don't care about the kid and that they're just trying to make money for themselves, it actually starts to reduce materialism.

Toni: There's also a great book by researchers at the University of Minnesota called *How Much Is Enough*? (*See Chapter 4 for an interview with Jean Illsley Clarke.*) The authors remind parents to give their kid chores.

Michele: I love chores. The University of Minnesota research is great: the more chores the child does, the more responsible the child will be.

The fascinating thing about all of this is, as I was writing *The Big Book of Parenting Solutions,* I found thousands of articles on late-breaking child development research. Some of it basically said that June Cleaver was exactly right. We know that regular family meals, for instance, help to reduce eating disorders, boost grades and create the happy factor.

I want to get back to a parent's daily word choices too.

Columbia University clearly stated, "Don't praise your kid for being smart, because when you praise your child for being smart it actually reduces motivation." The child begins to think it's all a matter of IQ. If you emphasize effort over being smart, it stretches the motivation and perseverance and actually helps the child learn to be empowered. They have the choice and the control regarding how far their grades are going to go.

Toni: You can check out my interview with Carol Dweck too. She's one of the researchers who discovered this phenomenon. *(See Chapter 9: Help Your Child Develop a Mindset for Success.)*

Michele: I love her.

Toni: We also have to be so careful about labeling our "gifted" and "talented" kids. The sad fact is that so many of those kids don't live up to their potential. I think labeling them may be part of the reason.

Michele: I used to teach gifted and talented kids, and I did a report for the Today Show on how to raise a really talented kid who is gifted. A University of Chicago study found that the labeling doesn't help the child and they don't appreciate it. A Columbia University study says you need to *teach* kids the process of learning.

The fascinating thing about really talented kids who succeed is that it doesn't really have anything to do with IQ; that's a very low correlation to success. One of the highest correlations to success, according to studies from Stanford, is the child who has *the ability to wait.*

Most kids have short attention spans, but what they discovered is that it's not just the impulse control that matters; it's the mother or dad who taught the four-year-old what to do so he could wait. "Stand there just a minute and sing the birthday song five times" or "Count your fingers upside down" or "Hop on your foot five times." Then he can do it any other time he needs to wait; it actually stretches the time. It's some of the best stuff I've seen in child development.

Toni: Isn't that great? I had a friend with four kids and she would make sure that her kids had to experience waiting every single day. We all rolled our eyes at the time, but Martha was way ahead of the curve!

Michele: I've never seen anything like this study. It's absolutely incredible because they look at four-year-old kids who were told, "Do you want to eat the marshmallow now?" or "If you can wait, I'll give you two marsh-mallows later." The researchers followed the kids and 15 years later found that the kids who immediately ate the marshmallow had SAT scores that were far lower than kids who could wait for the marshmallow and get two marshmallows later on. They're now following these same kids into their 40s and giving them MRI's. They're discovering that the kids who could wait and not eat the marshmallow at age four are now far more successful and happier in the real world.

There are lots of little ways a parent can do this. If your child is interrupt-ing you when you're on the phone, don't give in. Tell them what to do for three seconds to wait. Or instead of immediately giving in to opening presents right away, say, "No, you have to wait until after dinner to open the presents." All those are opportunities.

Toni: Michele, you've been a fabulous guest.

Contact Information:

Michele Borba:

Website: *www.micheleborba.com* (To find out more about Dr. Borba, her speaking topics, and media appearances, read her blog, and contact her for an appearance.)

Resources:

Michele has written 22 books. Here are the latest parenting books, all published by Jossey-Bass:

The Big Book of Parenting Solutions: 101 Answers to Your Everyday Challenges and Wildest Worries

Nobody Likes Me, Everybody Hates Me!: The Top 25 Friendship Problems and How to Solve Them

No More Misbehavin': 38 Difficult Behaviors and How to Stop Them

Don't Give Me That Attitude: 24 Rude, Selfish, Insensitive Things Kids Do and How to Stop Them

12 Simple Secrets Real Moms Know: Getting Back to Basics and Raising Happy Kids

Building Moral Intelligence: The Seven Essential Virtues That Teach Kids to Do the Right Thing

Help Your Child Develop a Mindset for Success

Meet the Experts:

Carol Dweck, Ph.D., is one of the world's leading researchers in the field of motivation and is the Lewis and Virginia Eaton Professor of Psychology at Stanford. Her research highlights the critical role of mindset in students' achievement and shows how praise for intelligence or talent can undermine motivation and learning. She's also held professorships at Columbia and Harvard Universities and lectures to groups worldwide. She's won the Klingenstein Award for Leadership in Education, the E.L. Thorndike Career Achievement Award for research in education, the Donald Campbell Award for research in social psychology, and the American Psychological Association's Distinguished Scientific Contribution Award, the highest honor in the field of psychology.

Her work has been featured in many major news publications; and her widely acclaimed bestselling book *Mindset: The New Psychology of Success* (published by Random House) has been translated into 18 languages.

Kristin Boileau, mother of three boys, is a school counselor in her 10th year at Osceola Elementary School. Kristin plays an active role in the social emotional development of children and strives to help students find a purpose in learning. She is active in her local PTA as a 10-year member, including three years as an officer. She is also very active in her community and believes that children's social emotional development is critically important to their academic success.

******

Toni: The current topic is "Help Your Child Develop a Mindset for Success" and the information we are sharing will help you raise a confident, successful child. I've invited two guests: Kristin Boileau, a school counselor in Osceola, Wisconsin, and Carol Dweck, one of the world's leading researchers in the field of motivation.

Carol, you've been doing research for decades and you've studied what factors contribute to a child's achievement and success. Your research has uncovered a "fixed mindset" and a "growth mindset," and it's the growth mindset that is critical to a person's success. First, define a fixed mindset for us.

Carol: The fixed mindset is when children believe their abilities and their talents are just fixed traits, something that they have a certain amount of and that is carved in stone. When they believe their traits are fixed, they become afraid of taking on challenges or making mistakes because they want to look smart. They don't want to look like they have deficiencies.

Toni: So with a fixed mindset they fear challenge and they feel that their innate qualities like intelligence and character won't change or grow over time?

Carol: Exactly. They think that their abilities, their talents, their character traits are all fixed and that they're on display when they perform. So they think they have to perform well and they worry about performing poorly.

Toni: So if I've been told that I have normal intelligence or high intelligence, or if I'm struggling in school, I have the belief that it's permanent, that I will be this way my whole life. If I'm the shy one, then I'll always be shy. So kids get stuck in these roles?

Carol: Yes. Those are the cards you've been dealt and there's nothing you can do about it. That's a fixed mindset.

Toni: It seems very limiting.

Carol: It is limiting, because even if you think you've been given a lot of intelligence, you still worry about it. When things get hard, you think, "Have I reached the limit? Maybe I'm not really as smart as I want to be. I better hide those mistakes."

Toni: Is there a danger in labeling kids as "gifted" or "high potential?"

Carol: Those are fixed mindset labels. They're saying some kids have high potential and some don't. I don't think we want educators to think that some children don't have high potential. Maybe they just haven't achieved as much yet. As educators, we should be looking to unleash their potential, not to label students as not having any.

Toni: I agree, and it's also harmful for the kids that are in the "high potential" groups, correct?

Carol: Yes. In fact, when I was in sixth grade, my teacher seated us around the room in IQ order.

Even the kids who were considered the smartest, and seated in the best seats, were nervous all the time. "What if we make a mistake? What if we take another test and we aren't the smartest ones anymore?"

So it was not an environment that was conducive to learning. We didn't care about learning; we just wanted to look smart all the time.

Toni: If you got a bad grade on a test, were you moved down a couple of seats?

Carol: Yes, that happened in math. If you did poorly on some tests, you had to sit in a worse math seat.

This teacher not only believed that intelligence was fixed and represented by an IQ number; she also believed that the IQ number represented your *character*. So only the top IQ students could carry the flag in the assembly or even wash the blackboard.

Toni: I'm astounded. It sounds so shaming. I certainly hope no one does this anymore… Now let's shift the conversation to the positive. Tell us about the growth mindset.

Carol: The growth mindset is the belief that abilities and talents can be cultivated and developed through passion, hard work, and instruction. It doesn't deny that people might be different … it doesn't say that anyone could be Einstein. But the growth mindset recognizes that even Einstein wasn't Einstein before he put in years and years and years of passionate and diligent hard work.

What's so exciting is that the fields of cognitive psychology and neuroscience are supportive of the growth mindset. They're finding that the brain has so much plasticity – the ability to change and grow – throughout the lifespan. Scientists are now finding that even the basic components of intelligence can be taught.

Toni: What I love about your definition are the words "passion" and "cultivating a quest for learning." It feels so optimistic. No matter what cards you've been dealt, you can improve your intelligence. Learning becomes an adventure.

Carol: Yes. Research is showing that people that we call "geniuses," and who have made great creative contributions, weren't always the most "talented" children early on. But they dedicated themselves to developing their abilities. On the other hand, some of the kids who we call "geniuses" really fizzle out later – because they've been called "geniuses" and they don't necessarily feel they have to work hard.

I was speaking to the top athletes in Scotland and they told me that not one of them was number one as a teenager. The number ones fizzled out. They were coasting on their natural talent, but the others who were number three or four or 10 knew they had to work hard – and they became number one.

Toni: So effort and practice are the most important qualities for success.

Carol: Yes, and a passion for learning. If you think that you have "natural talent," you may think that you can just coast. More and more research is showing that people who succeed are people who apply themselves and work hard, not necessarily the people who are born with the talent. And I think that often this idea of effort or having to work hard is not valued in our culture.

Toni: I agree. In fact, Mike Mann, from the National Institute on Media and the Family, was telling me that kids are exposed to a million ads a year and that the majority of those ads are giving kids the message that life should be "easy, fun, fast, and always getting more things." It seems to me that parents are really fighting an uphill battle if they try to emphasize effort and hard work.

Carol: Yet we must emphasize them, because our children really turn to us to see what we value. We have to value effort. Recently someone from another country said to me, "In your culture 'struggle' is a bad word," and I said, "You're right." People don't come home at the end of the day and say, "Honey, I had the most fantastic struggle."

Instead, we use the word "struggle" when we've had a terrible time. Yet, what does struggle mean? It means you're working hard for something you care about. It's something you should be proud of.

I tell parents they should sit around the dinner table and say, "Who had a fabulous struggle today?" And encourage kids to talk about the struggles they've been having in the service of things that they value.

Toni: It's really a paradigm shift. I agree that the dinner table can be a prime place for communicating these messages.

I want to focus on what parents can do to cultivate a growth mindset in their children. Let's start with praise. What are we doing wrong when it comes to praising our kids and how do we need to correct that?

Carol: The self-esteem movement taught us that we could hand our children self-esteem by praising their intelligence and talent, and that we had to do this at every opportunity in order to make our kids feel great about themselves and help them achieve. It turns out this was dead wrong.

As psychologists, we had been studying resilient and vulnerable children for many years and we realized it was the vulnerable children who were always focused on their intelligence. They were worrying: "Am I smart? Am I not smart?"

We thought praising intelligence put the spotlight on intelligence. It would say to children, "I can judge intelligence from your behavior and from your performance, and this is what I value you for."

So in our research we put this idea to the test. We gave children problems to work on. After they were done, some children were praised for their intelligence, and some children were praised for their effort or their strategies. We found that praise for intelligence really harmed the children.

After they got praise, they didn't care about learning anymore. They just cared about being smart. So they wouldn't take on a challenging task. They didn't want to make mistakes, even if they would learn something from it.

Then when we gave the "intelligent" students some harder tasks to do, they crumbled. They thought they weren't smart anymore. Their earlier success had meant they were smart, but the struggle meant they weren't. So they didn't like the task; they lost their confidence, their performance plummeted, and then they lied about it. When children are in that fixed mindset where intelligence is all-important, mistakes are humiliating and they cover them up.

Toni: So the exact words of praise that the researchers used in the two groups were: "you must be smart at this" for the first group, versus "you must have worked hard on this" for the second group.

And you found that in this experiment, words of praise that focused on *effort and hard work* had a huge impact on kids, even when complete strangers said those words.

Carol: Yes. When we praised the children for their effort and their hard work, they wanted to learn. Ninety percent of them chose a really hard task that they could learn from. They didn't care about making mistakes or looking dumb. When we gave them hard problems, they thrived; and many of them said those were their favorites. They taught themselves new strategies; their performance flourished; and they told the truth about their mistakes. So they either became or remained passionate learners, and in the end they did great.

And guess what, Toni … this was an IQ test, so by the end of the study, the kids who had been praised for effort were doing better on the IQ test than the kids who had been praised for intelligence.

Toni: It's really an amazing study. By changing a few simple words of praise, so many significant differences occurred.

Let's give a concrete example. If my child scores a few goals in a soccer game, how should I praise her?

Carol: The wrong way is to say: "You're brilliant." "You're so talented." "You're a soccer star." "You're the best one on the team."

We do that sometimes. We think it will make our kids feel great, but it's not a long-term strategy. The right way is to say things like: "Wow, I saw how you were really paying attention to where everyone was." "You kept your eye on the ball." "You really committed fully and you scored those fantastic goals."

When children learn about the process, it tells them how to be successful again and also what they have to do to overcome obstacles when things go wrong.

Toni: The thing I love about this is that you can identify a process for success in the smallest task that your child is doing. If your child is working on a puzzle, you can say, "Even though this was hard, you stuck with it until you found that piece." Or "I saw how you found the corner pieces first and then you looked for the colors to match. That seemed to help you." It doesn't necessarily have to be a big accomplishment, but one that recognizes the value of effort.

Now I'd like to shift to the idea of "failure." Should we strike that word from our parenting vocabulary? And should we have another paradigm shift regarding how we communicate "failure" to our kids?

Carol: In a fixed mindset, failure is so humiliating and kids want to erase it. I think parents are going too far in excusing the mistakes kids make and the failures they have. Then kids come to believe failure is so heinous

... so humiliating, and that failure can't be spoken about.

Instead, parents should really capitalize on setbacks to teach a growth mindset. They can say, "You seem to be having some trouble with this. What are some strategies we could try?"

Or let's say your child has a disappointing grade. You could say things like: "Let's talk about what went wrong. How did you study? What could you do now? Could you join a study group? Could you learn some new study strategies? Do you need to meet with the teacher?"

So setbacks present a learning opportunity.

And yes, strike the idea of failure, but don't stop addressing the issues. So many parents now are saying, "Oh, it's the teacher's fault" or "It's the coach's fault." They think they're helping their child's self-esteem. Instead, they need to work with the child about how to improve in the future.

Toni: I totally agree. After I read your book, we started having periodic discussions at the dinner table about mistakes. I asked everyone to share a mistake that they had made and I went first.

"Mom really made a blooper today." I told them what that blooper was and asked everyone what I could have done differently.

So I'm telling them that Mom's not perfect and that they can practice problem solving by helping to figure out solutions to mistakes I've made. I really want to model that and encourage those discussions in our family.

Let's also talk about constructive criticism. How can we do that with our kids?

Carol: Constructive criticism tells kids what they need to do differently in the future, and we should not withhold that. When the child strikes out in baseball, it's not the umpire's fault. Ask, "Were you keeping your eye on the ball? Make sure to do that next time."

For homework assignments ask, "Did you read through and outline your material?" So give suggestions and strategies that teach a process that the child can use in the future to do better.

Toni: Excellent advice. I think many parents have shied away from criticism due to the influence of the self-esteem movement.

******

All right, now let's talk to **Kristin Boileau.** Kristin is a mother of three boys and she's been a school counselor for 10 years at Osceola Elementary School. She works with kids every day and she's a firm believer that a child's social and emotional development is an important factor when it comes to the child's success in school.

So Kristin, as a school counselor, you know the importance of social and emotional skills. Tell us which of these skills we should try to nurture in our children to help them in their academic development?

Kristin: There are three that are probably the most critical.

The first one is helping children to recognize and label their feelings. And at the same time parents need to teach their children empathy skills so they can recognize and label others' feelings too and know how their actions affect others' feelings.

There are several ways you can help your children recognize and label their feelings. One is to simply label your children's feelings as you see them happen. So if you see your child angry with a sibling or frustrated about their homework, label that out loud: "You seem really frustrated right now with your homework" or "You seem really angry with your brother." Label the child's feelings and also label your own feelings.

If I'm driving along and a driver really makes me mad, and my kids ask, "What's wrong, Mom?" I'll say, "I'm just really angry at that driver that pulled out in front of me." Labeling our own feelings is important, so kids can understand that feelings are normal.

I also teach children to use "I messages" to communicate feelings. The child can state the feeling, why they're feeling that way, and what they'd like at the moment. Here's an example: "I feel mad when you take my things away from me, and next time I want you to ask me first."

Get the child to state her feelings rather than just holding the feelings in, and identify steps to help her move forward.

There are so many things that you can do around the dinner table. We do a "feelings whip." One person picks a feeling, like "excited," and then we all talk about something that excited us that day.

Another important skill to teach children is problem solving, so they can explore alternate possibilities in a situation. Teach them about obstacles and how to brainstorm solutions. When brainstorming, there's really no right or wrong answers; you just come up with a whole bunch of ideas. Then when you evaluate the ideas, ask, "What might happen if I were to do that?"

We also need to help children manage their anger. When I ask children if they think anger is a normal feeling that they should have, they tell me it's not okay to be angry. But, it really is okay to be angry; anger is a normal feeling that everybody has, and children need to understand that. And they need to understand that it's what we do with our anger that's important.

We need to teach kids where their anger comes from and what to do when they experience anger. Talk to them about the choices they have. Taking deep breaths and counting are useful activities for getting rid of anger.

You can also teach kids what their "hot buttons" are, and then teach them ways to avoid those hot buttons. Parents should also be able to recognize when their own hot buttons are being pushed.

Toni: Excellent ideas, Kristin. Thank you. And I have a number of resources to share:

I have a problem-solving form that parents can use. I call it the B-E-A-R problem-solving method. *www.getparentinghelpnow.com/myfreebookresources*

I've also included a goal setting form, since breaking down goals into manageable steps is an important part of success. *www.getparentinghelpnow.com/myfreebookresources*

For parents who would like help managing their child's anger and their own, I have a parenting program called, "8 Weeks to a Peaceful, Happy Family: Dramatically Reduce Yelling, Arguing and Fighting in Your Family," available at *www.getparentinghelpnow.com/programs.*

One other topic I'd like to raise, Kristin, is negative self-talk. When you meet with children, you hear them say negative comments about themselves. How can parents identify that behavior in their own children and correct it?

Kristin: I hear a lot of negativity from kids. They may say, "I can't do it." or "I hate this; I don't want to do it." or "I'll never win; it's not fair." or "I couldn't possibly do that." or "I can't calm down."

Parents can help their children change that negativity by coaching them to shift their thinking to more positive thoughts. Instead of "I can't do it," coach your child to say, "It's okay if I make a mistake; I'm growing and learning."

If a child says, "My homework is too hard; I don't know how to do this; I can't do this," coach them to say, "I can do this problem if I keep trying."

At a sports game, if your child says, "We'll never win," coach your child to say, "It's okay that we lost as long as I know that I worked hard; I gave it my best shot."

Toni: When you hear your kids using the words "always" or "never," that should raise a red flag too, because those are thoughts that typically lead to anger or hopelessness. Using those words can also trigger a parent's anger, so we have to be careful not to react negatively.

There's another critical point I want to raise, and that is kids not taking responsibility for their own actions and blaming someone else. When we hear kids blaming other people for their own mistakes, how can we turn that around? Carol, what are your thoughts?

Carol: Oftentimes, parents are modeling that. They don't want their children to feel bad, so they put the blame on other people to spare their children's self-esteem.

Instead, parents need to make it okay for the child to make mistakes, to take a wrong turn, or to fail at something. Discuss it honestly and without judgment; this teaches the child how to be open about what went wrong. Then do problem-solving together.

Toni: You can also stop kids point blank. With my own kids, I say, "I hear you blaming other people. I'd like to hear what you can do differently next time."

A lot of times parents will say to me, "I don't know who started it." When siblings argue, it doesn't matter to me who started it. It's more important to figure out: how did it escalate and how can we solve the problem? I require that each child contribute an idea for turning the problem around.

Carol, I want to return to your work on developing a growth mindset. The beauty of your work is that adults can make changes to their mindset and apply the principles to their work or their passions. How important is it for parents to model a growth mindset?

Carol: It's incredibly important that parents model a growth mindset. If, when we're stuck, we say, "This is fun" rather than "This is hard," kids will understand that stretching ourselves, learning new things, doing hard tasks, and taking on challenges is fun.

If we make a mistake and we say, "That's interesting; what should I do next?" or if we say, "I'm struggling and I'm enjoying it," those are things that kids pick up on, yet not many parents do that. Instead they say, "I'm not a math person" or "How could I be so stupid?" They don't hear what they're communicating to their kids.

The important messages we need to communicate out loud are: challenges are fun; struggle and effort are valued; mistakes are interesting; and setbacks are an opportunity.

Toni: You can incorporate some of those messages at mealtime. You can ask, "What did you learn today? What mistakes did you make today? Did you solve a problem today?" There's so much value in raising that type of question. If you're pursuing a goal, break it down and let your child know the steps you're taking to achieve it.

Creating a passion for learning is also a big part of the growth mindset. How can we create a passion for learning in our children?

Carol: We have a workshop that we call "Brainology" and we teach kids that every time they stretch themselves to learn something new, the neurons in their brain form new connections. Over time, they get smarter. This really stokes children's desire to learn. Many kids tell us that every time they're listening in class, studying, or reading a book, they actually picture these new connections forming in their brains. It gives them an impetus to study, and it helps make learning even more fun.

Toni: Another idea comes from the book *The Last Lecture*. The author's parents were very frugal, but the one thing that the parents bought was a set of encyclopedias. Every night at dinner the parents would raise a topic like the Fiji Islands or World War II. It could be any topic. Then they'd ask the kids to share what they knew about the evening's topic. If they didn't know anything about it, they were encouraged to look in the encyclopedia and share something that they found. The parents would share things too. This created an incredible passion for learning in the author, who became a very successful professor.

Not many people still have encyclopedias but we have the Internet, and we can create that passion for learning at the dinner table.

Carol, what points have we missed from your work that might be important to share with parents?

Carol: I think we've covered most things, but I'd really like to sum up by saying that people who have a fixed mindset believe that effort is a bad thing. With a fixed mindset, people believe that if you're smart or talented, you don't need effort; things should come to you naturally. This is one of the most destructive beliefs because instant success or genius without effort does not exist.

So I want to underscore the importance of letting your children know that you value effort, that you enjoy effort, and that effort is what takes your potential and creates learning and achievement.

Toni: In your book you also talk about many highly successful athletes like Michael Jordan. They've spent their whole life practicing their sport to become the best in the world. Even the most successful athletes still practice, still have coaches, and still strive to become even better. Breaking that down for kids would be really helpful.

Carol: Yes, these people not only practice what they're good at; they address their weaknesses. They keep ferreting out those weaknesses and working on them. So they never think: "I'm great. I'm talented. I'm perfect." They're always on a journey.

Toni: I think it's helpful for us to identify our own strengths so we can draw on those strengths to get us through difficult times. Identifying our weaknesses and the areas where we can improve will also help us grow as a person. And of course that goes for our children as well, as they get older.

I'd like to sum up some of the great points that Carol has made. We want to adopt a growth mindset ourselves so we can cultivate a growth mindset in our kids. We want to develop a passion for learning. We need to re-examine praise: we should praise our kids for their effort and teach them a process for working step-by-step and appreciating their progress. We should give our kids "constructive criticism" so they learn from their errors. Mistakes aren't a negative thing; we need to look at them in a positive light and grow from the mistakes we make. And as parents, we need to make our own mistakes transparent to get away from perfectionism.

We should also help kids set goals and break down projects into manageable tasks. I have a goal setting sheet and problem solving sheet, available at *www.getparentinghelpnow.com/myfreebookresources* that can be used to help kids learn a problem-solving method.

Carol, your work is incredibly important for all of us. Thank you. Thanks also to Kristin Boileau for all her great ideas.

Contact Information:

Carol Dweck, Ph.D.

Mailing Address: Department of Psychology, Stanford University, Jordan Hall, Stanford, CA 94305

Websites: *www.mindsetonline.com* and *www.brainology.us*

Kristin Boileau

Mailing Address: School Counselor, K-2, Osceola Elementary School, 250 10th Ave. E., Osceola, WI 54020

Phone: (715) 294-3457 x 305

Email Address: boileauk@osceola.k12.wi.us

Website: *www.myteacherpages.com/webpages/KBoileau*

Resources:

Carol Dweck, Ph.D.

Book: *Mindset: The New Psychology of Success*

Online growth-mindset training program for students: Brainology. See *www.brainology.us*

Better Sleep Equals Happier Kids

Meet the Expert:

Mary Sheedy Kurcinka, Ed.D., is a best-selling author and internationally recognized lecturer and parent educator. Her books, *Raising Your Spirited Child; Raising Your Spirited Child Workbook; Kids, Parents and Power Struggles;* and *Sleepless in America: Is Your Child Misbehaving or Missing Sleep?* have been translated into 10 languages.

The director of *www.parentchildhelp.com*, Mary provides training worldwide and private consultations for families and professionals. Licensed as a parent educator and early childhood teacher, she has pioneered efforts to bring temperament, neurobiology, the importance of sleep, and emotion coaching into homes, schools, medical practices and businesses.

Known for her real-life examples, Mary links research-based information with typical challenging behaviors and provides practical solutions that really work. Mary's work has been featured on Good Morning America, National Public Radio and many other national and local television and radio shows.

Meet the Parent Guest:

Tara Bishoff is a mother of two from St. Paul, MN who has worked hard to ensure good sleep habits with her children.

******

Toni: Mary, you have an astounding fact in your book. You said that 70 million kids are not getting enough sleep. This is really an epidemic in America, isn't it?

Mary: Yes, and unfortunately it's a *silent* epidemic. We have research showing that 80 percent of adolescents are not getting the sleep they need during the week. Sixty-two percent of children age two to 12, and even 40 percent of infants and toddlers, are short of sleep every week.

Toni: That's astounding. What are the sleep requirements for different ages?

Mary: For infants (from birth to about one year), the recommended amount of sleep is 14 to 18 hours. And obviously that depends on the age of the baby. Younger babies are going to be sleeping more. The big thing with seven-to-nine-month-old babies is they need a third nap. They need a morning nap, they need an afternoon nap, and they need about a 30-minute nap late in the afternoon, around 5:30 or 6:00, to really get the sleep they need.

Toddlers (from one year to about three years of age) need about 13 hours of sleep. Tiny toddlers from one year to 21 months or so still need their morning nap, yet parents often drop that morning nap much too early.

Preschoolers need 12 hours of sleep, and even kindergartners still need 12 hours. So if they get up at 6:30 in the morning and have no nap, kindergartners need to be asleep between 6:30 and 7:00 at night, which is obviously difficult to do.

School-age kids need 10 to 11 hours of sleep.

Adolescents need 9 1/4 hours of sleep.

Adults need 8 1/4 hours of sleep. Also, in the fall, we need a little bit more sleep than we do in the spring and summer.

Toni: What types of problems occur when kids don't get enough sleep?

Mary: You'll see four categories of behavior. The first is the inability to manage emotions. You may have kids who are losing it over little things and going into complete meltdowns. They're easily frustrated. They can't transition from one thing to another. They may be experiencing stomach-aches or headaches. They're very anxious and whiney. This may actually be a child who is short on sleep.

The second category is the body. They get clumsy and they trip. They fall. They have accidents. In fact, preschoolers who don't nap are 76 percent more likely to end up in the emergency room with an accident.

Also, kids may get very hyper at night. You put them to bed and they won't stay in their bedroom. They may be jumping on their bed. This can be a sign of an overtired child. They get a frenzy of energy which is also a sign of sleep deprivation.

Sleep deprived kids get sick more frequently. If you have to wake your child in the morning, they're not getting enough sleep. I think that's important to recognize. Now if you've got the little morning lark who wakes at six, whether you put him to bed at eight or 10 or midnight, he could still need more sleep; but for sure, if you have to wake a child, they're not getting enough sleep.

The third category is focus and attention. About 20 to 25 percent of kids who are experiencing focus and attention issues actually may have a sleep disorder. So if your child is experiencing those things, you may want to have that checked by a pediatrician.

The fourth category is social situations. Sleep-deprived kids may be getting into arguments with siblings and friends. Or they may be falling apart when you say "no."

So the bottom line is: we're seeing these challenging behaviors and our first thought should be "Is this child tired?" A lack of sleep may truly be the fuel for these behaviors.

Toni: So first calculate the number of hours your child is sleeping. Then by resolving the sleep issues, you may correct some of the behavioral issues.

Mary: Right. People will ask me, "How do you know if it's sleep?" You don't know 100 percent, because those behaviors can also indicate other behavioral issues or medical issues. But when I'm working with families, the first thing we look at is how much sleep is this child getting, because if we can stabilize that and increase the child's sleep, *a very high percentage of those behaviors simply disappear.* Then we can see what's left and what we need to work on from there.

Toni: How will these kids benefit when they're getting enough sleep?

Mary: Well, the interesting thing is: we live in a culture that really doesn't value sleep. People brag, "Oh, I can get by on five or six hours," but we actually now have research that shows a mere 41 minutes of sleep deprivation begins to affect kids' mathematical skills and reading skills. We know that children who get the recommended amount of sleep have higher grades. They have better mathematical skills and higher reading scores. They have better focus and attention. There are fewer fights. There are fewer accidents. They don't get sick. They even have fewer cavities and gum disease, and they're less susceptible to Type II diabetes and obesity.

Toni: That's an amazing array of benefits.

Mary: It's huge.

Toni: It is huge. You mentioned that 80 percent of teens aren't getting enough sleep...

Here's a comment from a parent of a teenager: "I talked to my pediatrician about my teen not getting enough sleep and the pediatrician just said, 'That's the way it is. It's difficult for teens to get to sleep when school start times are so early.'"

Do you have any advice for that mother to help her teen get more sleep?

Mary: There are a couple of things we know from recent studies. At puberty, the melatonin cycles shift in the body. (Melatonin tells our body when to go to sleep and our level of melatonin rises at night.) For adolescents, the melatonin begins to rise later. So at nine o'clock, their brain is saying they're not ready for sleep yet. Adolescents also *want* to stay up later and sleep in longer in the morning.

Another factor is a *community* concern. We need to be advocating for high schools to start at 8:30 or later. When schools start at 7:00 or 7:30 in the morning, it's comparable to adults having meetings at 4:00 in the morning.

In fact, studies have been done where they allowed teens to go back to sleep at 7:30. The kids put their head down on their desks and they immediately went into their deepest levels of sleep. They were physically in their seats at 7:30 but their brain was actually still asleep.

So a big factor is becoming an advocate for schools to change the start time of classes. Until the time changes, you can work with your teen to keep a more regular schedule. The challenge is: they're getting up very early during the week, so they're short on sleep and they sleep in on the weekend to catch up. While this has its benefits, it's also a problem. If they sleep till noon on Sunday, then they can't fall asleep that night. As a result, they're short of sleep on weekdays because they've got jet lag going on with this erratic sleep schedule. So try to equalize and stabilize their sleep schedule, even if it's just a little bit.

Toni: Should we wake a teen up on weekends at a time that's similar to the time they wake up during the week?

Mary: Well, obviously you're not going to haul them out of bed at 6:30 in the morning on Saturday or Sunday. Let them sleep in until maybe 9:00 instead of noon. Then suggest that they take a nap in the afternoon. Even after school during the week, suggest that they take a power nap of 20 to 30 minutes so they're not so sleep deprived when they get to the weekend.

Toni: I'm guessing that you're not a big fan of sleepovers, Mary.

Mary: I'm not. Of course every child is different. One child can go to a sleepover and they'll recover in a couple days and be fine. Another child goes to a sleepover, doesn't get their sleep, and it takes them three weeks to recover. There are definitely individual differences.

I'll be honest, though. With my own kids, I used to let them go to the sleepover and then we would pick them up early. They didn't stay past 11:00 or 12:00 at the very latest. Usually that was because they had sports the next day, so they had an excuse for their friends. It wasn't about being a mean mom; I was doing it to protect their sleep because it was so hard when they got only a few hours of sleep and got thrown off their schedule.

Toni: It seems that it's especially important to put your foot down and say, "No, sorry, we're going to keep the bedtime schedule" when viruses such as H1N1 are circulating.

Mary: Absolutely. We do know that you have a stronger immune system when you're getting the sleep that you need. It's during deep sleep that the immune system is strengthened. If you miss that and you're short on sleep, then you're more susceptible to infections.

Toni: You have a three-step process for helping kids to get more sleep. Let's break that down, starting with step number one.

Mary: Yes, there are three steps: *time, temperament, and tension.*

Step one is *time.* Our body has to know it's time for sleep. *Tension* is recognizing that we have to be calm enough for sleep. *Temperament* means we have to adjust for individual differences.

Let's talk about time. First of all, if your child is experiencing behavior or academic problems, the first question that we need to be asking is, "How much sleep is your child getting?"

When I work with families who have children experiencing behavior or academic issues, I'll say to them, "A good night's sleep begins in the morning. So let's just take a look at his day."

Our body clock runs on a 24-hour cycle. If we don't set it with regular wake and sleep times, and with regular meals, then we can innocently be putting our brain into a state of jet lag and we don't know when to sleep.

Toni: So providing the structure for sleep is a big part of step number one.

Mary: Right. I'll ask parents, "When does your child wake up and how many days of the week is that true?"

Let's say that the child gets up at 6:30 or 7:00 a.m. during the week but on weekends they wake up at 9:00 a.m. I live in Minneapolis so that's like spending the weekend in San Francisco. It can trigger our brain into jet lag. The brain won't know if it's supposed to be asleep or not.

Then we look at mealtimes. When is breakfast? Is that also true on the weekend? Or is there a big discrepancy? Meals help set the body clock.

Does this child nap? And how many days a week is that true? How long does the child nap and when? Is there consistency in the nap time?

When are they watching TV? When are they getting exercise? When are they getting exposure to light?

All of those things can innocently upset the body clock and make it harder to sleep.

If all of these time factors are going well, however, they can help set the body clock and put that body clock on our side to help us fall asleep more easily.

Toni: So first we examine those time factors. Then, step number two is *tension* management. What practical relaxation strategies can you provide?

Mary: First of all, recognize that even infants have elevated stress hormones when their parents are stressed. We might be thinking: well, this child can't be stressed; they're only an infant or a toddler or a preschooler; what would they understand that would create tension?

They don't have to understand anything; they just have to be living with an adult experiencing stress.

So, the first thing we can do to help our children's tension is to take care of ourselves and protect our own sleep. If we're experiencing relationship conflict, we should get some counseling or do the things that calm us, so we can be more nurturing and responsive to the kids. Kids physiologically pick up our stress.

Toni: What's step two?

Mary: Number two is to limit TV and video, especially in the evening. It can be very stimulating to children, plus the light can trick the body clock into thinking that it's not night time.

Baths, for some children, are actually alerting, rather than calming, because it's a fight getting them in the bath. Or it's a fight getting them out, or they streak down the hallway because they want to be chased. So we really have to look at our bedtime routine and ask, "Is this calming or is this stimulating?"

Toni: I think most people would think of baths as relaxing, so that's a good point. In your book, you also mention massage and creating a calming environment in the bedroom.

Mary: Yes. There are several pieces to that. Number one is to get the TV and computer out of the bedroom. For adolescents, get the cell phone and iPod out of the bedroom and make it a routine. The electronic gadgets can stay on the kitchen counter so they're not tempted to be checking them.

We do know that children with a television in their bedroom are getting less sleep than kids who don't have one. They also have lower reading scores. So look at the room. Is this a room where we shut down and go to sleep? Or is it a toy store or a media center?

The second thing we've heard so much about is that children must learn to self-soothe and put themselves to sleep. That doesn't mean we don't snuggle with them or rock them or read to them. It doesn't mean that we don't bring that adolescent a glass of water and sit down on the edge of the bed and talk to them. We still want to have a connection and a calming time with our kids before sleep. Then they can go to sleep and sleep through the night.

Toni: Tell us more about massage.

Mary: Massage is wonderful; and it has been shown to reduce stress hormones in the body. You can just do a little back rub or a little back scratch.

For kids that have trouble settling down, sometimes I'll just do a stroking of the eyebrows because if somebody strokes your eyebrows and runs their fingers down the side of your face, you naturally close your eyes.

Some kids really struggle with settling down; they're jumping around and not lying down. You have to notch those kids down gradually. You might take them up to their room and let them play with Legos or do puzzles or draw. Then you might snuggle and read to them or lie down with them. So give them time to wind down.

Toni: Let's talk about the third factor, which is *temperament*. Some kids, particularly the high energy kids and the intense kids, need more time to wind down.

Mary: They do, and the fact is that high energy kids have a very short window for sleep. If you miss it, they get a second wind, and then it takes another 45 to 90 minutes to get them asleep. You look at them and they're running all over. They might be wild and laughing. People will look at them and say, "Look at that kid, he's not tired." In fact, he's overtired.

Toni: Once your child gets that second wind, is there anything you can do?

Mary: Notch it down by letting them play a little bit in the confines of their room. You might sit in there and do some reading too. Then have them lie down, and maybe snuggle, and maybe rub their back a little. Once the second wind kicks in, it takes a while for it to work its way through their system. That's why we want to catch the sleep window and not let that surge of energy come into their system.

Toni: How far away from bedtime should most kids exercise?

Mary: A great time for exercise is in the morning before school. I really encourage the families I work with to not turn on the TV in the morning. There are several reasons for that. One is that kids will get up to watch their show, so they get up early when they would stay asleep if they weren't getting up for the show. The second reason is that they lie there half awake watching the show, so it's not a clear awakening in the morning.

A lot of kids will drink milk while they're watching TV; then they don't eat a good breakfast. They're also soaking up stimulation that they don't need. So I encourage people not to turn on the TV in the morning.

Instead, the child can go outside before the bus comes. Let them run. Let them ride a bike. Play catch with them. Let them do some physical things in the morning and then again in the afternoon.

On the other hand, cut off exercise in the early evening. We do know, especially for boys, that competitive events at night make it very hard for them to go to sleep.

Toni: That's tough because many sporting events and practices are on week nights.

I want to share a quote from your book that I loved. It's by Charles Osgood. "The two most important things parents can say to their kids are: 1) 'I love you,' and 2) 'Go to bed.'"

******

Toni: We have a caller named *Kirsten*, from Minnesota. Do you have a comment or question for Mary?

Kirsten: I just heard you talking about bedtime, and the best thing that we did with our son was to cut out the television before bed, just like you were talking about. We always thought that this would calm him down and help him wind down for bedtime. I didn't understand that TV actually stimulated him. I couldn't figure out why he couldn't fall asleep after he was so relaxed on the couch.

Toni: Did that make a huge difference for you?

Kirsten: Yes, it did.

Toni: Anything else you'd like to add about sleep, Kirsten?

Kirsten: We have a five-year-old and a three-year-old. The one thing we still struggle with at our house is that most nights my husband ends up on the couch because the kids are in bed with me.

Toni: So, the kids sleep in your bed?

Kirsten: They don't start there, but most nights they end up there. They start in their own beds, but a lot of times they wake up in the middle of the night and they come into my bed. It's rare that I wake up by myself in the morning.

Toni: Mary, is there any harm in our kids coming into our bed in the middle of the night?

Mary: First of all, there are real cultural differences in how we sleep, so there's not one right way. When I'm working with a family, I'll ask, "How's that working for you? Is everyone able to sleep, and is everyone okay with that?"

If mom and dad say, "Yes. We get time together before the kids get in there. We're fine as a couple. I sleep fine on the couch and I sleep fine with the kids," then it's fine. But if the family says to me, "No, I can't sleep with the kids there." or "We're fighting because my husband ends up on the couch." then we need to look at finding a way to make this better for the family.

Toni: Thanks for your call, *Kirsten*. We now have a call from *Kelly* from New Jersey. What's your question or comment for Mary?

Kelly: I have trouble with my kids. I have three of them and they were all such good sleepers as babies. Then at the age of three, they became afraid of the dark. They want their light on and it's a battle: turn the light off, turn the light on, turn the light off.

So we went to night lights and I don't even like that. It's always a battle with me, but we put the night lights in. Then they want flashlights too. Then they want their door open and the bathroom light on. I just keep giving in to everything.

Toni: This is such a common complaint. How do you respond when kids are asking for several things and keep calling you back and back again?

Mary: There are a couple of things. You can see that we offer them one thing and once that's taken care of, they need another and another. That pattern tells me that fear and needing the light is not necessarily the reason here.

What's probably happening is that something is creating a little bit of anxiety for them, so there are two things that I'm going to do. I'm going to take a look at the whole day. First of all, we're going to look at the schedule to make sure we've got the body clock on our side. Then we're going to look at the tension busters through the day. What is their day like? What is the schedule? Are they getting naps?

Kids who don't nap at three can often have more difficulty falling asleep at night because by the time they get there, they're overtired. There are always individual differences but we'll look at that too.

We'll see if there's a traveling parent. The research shows that if one parent travels every week – the first night the parent is gone, the kids experience more difficulty falling asleep.

We'll look at ways to set the body clock during the day, to soothe and calm during the day, so that when they go to sleep they really are in a state of calm. As a result, their brain is saying, "It's okay. You can go to sleep. You can stay asleep."

Toni: What do you mean by body clock?

Mary: The body clock is the hormones in our system that say, "This is when we go to sleep and this is when we wake up."

Toni: Does everyone have a pre-determined body clock?

Mary: There's a genetic element to whether you're a night owl or a morning lark. So, if you're by nature more of a night owl, but you have to get up for school or work, the challenge is that you have to keep that early schedule seven days a week because you'll naturally flip out of it if it's not your natural style. If you're naturally a night owl, you have to be stricter about adhering to a schedule to be able to get the sleep you need.

Toni: Kelly, does that help?

Kelly: Yes. One thing I've got to stop doing is letting them watch a TV show before we start our bedtime routines. I thought it was a relaxing way to end the evening, but apparently it's not.

Mary: A family I worked with said watching TV is how the kids fall asleep. They said it really works and I always respect what works. It's not what I would recommend, but if it's working, I'm not going to try and change it. I did suggest, however, that they get the TV out of the bedroom.

Well, they moved, and when they moved the mom decided no TVs in any bedrooms. She emailed me two weeks ago and said, "I cannot believe the difference in my daughter's behavior. She's falling asleep so easily. She's sleeping so much better now that we've taken the TVs out of the bedroom. I had no idea how much it was affecting her."

Toni: So it seems that, if sleep is a problem for your family, you really have to put some structures in place to protect sleep.

In your book, you have a graph that breaks down the day. First, you start with the amount of sleep your child needs. Then you back track from there and plan activities, TV, exercise and meals, all around the sleep schedule.

Mary: It is helpful. People don't want to become so rigid that they feel they can't do this or that, so what I stress is to become aware of your decisions.

If you just got tickets to the hockey game and you have never had tickets before, then it would be a really special night. You ask, "Is it worth it? We're going to pay for this with the kids losing sleep." Maybe it's worth it because you're a hockey family.

Or maybe you get a sitter. Let the kids get their sleep, and you have a date.

When signing up for sports, check when the practices are. And when are the games?

If you're going on vacation, do you save the money by taking the 6 a.m. flight, which means you get up at 4 a.m. to get there? Or do you say, "That's not how we want to start our vacation. We're going to pay a little bit more to go later, or we're not going to be able to go."

Toni: Many of the sporting activities are during the evening, especially for the older kids, so what do we do about that?

Mary: This is where we work as a community to advocate and begin to change attitudes. For example, Mothers Against Drunk Driving, or MADD, has totally changed our paradigm of how we see drinking and driving. So hopefully, if we come together and say: "What do you mean we have hockey practice that starts at 9 p.m. three nights a week, for 11-year-olds?" it will create an uproar in the community.

Toni: Mary, will you organize our community regarding that?

Mary: In every workshop I do, the closing activity is: How do we take this information to the broader community and begin to build that community support? The fact is that it begins with individuals. We can talk to our friends and neighbors and spread the word. You wouldn't skip a meal, so why would you skip sleep?

******

Toni: We're being joined by **Tara Bishoff**, a St. Paul parent with a nine-year-old and a six-year-old. Tara took an Early Childhood Family Education class from Mary in St. Paul a long time ago.

When you took Mary's class, you charted out the sleep your kids were getting. What solutions did you find that were really helpful in managing your kids' sleep?

Tara: I know that it was a revelation that even a little baby would need so much free time. My son wasn't even crawling yet, but I learned that he needed floor time and lots of playtime to wiggle.

He had a lot of energy already, and when we did a sleep log, I was amazed to find out how much time my child might be sitting in a car seat or cooped up in a high chair and other places where he couldn't move freely.

When I realized this, I tried to reduce that time whenever possible so he could have his freedom. When I did that, he napped better. He would use up his energy differently and be calmer for napping.

Toni: Good point. You also found some creature comforts that are really important to your kids.

Tara: That's true. Our children are different in some ways, but they're both quite sensitive to things like the right temperature in the room. It became important in the winter to have fleecy pajamas with feet on them.

Or if it's even colder, they can wear socks or a T-shirt underneath those footed jammies and then sleep with a warmed-up bean bag. You can buy bed buddies at Walgreens. You just pop it in the microwave for a minute and let the child cuddle with it.

When I was a kid, I used to sleep with my cat and there's nothing more soothing than a little bit of heat.

Toni: Isn't that sweet? It sounds like you've done a really good job of creating the right sleep environment for your kids based on their needs.

Tara: Well, we've been highly motivated because it's been highly challenging. Both of our kids have asthma and trouble with sinuses. So we really want them to get their sleep.

Mary: Both of your kids are in school now. Does homework have an impact on the nightly schedule?

Tara: It sure can. When my older daughter was in kindergarten, I would make sure that she got her homework done each night. What I've learned now, though, is that most teachers are quite humane about kids not completing homework if you speak to them or send a little note.

I explain that the math worksheet is not complete because there was a family birthday party last night, my child was tired, and I wanted him to get enough sleep. Most teachers are quite understanding about that.

Toni: That's such good advice. You're being an advocate for your kids, and let's be honest – kids will function better in school the next day if they've had enough sleep. In the end, the teacher and the child will benefit.

Tara: That's true. I've worked as a tutor, and one of the kids said to me, "Well, I watch TV until 12 or 1 at night." So no wonder he was yawning and couldn't read; he was exhausted.

Mary: We have research demonstrating that, in order to learn to read, you have to be able to manage your emotions so you can focus and attend to the detail necessary for reading. If you haven't had enough sleep, you can't do that.

The ability to regulate your arousal system and your emotions is actually very important for learning cognitive skills like reading, writing and mathematics. Without adequate sleep, you'll have more difficulty.

There are other studies that have shown that sleep and the ability to regulate the arousal system is more influential than IQ and economic levels.

Toni: That's important to know. Now, Tara, your kids share a room and that's common in many families. Mary, can you provide some tips on that?

Mary: I think the most important thing that Tara is pointing out is that she knows her children as individuals. She knows what each of her kids needs in order to feel safe emotionally and physically, to be calm enough to go to sleep, and to do their best in school.

In many cultures, kids share a room, so some people think we're crazy when we have kids sleeping alone in their own room. The important thing is knowing your own kids. Does sleeping alone work for them or is it a comfort to have their sibling there? Or is this a source of stress for them? If so, then it doesn't work. There isn't one right answer. It's knowing your child and what helps their brain say, "It's okay; I can sleep."

Toni: Tara, what has been your solution for sharing a room?

Tara: We have our daughter rest on our bed while her younger, more talkative brother goes to sleep. Then she goes back to her nice, quiet room when her brother is asleep.

Toni: For more information on developing great sleep habits for your child, check out Mary Sheedy Kurcinka's book: *Sleepless in America: Is Your Child Misbehaving or Missing Sleep?*

<u>**Contact Information:**</u>

Mary Sheedy Kurcinka, Ed.D.

Phone: 651-452-4772

Website: *www.parentchildhelp.com*

<u>**Resources:**</u>

Books by Mary Sheedy Kurcinka:

Sleepless in America: Is Your Child Misbehaving or Missing Sleep?

Raising Your Spirited Child

Kids, Parents, and Power Struggles

18 Secrets for Cutting the Family Budget

Meet the Expert:

Melissa ("Liss") Burnell is the founder of *www.Budget101.com*, a website that provides cost-effective, time-saving budgeting techniques that can be utilized by anyone working in or out of the home. As a busy wife, mother of two active young men, and full time computer consultant, Liss understands the value of time and money. Liss is the author of *How to Feed a Family of Four or More for Less than $200 a Month*. Her website, Budget101.com, strives to help people utilize the tools and resources they have available to dig themselves out of debt. Budget101.com was initially created in 2001 at the request of several lively ladies who yearned to live within their means and get out of debt utilizing the resources they currently had on hand. What started as a handful of people has grown to thousands, and the website now ranks in the top 30,000 U.S. websites online.

******

Toni: We're going to share 18 tips for cutting the family budget. I've gone to your website and I've already started using some of the great ideas you recommend on your site.

You've said that the best way to cut the family budget is to cut the grocery bill, so we're going to provide four tips and **Tip No. 1 is buy cheaper cuts of meat.** Tell us more.

Liss: There are lots of ways to cut your budget, and the grocery budget is the easiest way to cut expenses. You want to buy cheaper cuts of meat, and meat that's been reduced for quick sale. When they're on sale, you can usually get more expensive cuts of meat for half the price and then freeze them for later. They don't lose their quality and they'll last for about six months in your freezer.

There are three different methods you can use to cook the cheaper cuts of meat, such as flank or skirt steak. The first way is to use the old hammer method which you may be familiar with. You defrost your meat overnight, put it in a clean plastic bag, and tenderize it with a wooden mallet or meat tenderizer. It makes delicious meals, and you can even grill it.

The second way is to marinate the meat prior to cooking it. There are a number of recipes. You can use anything from homemade Italian dressing to store-bought dressing to a little bit of lime juice to take the toughness out of the meat. Lime juice works wonderfully.

The third way is to cook the meat in a slow cooker or pressure cooker.

Toni: I love slow cookers.

Liss: They're great for busy parents. With a slow cooker, you can also feed a larger number of people with less meat. If you need to stretch a single steak to feed several people at once, you can actually do that by cutting it into thin strips. Just lay the meat on a flat surface, hold your knife at an angle, and cut really thin strips against the grain of the meat. Using that method, you can end up with enough meat from one large steak to feed four to six people.

Toni: I like making kabobs, fajitas and stroganoff for that reason.

Liss: If you want a healthier meal, you can put steak tips over a fresh garden salad.

Toni: Tip No. 2 is make meals ahead. What do you mean by that?

Liss: I like to have prepared leftovers. When you're making dinner, plan to have enough food to serve two full-size portions. Eat one portion that night and then freeze the other portion for later use.

I can hear people say, "I don't like leftovers." Well, if you're running late and you have a portion of leftovers in the freezer, you can simply take the item out, put it in the oven at 350 with foil on it, go take your shower, unwind, spend a few minutes catching up with the kids, do housework, and in less than 35 minutes dinner's ready.

It saves you from ordering takeout. It saves you from running down to the store because you only have half the ingredients for dinner. So you save time and money.

If you want to get really creative with the kids, you can play restaurant by making menus on your home computer and letting them pick various entrees. It gives them options.

Toni: When my husband and I were in graduate school together and working full time, we would always double our recipes. We'd only cook three days a week, have leftovers three nights a week, and then serve pizza every Sunday night. It saved us so much time. Your idea of freezing the meals, however, will appeal to those people who don't like the idea of leftovers.

Tip No. 3 is buy food when it's in season. How does that help us?

Liss: Fruit and vegetables are readily available during certain seasons. For instance, strawberries and asparagus are usually inexpensive in the spring. Various types of squash are available in the fall, but if you try to find them in the spring, you're paying more.

Purchasing the item when it's in season and preserving it by freezing, dehydrating, or canning will drastically reduce your grocery bill. If you're new to canning and preserving, you can visit my site at *www.budget101. com* for step-by-step photo directions and it will explain how to begin. Here are two links:

Preserving Foods at Home:

www.budget101.com/frugal/dehydrated-dried-food-mixes-186

Step by Step Canning Help:

www.budget101.com/sbs/sbs2.htm

The best grocery budgeting tip that I can offer you regarding buying in season is to help you understand sale cycles. Think of your shopping on a 12-week cycle rather than a weekly one. Sale categories rotate, so most items are on sale just once every 12 weeks. That means if you stockpile items short-term, meaning a three-month supply, you're saving a considerable amount of money.

I can give you an example. About a week ago Charmin bath tissue was on sale for $5.99 each, whereas it's normally $9.99. I bought three – that's a three-month supply – and saved $12.00, which is 40 percent.

Toni: That's excellent. So don't be embarrassed if you have a whole cart full of toilet paper when you're leaving the store.

Liss: Right. But you're only buying a three-month supply. As I said, your typical sales deals rotate. For example, in October, candy, Halloween treats, baking supplies, chocolate chips, flour, sugar, apples, pumpkins, and pet products are typically on sale.

Toni: So we'll stock up on those items in October.

Tip No. 4 is make homemade mixes.

Liss: Homemade mixes are wonderful for your budget. Sometimes it's great to have the convenience of a quick mix – who doesn't love being able to grab a Betty Crocker cake mix and have a chocolate cake in less than 35 minutes? But the convenience doesn't have to end there.

On *www.budget101.com* we offer over 2,000 mix recipes in various categories to help you save money: *www.budget101.com/frugal/convenience-mixes-181*

These are items you can make in your home for just pennies and keep on hand – like sun-dried tomato and basil pesto mix, or your own gourmet popcorn seasonings. Or you can make rice mixes like Alfredo mix or cream-based sauce mixes.

Another plus is that homemade mixes are wonderful if you have dietary concerns like a gluten-free diet or diabetes.

Toni: Do you make big batches, divide them up, and then store them?

Liss: No, what I generally do is make about five mixes while I'm chatting on the phone with a friend for 15 minutes.

Take five Ziploc baggies, line them up, and then add each ingredient to each of the five baggies down through your list of ingredients. Then take a permanent marker and write on the baggie how to finish the recipe.

For example: add 1 cup of milk and 1 tablespoon of butter to a small sauté pan and cook for eight to 10 minutes.

Toni: When you first started talking, I was thinking, "How much more work is this going to be?" But you make it sound so easy.

Liss: It really is. You just print the recipe from the site, follow the recipe, and add the ingredients to each bag.

For example, in the noodle mix, add 1 cup of noodles, 3 tablespoons of powdered milk, and 1 teaspoon each of salt and pepper to each of the five bags. Even your children can make them. My sons help make mixes all the time.

Toni: Tip No. 5 is save money on Halloween costumes. How can we cut some costs there?

Liss: Halloween is a great time of year, but the costumes in the stores can empty your wallet in no time. The fun in Halloween is the creativity of your costume. With a little help from your pantry, you can make your kids look spectacular.

You can learn how to make your own special effects such as guts, scabs, scars, and boils. You can actually make your own broken and protruding bones! I have a number of recipes on my website, and these are just items you find in your pantry. For example, you can make warts using peppercorns, food coloring and a little bit of corn starch.

Actually, there are 16 different categories with 150 homemade costume ideas to choose from.

For example, you can choose from one of our Frightful categories at:

www.budget101.com/frugal/homemade-halloween-costume-ideas-141

You can also check out our Make-up Recipes:

www.budget101.com/special-effects-halloween/happy-halloween-make-up-recipes-2801.html

Or look at our Spooktacular Party Games:

www.budget101.com/frugal/frugal-halloween-party-games-144
Or check out our Eerie Edibles:

www.budget101.com/frugal/halloween-food-143

Toni: So there's a huge variety of creative things you can do for Halloween at a low cost.

Next is **Tip No. 6: eat out less.**

Liss: The average family eats out twice a week. Generally, one is at a sit-down restaurant and one is takeout.

Here are some tips for dining out, getting the most for your money, and having a fine dining experience without spending a lot of cash.

The first tip, if you're going out with your spouse, is to order one entrée and one appetizer and then split them. Restaurants typically serve way too much food, which is costly for you and also unhealthy if you try to finish the too-large meal.

The other thing is to eat breakfast or lunch out because they're generally cheaper than dinners. Also try the lunch specials. They're usually a good deal and you can typically get a meal for $5.00 or $6.00.

Toni: Our whole family loves a restaurant up in northern Wisconsin, and they do give those huge portions that you mentioned. We discipline ourselves and only eat half, so we get a second meal out of it. Although it may cost us $50.00, we get two scrumptious meals for a family of four.

Liss: That's an excellent way of doing it. Another suggestion is to just order side items, like a salad and an appetizer, that are affordable.

Toni: You also have some copycat recipes available on your site. Correct?

Liss: Yes. Sometimes you travel a long distance to go to your favorite restaurant and what you really want is just a taste of something, like a fried onion ring or maybe an onion blossom from the steak. If you go onto *www.budget101.com* and go to the Copycat Recipes, you can find recipes for all of your favorite restaurant dishes: *www.budget101.com/ mixes-myo-copycat-etc*

For instance, you can get recipes for fried onion rings, the Toscana soup from Olive Garden, or the Big Mac sauce at McDonald's. Just go to the forums, post what you're looking for, and someone will come on and give you that copycat recipe.

Toni: What a great idea!

Tip No. 7 is make your own cleaning products.

Liss: You can make almost any type of cleaner that you need. We have over 1,500 cleaner recipes on the site. You can make ceramic tile cleaner, concrete cleaner or brass polish. As an example, basic window cleaner is just 3 tablespoons of ammonia, 3/4 cup of water and 1 tablespoon of white vinegar. Then you can add blue food coloring so everyone knows not to drink it.

You can also make green cleaners that don't contain any bleach or ammonia, using baking soda, lemon juice, and salt.

Here's the link for making your own cleaning products: *www.budget101. com/frugal/household-tips-n-tricks-204*

Toni: So you're helping the environment, keeping toxins out of your home, and saving yourself a bundle.

Liss: It really does save money when you factor in the average cost of a cleaner, which is $4 a bottle.

Toni: Tip No. 8 is coupon use. I've been waiting for this one. I want to use coupons more easily and effectively.

Liss: Coupons are wonderful. A lot of people think they can't get fresh produce like fruits or vegetables with coupons, but you absolutely can.

What you need to do is watch your weekly circulars.

First, to start using coupons, grab your Sunday paper; it has the inserts in it. You'll have either Red Plum, Smart Source, or Procter & Gamble. Those are your three big inserts.

Browse the circulars and match the coupons that you like to the sales that are in your area. You can also use the grocery guide on Budget 101 to match up the sales from your favorite local shopping spot. Go to the site, type in your zip code, and it will tell you what stores are available in your area, like Aldi's, Shop and Save, or Walmart. You just click the box beside it, and it will tell you exactly what's on sale that week.

Toni: No kidding?

Liss: Then you match up your coupons to those sales.

Toni: So you can use the coupons with the sales?

Liss: That's correct, and you save a bundle.

Here's my favorite trick for saving 80 percent or more. A lot of stores will allow double coupons that are under $1.00 and you can use a double discounter.

For example, suppose you normally pay $1.85 for a jar of Ragu spaghetti sauce. You discover that your local Stop and Shop is running a special on Ragu for $1.00. Bring your 35-cents-off coupon for Ragu, and it's doubled, so that's 70 cents off. You just bought that jar of sauce for 30 cents.

Toni: So the key is to find a grocery store that lets you double your coupon?

Liss: That's right. Also, a lot of times, even if the stores won't double, they'll accept competitor coupons. Walmart will price match any competitor's ad or coupon and Target will as well.

So if you're shopping and the only thing you have locally is Walmart, but you have another store within 40 miles that doubles, bring that coupon in with the flyer, and it will get doubled for you.

Another tip is to buy smaller when you use your coupons. Coupons make the smaller sizes a better deal because you're getting a larger percentage off.

For example, Gold Medal is $2.55 for a 5 lb. bag and its $4.88 for a 10 lb. bag. That makes them both 3 cents per ounce. If you use a 25 cent coupon for the smaller bag, you get a 10 percent discount, whereas on the 10 lb. bag you only get a 5 percent discount.

Toni: You've thought of all the angles. Can you go shopping with me next time?

Liss: Sure, I'd love to. I'll show you how to find the best deals. Here are the links for coupon use on my site:

How to organize your coupons:

www.budget101.com/coupon-deals-printables/organizing-your-coupons-513.html

Free online coupons:

www.budget101.com/coupon-deals-printables/free-printable-coupons-508.html

Toni: Tip No. 9 is save money on children's clothing.

Liss: For back-to-school clothing, the best thing to do is to shop at resale clothing stores. They offer good quality clothing at a fraction of the cost. Savings are especially good for the younger kids.

Teenagers are a little harder to satisfy. However, jeans are still in and the worn look is still in style.

Another idea is to hold a swap party. Don't throw out your kids' clothes; they outgrow them so quickly. Instead, have a few moms over for drinks and appetizers, throw all your unwanted clothes in a big pile and swap away. This works really well with teen girls.

Toni: I bet they'd have a blast.

Liss: Another thing is to use coupons. Google your favorite stores for printable coupons and codes. I know T.J. Maxx and JCPenney offer huge deals. You can get jeans for $5.00 a pair at both places.

Toni: I love Penneys. I never thought I'd say that. It was a store my Grandma shopped at, but I have to tell you the deals that I've gotten there are just fabulous. Tell us about **Tip No. 10: save money on birthday parties**.

Liss: We tend to spend a lot on birthday parties because we want to give our kids everything that we can. First, try to decide how much money you're willing to spend on the party. It's really easy to start spending and spending without realizing how much money is actually leaving your pocket. Set up a party budget and allot a certain amount of money for each item, like the cake, the food, the party favors, and the games, and stick to it.

Keep the guest list small and don't feel guilty about limiting the size of the party. The number of kids on the list should match your child's age.

Toni: I set up a budget for my daughter's last party and it really helped us rein in the costs.

Tip No. 11 is save money on flu shots. Flu season is here. We're supposed to get our flu shot. How can we save money on shots, Liss?

Liss: If you're insured, call your doctor, because usually there's just a small co-pay. For a great number of people, insurance isn't an option, however. You can check your local or state health department information regarding free or low-cost shots.

For Walgreens locations, you can go to www.Walgreens.com, or visit the forums at budget101.com for locations: *www.budget101.com/ freebies/67979-free-flu-shots-people-w-out-insurance.html*

Toni: Very important information. Thanks, Liss.

I had sticker shock in September. My youngest is a competitive dancer and I just about had to re-mortgage the house for that bill. **Tip No. 12 is save money on extracurricular activities for the kids.**

Liss: My number one tip for cutting children's extracurricular expenses is to start cheap. We all hate to skimp on our kids, and I know when I've watched other parents shop for sports gear, they seem pretty eager to lay down large sums of money for the best equipment they can buy.

As a mom, I understand the sentiment. I only want the best for my kids, too, but it's too easy to get in our own vicarious field of dreams.

Start by finding less expensive equipment and lessons. At first, you're not sure if they're going to stay in the activity, so don't spend a lot of money on it – it may have a shelf life of just days.

The other thing is to check your local Freecycle. If you're not familiar with Freecycle, it's a national site dedicated to keeping items out of landfills. It's a free swap board. You visit *www.freecycle.org*, pick your city and your state, and check for used sports equipment, building materials, clothing, kitchen supplies – you name it. Then you go and pick up your items.

Toni: That sounds like a great idea.

I have a cute story to share. My daughter is starting guitar lessons, and a friend of mine tipped me off to an instructor and offered to let us borrow a guitar and amp from her son. When I went to pick them up, the guitar was broken. She said, "Wait a minute. Our neighbor just had a garage sale, and I think I saw a guitar and amp over there." She called Nick and I got a guitar, an amp, a case, extra strings, and a guitar book, all for $50.00!

Liss: What a deal!

Toni: So networking can be so helpful.

Liss: Yes, and of course another source is Craigslist. It's wonderful for finding gently used equipment.

Toni: Tip No. 13 is find cheaper movies.

Liss: First, check your local library. Most libraries have hundreds, if not thousands, of movies you can watch for free, including new releases. It's often an overlooked resource.

Second, Redbox and Blockbuster both offer $1.00 rentals that are located in entryways at the big box stores such as Walmart, CVS and Walgreens.

Also, if you go online and Google "Redbox code" you can regularly get discount codes for free rentals.

Toni: Free?

Liss: Free rentals. When you're at your local Redbox kiosk, just before checkout you simply enter the coupon code on the main screen and you'll receive a free one-day rental. To find free Redbox codes, visit: *www. forums.budget101.com/freebies*

Toni: I'm so glad I interviewed you. The dollar bills are growing in my wallet as we talk.

Liss: If you like theater productions, you can volunteer as an usher. Most local theaters need volunteers to serve as ushers during performances, and in return you get to take in some free theater. It's a great way to soak in some culture without emptying your wallet.

Toni: I love it! Now for **Tip No. 14: save money on craft items.**

Liss: Most of your kid's craft items, like glue, paste and play dough, can be made with basic ingredients in your pantry. Even scrapbooking supplies and rubber stamping supplies like embossing ink and ink pads can be made at home. They're really easy to make.

Scratch-and-sniff paint is wonderful and it's simply made with a little bit of water color, vinegar, and Jell-O. And you can make scented playdough using Jell-O. Just visit the tips and tricks section of our site and view those recipes.

Craft Ideas and Recipes:

www.budget101.com/crafts/pcwindex.htm

Craft Ideas and Recipes for Kids:

www.budget101.com/frugal/kids-babies-206

If you need actual craft supplies, *www.freecycle.org* is a wonderful site to find them. People are often giving away cross-stitching supplies or knitting supplies.

Toni: What I'm learning about your ideas is that they're going to save people money *and* help the environment.

Liss: Well, thank you.

Toni: The holidays are looming and everyone wants to have a lovely celebration and presents for their kids, despite the recession. **Tip No. 15 is save money during the holidays.**

Liss: The easiest thing to do is to make a list of everyone that you plan on giving a gift to this year, and then plan for one or two extras because we always seem to forget somebody.

When going through your list, you need to determine whether the gift should be an individual gift or a family gift. For instance, for your own kids you choose personal gifts. But if you're choosing a gift for a neighbor's child, you might choose a family gift for the whole household to enjoy. Then you could do a family gift basket like a movie gift basket with popcorn and the homemade popcorn seasoning mixes.

For each person, jot down a few things that they enjoy. For instance, write down their hobbies, occupation, favorite sports, and whether they pamper their pets, to give you some ideas of what to choose for a gift.

Then comes the tough part: determining a dollar amount that you plan to spend on individuals and a total for the whole holiday season.

For instance, you might spend $25 on your parents, $50 on your children, and $5 on a neighbor. But you need to be realistic, and don't allow for gifts on your credit card!

Toni: What can be done for people who are really low on cash?

Liss: If you're really low on cash, you can make gift coupons. You can give a gift of time – and this works great for kids of all ages. For a teenager, you could give a manicure, or a ride in mom's taxi service, arriving at the destination of their choice with no grumbling.

Here's a link with more ideas on how to avoid the holiday cash crunch:

www.budget101.com/frugal-living-articles/holiday-cash-crunch-how-avoid-2180.html

Toni: Back massages make a good gift coupon as well.

Tip No. 16 is cut babysitting costs.

Liss: My children are older now, but I do remember how difficult it was trying to balance the budget *and* pay for a babysitter and an evening out. Every parent longs for a night out with their spouse, or with friends, or even alone time to get their sanity back.

Most parents, whether single or married, also know another parent that feels the same way. Rather than spend a fortune on babysitters, consider setting up a trade. One evening per week or bi-weekly, your friend watches your children, and on another evening you return the favor by watching her children for the same period of time.

Just set some ground rules. Make sure you know how many children you're watching and the amount of time allotted per swap. Is it going to be four hours, eight hours, or 24 hours?

Toni: I love that. My friend Sue and I do that. Once a year we give each other a 24-hour getaway.

Liss: And it's wonderful!

Toni: It's wonderful! I love swaps. If you have a lot of energy, you can also start a babysitting co-op with people, where you log hours watching other people's children and then you get that number of hours of free babysitting.

Liss: If you can't afford to go out on your night off, you can hike a nearby trail and have a picnic. Or have a candlelight dinner at home. There are other ideas here:

www.budget101.com/frugal/3-frugal-living-articles/index4.html

Toni: Tip No. 17 is save money on your child's lunches. Do you think that we should sign our kids up for school lunches or make them bag lunches?

Liss: School lunches are wonderful if you can afford it. It's a balanced meal because they have to meet standards. At the same time, it's pretty easy to make your own lunch in the morning for the same price.

You can make a lunchable-style lunch with crackers, cheese, and sandwich meat, and then, in a separate container, cut veggies or fruit into cubes. Or you can use leftover dinner items like meat loaf.

For the younger kids, you can make the food more appealing by using cookie cutters and cutting sandwiches into shapes or triangles.

Kids love tortillas spread with fruit butter and then rolled up. Apple butter with a little bit of cream cheese rolled up in a tortilla is my kids' favorite.

Toni: The presentation and shape of food is really important to kids. My daughter would never eat oranges, yet when I sliced them in a circular fashion she loved them. So experiment and find out what your child likes.

Liss: Exactly. You can make a wonderful fruit dip by taking cream cheese, a little bit of brown sugar, cinnamon, nutmeg, and a handful of walnuts. You can dip every kind of fruit or even celery and carrot sticks in it.

You can also get a thermos for less than $5.00 at Walmart. Use it for chop suey, pastas, mac and cheese, or even ramen noodles.

Toni: I just sent ramen noodles with my daughter last night. She wanted a warm dinner and you can't beat it at 10 cents a bag.

Liss: Yes, it's the easiest meal. Here are the links for tips on school lunches and snacks:

Lunch Ideas:

www.budget101.com/frugal/3-frugal-living-articles/index2.html

After-school Snack Ideas:

www.budget101.com/frugal/3-frugal-living-articles/index2.html

Toni: Tip No. 18 is decorate for fall.

Liss: Fall's a beautiful time of year and nature offers an abundance of inexpensive decorations so you can enjoy the full beauty of the season indoors or out.

Inside, you can take some cut wheat or sunflowers, place them in a wicker basket, and attach a bow or cornhusk dolls.

On our site we have step-by-step directions with photos so you can make your own kitchen witch cornhusk doll out of just a few cornhusks and a little bit of yarn. She's adorable.

Cornhusk Kitchen Witch:

www.budget101.com/halloween-decor/enchanting-corn-husk-kitchen-witch-2788.html

You can also take dried apple slices and make beautiful wreaths or garlands. To prevent them from browning, dip them in lemon juice and add some cinnamon sticks. For centerpieces, use pint-size mason jars filled with cracked corn.

Or you can take a few apples and in the center of each apple carve out enough space for a green tea light candle. Then place the apples in a row for a beautiful addition to your table.

Toni: Last year we hosted a wine-tasting party. Everyone was asked to bring a bottle of wine and an appetizer to share. We ended up with 50 people and 25 bottles of wine to taste, along with 25 great appetizers.

My centerpiece was a grouping of colorful vegetables. I loved the color and the bounty that it added to the table. And it was a blast tasting all the appetizers and fabulous wines!

Liss: What a wonderful get-together, and an inexpensive party idea.

It's the simple things that stand out and people really notice. Centerpieces with gourds are inexpensive and add a lot of color. You can also make fall swags. Take branches with beautiful fall color, like oak or maple, then snip a few of the leaves off and place them in a mix of glycerin and water and soak them for two weeks. The leaves will keep their color, and you can make gorgeous centerpieces and swags out of them.

Halloween Décor Ideas:

www.budget101.com/hw6.htm

Enchanting Witches Broom Favor Bags:

www.budget101.com/halloween-decor/enchanting-witches-broom-favor-bags-2760.html

Autumn Décor:

www.budget101.com/autumndecor.htm

Toni: Liss, you are fabulous. Thank you so much!

Contact Information:

Melissa 'Liss' Burnell

Mailing Address: P.O. Box 3 Westville, SC 29175

Email Address: contact@budget101.com

Websites: *www.Budget101.com* ; *http://www.GroceryBudget101.com*

Resources:

How to feed a family of four for under $200 a month: *www.budget101.com/frugal/3-frugal-living-articles/index4.html*

Do it Yourself: Time and money savers for the busy family:

www.budget101.com/frugal/do-yourself-113

$50 Weekly Menu Plans for a family of four:

www.grocerybudget101.com/content.php/8-menus

Mealtime Dilemmas Solved

Meet the Expert:

Ellyn Satter is an internationally recognized authority on eating and feeding. Ellyn pioneered the concepts of the feeding relationship and eating competence, as well as the division of responsibility in feeding.

Practical, warm and empowering, Ellyn integrates her 40 years of experience into helping adults be more positive, organized and nurturing in caring for themselves and their children. She emphasizes competency rather than deficiency; providing rather than depriving; and trust rather than control. Her theoretically grounded and clinically sound methods allow the individual's own capacity for effective and rewarding food behavior to evolve.

You can find Ellyn's materials and other resources at *www.ellynsatterinstitute.org*. Ellen's books include: *Secrets of Feeding a Healthy Family; Your Child's Weight, Helping Without Harming; Child of Mine: Feeding with Love and Good Sense;* and *How to Get Your Kid to Eat…But Not Too Much;* as well as the *Feeding with Love and Good Sense* series of condensed booklets.

Meet the Parent Guest:

Beth Weiss raised five children as a single mother in Arizona, where they had a thriving vegetable garden. She started teaching her children to garden, cook, and plan meals when they were young. She now lives in Minnesota and has seven grandchildren.

******

Toni: You have a number of books, Ellyn, but we're going to focus on *Secrets of Feeding a Healthy Family*. You have a "golden rule" that defines how parents should approach eating.

The "golden rule" is: "parents are responsible for the *what, when and where* of feeding. And children are responsible for the *how much and whether* of eating."

Let's break that down.

Ellyn: The critical issue is that children need to know that they're going to be fed and parents need to be reliable and trustworthy about feeding them.

Parents need to provide kids with three meals a day, and younger children need to have snacks between meals. By snacks, I mean planned snacks where the parent makes up her mind what the snack is going to be and puts it on the table and rounds everybody up as if it's a little meal.

Then the parent is controlling the *when* and also the *where* of eating. The child isn't allowed to graze and the parents make up their minds on what the food will be. So, it's the parent who is in charge of the menu, and the child grows up gradually learning to like the food that the parents eat, whatever it is.

As far as I'm concerned, there's really no right or wrong food. I don't get hung up on finger shaking and saying you should eat this and you shouldn't eat that.

I think it's extremely important that parents put together meals that they find rewarding, and that they enjoy planning, preparing and eating. Enjoyable meals will be different for everyone. Eating family meals is absolutely critical, not only for children, but also for grownups; but for those meals to be self-sustaining, meals have to be enjoyable.

Toni: Your mantra is to enjoy food and share that love with your children.

Ellyn: Absolutely. To help parents develop a meal habit, I often say to them, "You know, you're already feeding yourself and your children. Even if you're not having organized family meals, there's food there and people are eating it. So, why not start with putting structure around what you're eating now?"

In other words, to get started with family meals, change *how food is being served* first, and think about *what the foods are* later. Start out by eating what you're eating now, but have it at regular meal and snack times when you round up the family to eat together. Then you let your child decide *what foods to eat* and *how much to eat* from what's on the table.

That way you make meal times pleasant. You talk and enjoy each other. You don't scold or fight.

Many times people who have been grazing on pizza, chicken nuggets, and French fries are a little shocked at that advice. They say, "You don't really mean that we're supposed to go to the table and eat that?"

And I say, "Yes, if that's what you like and that's what you've been eating." Just put some structure around it. Get yourself started with family meals using the food that you currently eat and enjoy.

Toni: So step one is to put structure in place by deciding what time meals will be served and then gather your family for that meal.

Ellyn: Once people do that, a funny thing happens. Once they sit down and pay attention to the few basic meals that they've been eating, they begin to realize it's kind of boring.

They aren't enjoying those foods as much as they did when they ate them on the run. They begin to look around and say, "Well, what other foods can we add? What would be good with this? How can we make this meal more interesting?"

At that point, people start to add things like vegetables or a new bread. They begin to diversify their menu.

Toni: You advise that children should be responsible for *how much* they eat. Do you recommend serving meals family style so kids can pick their portions?

Ellyn: Yes. When food is served family style, you put the food on the table in bowls, you pass it around and kids can pick and choose. They can take a particular food on their plate or not, and they can ask for seconds. That's really important.

It's so important at every stage of the game, whether you're just getting started with family meals or you have them well established, that you let children pick and choose from what you've put on the table.

Being kids, especially young kids, they won't eat some of everything that's put before them. They'll probably eat only two or three food items. But, the two or three food items they eat today will be different from the two or three food items they eat some other day.

Toni: Last night we were eating leftovers from Famous Dave's restaurant. Our teenager chose what to eat. She ate half an apple and French fries. She didn't bother to eat the ribs, chicken, or coleslaw.

Ellyn: That's great. That's what she was hungry for and what tasted good to her.

Toni: I knew I was interviewing you soon, so I thought, "Toni, stay quiet. Ellyn doesn't want you to interfere with what she's eating."

Ellyn: Good for you. You got the message.

In *Secrets,* I write about the feeding relationship. Parents need to stay on their side of the division of responsibility. Don't interfere with children's prerogative of *what* and *how much* they eat.

I also talk about adults and their eating. I wonder if you've been giving yourself a little more leeway since you've read *Secrets.*

Toni: Yes, I think that's fair to say. I know that you're not a fan of the food pyramid, but it helps me set guidelines for meal planning. I try to get fruits, vegetables, calcium and protein in most meals. Are you advising people just to serve a balance of foods?

Ellyn: Yes. In fact, we're up to step four of family-friendly feeding: Building Family Meals – which is on my website: *www.ellynsatterinstitute.org.* I use meal-planning strategies, rather than the pyramid, for getting the meal on the table.

To me, the pyramid gets in the way of the practicality of putting meals on the table. So here's what I'd recommend. Once you're comfortable with the other steps, include: all the food groups including meat or another protein; a couple of starchy foods like bread; a fruit or vegetable or both; butter; salad dressing or gravy; and milk.

Always offer plenty of bread or some other starch that family members like and can fill up on. In Africa they eat a polenta-like food at almost every lunch and dinner. They consider that their staple starch. Every culture seems to have a staple starch that they consider essential at a meal.

Then you include high and low-fat food so you can satisfy both the big and little appetites. You include butter and salad dressing and gravy along with bread, all of which are relatively high in fat. And you include vegetables or fruits, which are low in fat.

There's a helpful series on my website. It's called "Mastering Family Meals Step-By-Step" and it's available here: *www.ellynsatterinstitute.org/hte/howtoeat.php.*

Then I encourage people to regularly offer forbidden food.

Toni: I love forbidden food. Tell me the plan.

Ellyn: Toni, tell me what you think of when you think of forbidden food.

Toni: Decadent chocolate, chips, candy...

Ellyn: Yes. You're doing well.

Toni: All right! I know my forbidden foods!

Ellyn: Well, everybody has a different food that they love.

Forbidden food is something that grown-ups really struggle with, so I came up with a set of guidelines for parents to use with respect to forbidden foods.

Forbidden foods, or, as one of my patients called them, "controlled substances," are high fat and high sugar. They're relatively low-nutrient foods, like sweets, chips, and sodas.

So how do you use them? You don't want to give your kids (or yourself) unlimited access to these foods because they'll fill up on them. Then their dietary balance will be all screwed up and they won't learn to like other, more challenging foods.

On the other hand, if you restrict them, the research is very clear that children will eat more of them when they get the chance and be fatter than they might be otherwise. So it's very important to find the middle ground.

Toni: How do we do that?

Ellyn: Here's what I recommend: include chips or fries occasionally at meal time and see how well you do. Arrange to have enough so everyone can eat as much as they're hungry for.

The thing with those fatty foods is that they really don't compete with other mealtime foods. Sweets do, though. If you let kids eat as much dessert as they want to, most kids are going to fill up on it.

Have sweets for dessert, if you like dessert, but limit everybody to one serving. Now, this violates the division of responsibility in feeding, but there's a reason for it. If you let kids eat as much dessert as they want, they won't be interested in their vegetables or anything else, and that creates a deficit.

However, if you're only going to allow one dessert, you're imposing scarcity on your child, so at some time your child needs to be able to eat as much as they want of sweets. That's where snack time comes in. Earlier I talked about the planned snack, and I recommend that periodically, at this planned snack time, you offer unlimited sweets.

For instance, you put cookies or snack cakes on the table and you let your child eat as many cookies or cakes as she wants.

Toni: How often do you do this?

Ellyn: It's up to you. Some parents are still kind of freaked out by this. Some manage to do it once a week and that's as good as it gets. Others will do it two or three times a week. The thing is, the first time this happens, the child is going to eat sweets like there's no tomorrow, but soon they get used to the idea and they'll eat one or two or three and then lose interest.

Toni: What do you think of the old adage "eat your fruits and vegetables and then you can have dessert?" A lot of parents still say that. Should we be quiet?

Ellyn: Eighty or 90 percent of parents pressure kids to eat.

Toni: That's astounding!

Ellyn: It's scary, because when you pressure children to eat, they eat worse, not better. They'll be less likely to learn to genuinely enjoy fruits and vegetables when you stipulate that they need to eat them first before they can have dessert. It takes away trust.

You see, it's perfectly legitimate to trust your child to grow up to eat the foods that you eat. They'll do that because they admire you. They see you eating well and they assume, on some level: if mom does it, someday I'm going to do it, too.

Toni: So it comes back to modeling. We need to enjoy food and trust our child.

Ellyn: Yes. There's a way of modeling so elaborately that it chases kids away, however.

Toni: So don't be a health nut.

Ellyn: Yes, really! Don't say, "Oh, this is so good!" over the top. Kids can see through you. They're not dumb.

Toni: Ellyn, I have to ask you this. Sometimes kids don't want to eat at all. You've made a lovely meal and they either pick at it or don't want to eat it.

It seems there's so much emotion around a parent preparing a meal for a child and parents take it personally if the child doesn't eat. If your child doesn't eat a thing, should you just say, "Oh, well, I guess you're not hungry"?

Ellyn: Yes. And you can say, "Well, that's it for now. There'll be more at three o'clock for snack time."

Kids will try to do things like not eating a thing and then get up from the table and want ganache-topped brownies. So you have to be able to say, "No, that's it for now. You've had your chance to eat and the next time is 3:00. You can have something to eat then."

Toni: If it's at dinnertime, should you give in to snacking later?

Ellyn: For young kids, I think it's a good idea to let them have a bedtime snack because many of them eat really poorly at dinnertime. They're tired of eating; they've been eating all day.

At dinner, the foods are often more challenging because both parents are home and they want a good, hearty dinner. So kids may not eat much. In that case, the planned snack is the ace in the hole for beleaguered parents.

If you don't have a bedtime snack to fall back on, it's going to be pretty hard for you to send your child to bed hungry. So, the snack is really helpful for both of you. It helps you to hold the line on short-order cooking at dinnertime.

It also helps you to be more matter-of-fact about letting your child get something to eat before he goes to bed, but you don't want to make the snack exciting. Don't serve ice cream or brownies at bedtime; instead, offer toast, milk or cereal.

Toni: I shared your idea of serving meals family-style with a parent who has a picky eater. If a child eats only the bread and fills up on that, you recommend just letting it go, and that's what I said to her. She thought I was crazy. She said, "You want me to just let him eat bread?" I said, "Yes" and I blamed you!

Ellyn: Well, that's hard for some parents. They'll say, "What if he eats two slices of bread?" I say, "Let him have three or four slices." It tastes good to them. It's really accessible. It's easy to like and enjoy.

At first, when you offer them unlimited bread, they're likely to eat a lot, but then that wears off and they'll take an interest in something else. Something that children do way better than grownups is pay attention to what tastes good to them. And what tastes good one day is going to be different from what tastes good another day.

Toni: I hate food jags.

Ellyn: I don't comment on a food jag. To me a food jag is when you're trying to outguess what your child is going to eat.

What I'm talking about is just keeping the day-in-day-out routine of menu planning going. You serve a protein, a starch, vegetables and fruit, and you're undeterred. Don't serve hot dogs day after day because a child happens to have a yen for hot dogs. Do your menu planning and your child works within that framework.

Toni: What I hate is when my kids like a food or beverage, like V8 Diet Berry Blend juice, so I'll buy six of them when they're on sale. Then they don't like them anymore and I'm stuck with six juices I don't like.

Ellyn: I hate that too. I've done that with green beans. One day they ate them all up and I thought, "Oh, this is great." The next day I made them and nobody touched them.

Toni: We have to talk more about picky eaters. You advise against making separate meals. You also suggest serving food family style. What else can be done?

Ellyn: The question is: is the picky eater born or made? And the answer is that it's both.

Almost all children are picky to some extent. When they're young, they're inexperienced with food so most kids don't like a food the first time they eat it. It takes them five to 20 times to learn to like it, but some kids are particularly cautious. It seems they have a strong reaction to texture and taste.

Some people actually have more sensitivity to the bitter taste in some vegetables, so they have more to overcome to learn to like new foods. But they do it. They do learn to like new foods if the parents are able to hang in there with the day-in-day-out division of responsibility and feeding.

Parents decide *what* foods to serve, *when* to eat and *where* to eat. Kids decide *whether* they will eat and *how much*.

If parents can hang in, they're doing two things for the child: 1) they're giving him exposure to unfamiliar foods, which means that the child can slowly warm up to them; and 2) the child can see you eat the food, he can touch it or taste it, and eventually he'll learn to like it.

The other thing parents can and must do in order to avoid having a picky eater is not get pushy. They simply need to give the child the autonomy he needs to learn to like the food.

Toni: It took our oldest child 13 years to like asparagus, so sometimes you have to be really, really, patient.

What else do you want to tell us about picky eaters?

Ellyn: You need to sit down and have regular meals together with your child. You need to give them exposure to a variety of foods so they can get comfortable with them and learn to like them. Then you need to avoid pressure of any sort. Pressure includes reminding, badgering, rewarding, applauding, and withholding dessert until she eats what you want. Don't try to get your child to accept more food or trick her into eating – because that will make her pickier.

Toni: Great advice. So what does a healthy eater look like, Ellyn?

Ellyn: Well, a healthy eater comes to the table happily, is willing to be there, enjoys what goes on at the table and enjoys the sociability. She's comfortable with the food that's on the table, picks and chooses from what's available, doesn't necessarily eat some of everything, doesn't whine, doesn't complain about eating certain foods, and doesn't beg for other foods. She is able to come to the table, be a pleasant person to have there, and cope with the food.

Toni: Very good.

Ellyn: Interesting, isn't it? I didn't say a thing about eating their vegetables.

Toni: No, not at all. We really have to keep the big picture in mind, don't we? It goes beyond, "Gee, my child didn't eat the vegetable tonight." We need to get out of the single meal mentality and think in terms of a week or two – did my child get the nutrition she needs?

In your opinion, does raising a healthy eater take years?

Ellyn: I just described what a good eater looks like when they come to the table. If the table is a pleasant place to be, which allows the child to master those skills, then gradually, over the years, the child will increase her food repertoire. She'll learn to like an increasing variety of food and she'll hang on to her positive attitude about eating, which means that in the long run she'll be able to eat the food that is out there in the world and enjoy it. She'll be comfortable going to an unfamiliar table, know that she can manage the food there, and do a good job of seeing to it that she gets fed.

Toni: All right. Let's talk about family-friendly meal planning tactics. I think for some people it feels overwhelming after working all day. What's your advice for parents who struggle with meal planning?

Ellyn: Well, the first thing is to forget about Ozzie and Harriet and think about what's possible. What can I do?

Some families do scratch cooking. Other families stop by the drive-in and pick up bags of food. If they sit down together at the drive-in and eat it, that's great. If they eat it at the kitchen table, that's great. If they do use pre-prepared food or pre-prepared ingredients, that's all just great.

In order to get meals on the table, it takes a lot of different strategies, and it does take some pre-planning.

I really worked hard and racked my brain in *Secrets of Feeding a Healthy Family* to come up with mealtime suggestions for "quick and dirty" menus that you can grab and serve. This includes ingredients you can keep on the shelf and meals that can be made ahead and frozen.

The bottom line is that you have to think ahead and do some planning, rather than trying to create something at 6:00 when you're exhausted.

Toni: I know that each family has to do what will work for them, but do you recommend sitting down once a week to plan some menus for the week? What strategies have worked best for parents?

Ellyn: All different ways work best for parents. Once-a-week meal planning helps a lot. In *Secrets* I did a three-week-cycle menu, which is quite ambitious but once you've got it in place, you use it every three weeks and it's good to go. You just start all over again.

Some people have told me they like it. It depends on what works for the individual. And where you start isn't where you're going to end up. If you can start by doing some short-term planning and be successful with it, then you're going to find as you go along that you get more "plan-ful" and more organized when it comes to getting meals on the table.

Toni: In FamilyFun magazine, which is one of my favorite magazines, I read about a mom who planned a 30-day meal rotation. At least once a week she made each family member's favorite meal, and she even had standard grocery lists. I thought it sounded like such a great idea.

Ellyn: I agree with you. I think it's a marvelous idea.

Toni: In your book, you also suggest having at least one food that a picky eater likes at each meal.

Ellyn: Yes. Always try to match a favorite food with a not-so-favorite food. If you have a picky eater, serve a food that the child can manage, without making a big deal of it. Make a big enough dish so everybody in the family can have some. You don't make it apparent that you're short-order cooking for this child or making special food, because you want them to feel capable.

Toni: I've also found that involving a picky eater in selecting the food or preparing the food is very helpful. One time I put some salad dressing in little bowls and I called them "dips." Then I said, "Here, try this lettuce with the dips." She'd never eaten lettuce before, but when I called the dressing a "dip," all of a sudden she was interested.

Ellyn: Is this the 13- year-old that finally ate asparagus?

Toni: Yes.

Ellyn: The research does point out that there are three different kinds of kids in terms of food acceptance. There's the one who is enthusiastic about every new food and will try it right away and frequently like it. Then there's the one that's more cautious and will say, "I don't like that," but if you say, "Try it, you might like it," they'll generally like it. Then there's the one who just doesn't try it, and doesn't like it, until they get to be 12 or 13 years old.

Toni: Bingo!

Ellyn: Then they start to wake up to the fact that they're missing out, and they begin to add these other missing foods to their diet. You surely can't hold your breath, can you…?

Toni: No. The good news is that they will eventually like more foods.

I love your philosophy of making meals enjoyable. It's about conversation. It's about being together as a family. It's about manners. It's about enjoying good food together. I think if we keep those goals in mind, it takes a lot of pressure off our expectations for our kids.

Ellyn: Absolutely. The bottom line is that parents need to know how important family meals are. Having regular family meals is a venue for parents to give reliable, undivided attention to their children, and children really depend on that.

Toni: There are so many protective factors that having family meals provide. The research tells us that those factors include higher grades, lower alcohol abuse rates, and lower pregnancy rates for teen girls. The bottom line is that we just have to relax and make meals an enjoyable family experience.

✶✶✶✶✶✶

Okay. I'd like you to meet **Beth Weiss**, a single mom who raised five children and now has seven grandchildren. Beth thought of mealtime as a time to connect and have fun with her kids. Beth, what were some of those fun things that you did with your kids during the dinner hour?

Beth: Well, one of my favorite questions was, "What was the worst thing that happened to you today?" Then I'd say, "Tell me the best thing that happened today."

I'd also pick an easy topic that each child had to talk about for one whole minute, non-stop. It's harder than you think. I thought it was a lot of fun, but the kids had a love-hate relationship with it.

I'd pick questions like, "What was your favorite vacation?" or "What would you like to do on a vacation if there were no restrictions and money was no object?" or "What would you do if you were President of the United States?"

It helped to develop their speaking skills, but it was also a time when everybody had to pay attention and listen. It also took the focus off the food.

Toni: Are your kids good public speakers now as a result?

Beth: They are. Mealtime is so valuable because of the undivided attention that they get from the parent or parents.

Toni: Yes. Connecting emotionally through the conversations you have at mealtime is just as valuable as the meal itself.

You also had a garden. Tell us about that.

Beth: Yes, we had a 10 foot by 10 foot garden. We put ropes up and divided the garden into sections. The three younger children and I each cultivated and weeded our own section.

We lived in Arizona and we'd try to grow whatever we could. We succeeded in growing okra, snow peas, tomatoes, corn, and even Swiss chard. Believe it or not, if they grew it, they ate it.

One year the tomatoes were so amazing that we went door-to-door with our tomatoes and shared them with the neighbors. We have a lot of good memories, and the children did become good vegetable eaters.

Toni: I'm sure the garden helped with that.

We planted our first garden this year. We live in Minnesota and we planted the carrots too late. One night in the fall, we had a frost, so we went out to pick the lone carrot that had grown. It was maybe an inch and a half in length and we ceremoniously cut it into four pieces.

I said, "Okay everyone, here's the fruit of our labor" and we had a giggle over the lone carrot.

Ellyn: What a great story!

Beth, were you a single mom when your kids were little?

Beth: Yes.

Ellyn: I hear a lot from single parents. They tell me that it's just too hard to have family meals for kids when you're single. How did you cope with it?

Beth: When they were old enough to stand on a chair, they helped me cook. By the time they were age 12, I wanted them to be able to run a household, so I got them involved in meal planning.

They would write up the menu, shop and cook. Of course, they could choose what they liked the best.

My goal was to have them plan a meal one night a week, but I wasn't always successful at that.

When I planned the menu myself, there may have been a food they hated, but then I'd try to serve one food they liked. For instance, if I served fish with the bones in it, I'd always make French fries.

Toni: My guess is that with five kids you were not a short-order cook. Am I right?

Beth: Yes, they never knew that was even a possibility.

Toni: So you have to teach kids that it's not an option to make another meal.

Ellyn: Yes, you must make a strong commitment to family meals right from the get-go.

Beth: We were pretty structured. There were chores before breakfast, then breakfast, and then school. I didn't serve many snacks.

Ellyn: That's impressive. You were able to see and act on your own values. Even though you were the only adult in the home, you made it clear that meals were important. You made them happen and your kids had access to you on a regular basis.

Toni: Yes, that is very impressive, and I bet you now have very responsible children. You gave them chores, structure and meal-planning skills, so they now have those life skills. Thank you, Beth.

Contact Information:

Ellyn Satter

Mailing Address: 1670 Don Simon D., Sun Prairie, WI 53590

Phone: 608-318-1600

Email Address: *Clio@ellynsatterinstitute.org*

Website: *www.ellynsatterinstitute.org*

Resources:

Secrets of Feeding a Healthy Family: How to Eat, How to Raise Good Eaters, How to Cook www.ellynsatterinstitute.org/store/index.php?route=product/ product&product_id=50

Child of Mine: Feeding With Love and Good Sense

www.ellynsatter.com/books-child-of-mine-feeding-with-love-and-good-sense-p-786.html

Your Child's Weight: Helping Without Harming

www.ellynsatterinstitute.org/store/index.php?route=product product&path=59&product_id=52

Ellyn Satter's Feeding With Love and Good Sense II DVD

www.ellynsatterinstitute.org/store/index.php?route=product/product&path=61&product_id=57

Feeding with Love and Good Sense: The First Two Years

www.ellynsatterinstitute.org/store/index.php?route=product/product&product_id=79

For handouts and articles, see *www.ellynsatterinstitute.org*. See especially "Resources/Just for Fun/From the Cook" at *www.ellynsatterinstitute.org/res/justforfun.php*.

10 Tips for "Going Greener" as a Family

Meet the Expert:

Micaela Preston is a freelance writer and marketing professional with a passion for all things green and healthy. She has a practical take on "green living," which she applies in her popular blog Mindful Momma. Like many parents, Micaela cares deeply about the health of her family as well as the health of the earth. Yet, she knows first-hand how hard it can be to keep on top of all the latest eco-friendly products and the most recent health scares … while still keeping the reins on the family budget.

Micaela's book *Practically Green: Your Guide to Ecofriendly Decision-Making* includes essential information to help you make smart, green choices for your family, as well as over 30 do-it-yourself projects and ideas for making your own earth-friendly products. Micaela is available as a writer and speaker on green living topics and as a brand champion for your sustainable product or service.

Micaela lives in Minneapolis with her husband and two boys. When she is not writing, she is busy whipping up a healthy meal or the eco-craft du jour.

******

Toni: Our topic is "10 Tips for Going Greener as a Family." There are so many reasons to go green, but keeping our families healthy by limiting the amount of toxins we're exposed to is one of the most important, along with keeping our wonderful earth healthy.

There have been more reports recently about toxins in toys, lotions, jewelry, cleaners, and many other products that we have in our homes. Micaela, your book *Practically Green: Your Guide to Ecofriendly Decision-Making* gave me practical information that I could use right away.

I found the book very easy to navigate, and I loved the graphs and visuals because I could get the essential information even if I didn't have time to read a whole chapter. Congratulations on putting together a great guide.

Micaela: Thank you.

Toni: I want to start out by talking about the latest scares. First, China is producing kids' toys with lead in them. Senator Amy Klobuchar did get some legislation passed in Congress to limit that, but now the latest scare is that cadmium has been found in jewelry sold in stores like Walmart and Claire's.

The jewelry contains cadmium levels ranging from 10 percent to 90 percent. Cadmium is a known toxin and is seventh on a federal government list of most hazardous substances. So I'm just wondering: who the heck is monitoring toys, jewelry and other kids' products?

Micaela: Well, that's a very good question, Toni. It is supposed to be the Consumer Product Safety Commission, which is the federal agency that monitors the safety of the products that we buy and the things that are sold in the United States. But, as we know, there have been some issues with products getting through the cracks.

Recently, the Consumer Safety Product Improvement Act helped to make improvements by banning lead and certain foliates in any product for children. That was a great move. Unfortunately, what's happened now is that some of the manufacturers have found a loophole; instead of using lead they're using the heavy metal called cadmium, which is not yet banned. So that's tough, because now we need to watch out for that.

For our families to stay safe, it takes a combination. We have a federal agency watching out for us, but we *also* have to keep tabs ourselves on what's going on.

Toni: But how do we do that? When you pick up a toy to buy for your child, there isn't a list of ingredients on the back that says "cadmium" is in that toy.

Micaela: No, there isn't.

Toni: So tip number one is: How do we figure out what toys are safe to buy for kids?

Micaela: My best advice for parents is to shop for toys at a local toy store that you trust. Where I live, in the Twin Cities, we have a couple of great local toy stores that carefully research the products they carry.

They have sales people that are well informed and very helpful. So I can feel confident purchasing toys from a place like that versus going into a Toys "R" Us, where it's a lot harder to know what you're buying.

Toni: So find a smaller toy store and ask them, "Do you monitor the safety of toys?" and see if they come up with a good answer.

Micaela: Yes. Then you gain a level of trust by getting to know the sales people. Now, I know that parents can't always do that, but that's my first recommendation.

Another thing: I highly advise staying out of the dollar stores, because that's where the cheapest of the cheap toys get to.

Toni: I'd also like to provide parents with a link to a reliable website: *www.healthystuff.org.*

Micaela: Yes, they're a great resource because they do research on the top hazards and metals that are in toys, and they test them.

On their website, you can look up toys by type or by brand, or you can even check to see if they have tested a particular toy.

Toni: Now let's shift to BPA and plastics. **Tip number two is: What plastic products should we avoid?**

Micaela: BPA is also known as bisphenol A. It's a chemical that is used in the manufacturing of certain plastics, and it's commonly found in plastic bottles. All plastic bottles that contain BPA will have a "7" recycling designation on the bottom, but not all plastic bottles with a "7" designation contain BPA, so it can be confusing. Some bottles will have a 7 plus "BPA free."

Many manufacturers are now moving away from using BPA in their products because it's gotten such a bad rap; and the FDA finally agreed that this is a chemical of concern to them. So we're probably going to see more legislation around BPA. But currently, BPA is also found in the lining of cans, which is something that not everyone knows. So when you buy canned food in the store, there's a lining in that can that contains BPA.

This isn't good. Eden Foods, often listed as Eden Organic, is one brand that I know of that doesn't use BPA. I buy their products whenever I can and stock up when they're on sale.

Toni: Baby bottles and children's sippy cups contain BPA, correct?

Micaela: Baby bottles, children's sippy cups, and water bottles all contain BPA, unless otherwise indicated.

Bottles with a recycling code on the bottom of 1, 2, 4, or 5 are considered the safer bottles. There are still some recommended guidelines for plastics, though. The biggest one is not to microwave plastics, because when plastics are heated, the chemicals migrate and leech into the food.

Toni: So, definitely use glass containers for reheating food in the microwave.

Okay, time for **tip number three.** A healthy diet includes fruits and vegetables, yet many of them have pesticides on them that don't wash off. You have a list of the "dirty dozen" that will help us determine which fruits and vegetables to buy organic. **What are the "dirty dozen" fruits and vegetables that have the most pesticides?**

Micaela: The Environmental Working Group put together a great guide each year, and it's called, "The Shoppers Guide to Pesticides." It's available on their website at *www.ewg.org/foodnews/summary.php*

In the guide, there's a list of the fruits and vegetables that are the most contaminated with pesticides, and those are known as the "dirty dozen."

Unfortunately, they are some of the fruits and vegetables that families with young kids tend to eat the most: apples, strawberries, grapes, cherries, peaches, tomatoes, cucumbers, bell peppers and celery. It's really recommended that you make a choice to buy those things organic.

Then you can check out the fruits and vegetables that are lowest in pesticide residue. I was happy to see that cantaloupe, mangos and pineapples are on the list, as well as corn, asparagus, avocado, sweet peas and onions.

When you're making choices in the grocery store, it helps to know which foods are most contaminated and least contaminated with pesticides.

Toni: What an irony that most kids tend to like apples and strawberries and grapes, yet they are high in pesticide residue.

Micaela: Right. I recommend that parents purchase organic when they can. I know it can be very hard to spend the extra money, so I just try to focus mostly on apples because we eat a lot of apples. Then I buy whatever I can on sale. As a parent, I feel that we're constantly making choices and tradeoffs, so we just do the best we can.

Toni: That's great practical advice.

Tip number four: Give us some tricks for sneaking more healthy nutrients into our kids' meals.

Micaela: I was just at a cooking class with an instructor who teaches kids in the school district about healthy eating.

The biggest tip was to get kids involved with cooking, because then they take some ownership and build enthusiasm about food. I think we often forget about that because we're so busy just trying to get the meal on the table.

Toni: I want to share a story. Our oldest daughter had never touched lettuce. She just refused, saying she didn't like the look of it or the texture. So, when she was nine years old, we did an experiment at the cabin. Both kids washed the lettuce, ripped it and used the spinner to dry it. I think kids love to use gadgets. Then I put different dressings in custard cups and called them "dips," and let them dip the lettuce into different containers. After that, she started eating lettuce. So I think we have to be a little creative sometimes.

Micaela: That's a perfect example.

Toni: Packaging is important to kids, too. They may eat yogurt from a tube they can squeeze rather than from a carton.

Micaela: Here's another tip: when I bake, I buy white whole wheat flour. It's a cross between basic all-purpose flour and regular whole wheat flour. It's not as heavy as regular whole wheat flour, but it does have most of the same nutritional content. It's great to mix into cookies, breads or cakes, and I find that my kids don't notice the difference so I can sneak in a few more nutrients.

Toni: Great idea.

There's a lot of discussion these days about our "ecological footprint" and how our daily actions impact the earth. Buying products from other countries like Guatemala or water from Fiji, versus buying locally, really makes a difference.

Give us some advice on buying locally, which is tip number five. Why is this important?

Micaela: It's important for a number of reasons. When you buy locally, versus having things shipped from all around the world, it's better for the environment, there are fewer transportation costs, and the food is fresher. It's also important to make our children aware of this.

A lot of kids grow up not knowing where their food comes from. They think it all comes from the grocery store and they don't really give it much thought. So I try to get my kids to understand where the food comes from, whether we're shopping at a grocery store or a farmers' market. And we grow some food ourselves; I find that kids just love to help grow their own food.

Toni: It really is fun, particularly when you start from seeds and nurture the plants the whole way. When you're buying food in a store with your kids, do you point it out to them when the food comes from another country?

Micaela: Yes. More and more stores are getting on the local food band-wagon, and they're making signage, especially in the produce section, to let you know what is locally grown.

Toni: We live in Minnesota, so if we just had locally grown fruits and vegetables, we would not have much to eat in the winter. What do you suggest for people that live in climates like ours?

Micaela: You can freeze many vegetables and fruits. So, if you're really industrious and you have the time, you can purchase a lot of things at the farmers' market, flash freeze them, store them, and eat them in the winter.

You can also do without some things. I've met people who simply don't buy bananas because they don't grow here and they never will.

I don't suggest that everyone's going to take that position, but you could stop buying strawberries in the winter, for example, because that's a summer food. Tell your kids that and they'll understand it's a seasonal fruit.

Right now we've been eating a lot of root vegetables, like potatoes and rutabagas, that can be stored for longer periods of time.

Toni: Another big topic is cleaning products, so let's get to **tip number six**.

If I'm in a small room and I open up certain cleaning products, I have trouble breathing; I can feel the impact in my lungs. **What are some cleaning products that you don't even want to have in your house?**

Micaela: Some products are worse than others. Some that are especially bad are oven cleaners, drain cleaners and toilet bowl cleaners. The conven-tional ones have some particularly nasty chemicals in them; they contain ingredients like lye and hydrochloric acid, which are highly corrosive ingredients and can burn your skin.

You don't want to risk having your kids get hold of those kinds of products, so if you do have them, keep them out-of-reach of children. But even for adults they're nasty.

There are more natural and much safer versions of these types of products that you can buy, so I do recommend switching to safer brands for those three cleaning products.

Toni: What's a good brand of cleaner we can buy without all the toxins?

Micaela: A very simple scouring product called Bon Ami is a great product for cleaning ovens.

Toni: You also have some recipes for making your own cleaning products.

Micaela: You actually don't need to *make* your own cleaning products. A lot of the ingredients that you already have in your kitchen cupboard – like baking soda, lemon and vinegar – work well. Vinegars are antibacterial and baking soda is a non-abrasive scrub, so they're great for making scrubs for counter tops or bathtubs. They're the super-cleaners.

Toni: What do you like to use to clean your windows?

Micaela: I have a recipe for my own window spray in my book. It's 1/3 cup of vinegar, 2 cups of water, and 1/2 teaspoon of a natural dish soap or castile soap.

Toni: Excellent, thank you. Next, we're going to talk about body products like lotions. I read a book called *Anticancer* and became aware of "parabens" and some of the other potential toxins that are in things like moisturizers and lotions that we've been lathering on our bodies for years.

For tip number seven, tell us what ingredients to avoid when buying body products.

Micaela: The scariest thing about our beauty product routines is that, on an average day, most people apply over 100 ingredients on their bodies – because there are so many ingredients in the products that we use and we use many types of products. A lot of these chemicals haven't been thoroughly tested and so there are risks.

Parabens are used as preservatives in body care products and they have negative repercussions that are linked to hormone disruption and breast cancer. In fact, parabens have been found in breast cancer tissue, but these products are still allowed in our beauty products. So, avoid parabens.

Also try to avoid phthalates, which are used to fix the fragrances in place. Those can also be harmful and they cause a lot of allergic reactions.

There are certainly many ingredients in conventional beauty products that one should avoid; but fortunately, there are also a lot of great natural products available.

Toni: Parabens can also be listed as "methylparaben" or "butylparaben;" just look for "paraben" at the end of a long word…

Micaela: My best recommendation when it comes to buying body products is to find a retailer that you can trust and find sales people that can recommend products for you. If you go to a Whole Foods, for instance, or to your local food co-op, there are lots of products there, and it can be overwhelming to try to figure out what to buy.

Express your concerns about specific ingredients and then go with the recommendation from the sales people who are the most knowledgeable.

Another resource that I definitely want to mention is called "Skin Deep." *www.ewg.org/skindeep*

It's a beauty products and cosmetics database, and it's a wonderful resource because you can check specific products against the database to tell you how safe they are based on a number of measures. It's a very thorough rating system. Like the "dirty dozen" food list, it's from the Environmental Working Group (EWG).

Toni: Tip number eight is about cosmetics safety. Cosmetics are not monitored by the Food and Drug Administration, right?

Micaela: Right. They do have some regulations, but they don't have the budget to monitor all the thousands and thousands of chemicals that are out there. Only a miniscule number of chemicals are actually monitored and properly tested.

Toni: There was an article in the Star Tribune stating that many lipsticks and mascaras, cosmetics that women use daily, have lead, mercury and parabens in them.

Lead and mercury are known to be human carcinogens, so the FDA tested 22 lipsticks and all of them contained lead. We're putting these lipsticks on our lips every day and there's lead in them!

In another study, they tested the blood and urine of teenage girls and they found there were 16 toxic chemicals inside their bodies. Some of those are commonly found in cosmetics. So, every day people may be putting toxins in their body without even knowing it.

Micaela: One of the biggest concerns is not necessarily an individual chemical, but what's called the "body burden." The question is, "What are the repercussions of having all these different toxic chemicals combine and accumulate in your body over time?"

A lot of chemicals don't disappear. They stay and they accumulate. So it's best to stick with products that are as natural as possible and that have the least amount of chemicals, in order to try and keep that body burden down.

Toni: It sounds like a mad science experiment.

Micaela: It does, and it feels like we shouldn't have to be the ones worrying about this, but we must protect our families.

Toni: Let's mention that helpful website again: *www.ewg.org/skindeep*

Micaela: Yes. They rate cosmetic products on a scale from zero to 10. Zero is the best and 10 is the worst. It's just a great way to find products. Buying products in the zero to three range is the best. If you check your lipstick on the site and it rates a nine or a 10, for example, you probably want to get rid of that lipstick.

Toni: I remember reading that red lipstick is the worst, along with nail polish. Another safe site is *www.organicdivas.com*

Micaela: Yes, on that website the owner's mission is to make sure that all the products don't contain bad chemicals.

Toni: Tip number nine: Help us understand the different advertising labels on foods. They may say, "organically grown" or "healthy" or "family grown." Which labels can we trust so we know that the product is organically grown and free of chemicals and pesticides?

Micaela: The gold standard is the USDA Organic seal. It's the circle that says, "USDA Organic." There are very stringent guidelines for food manufacturers to be able to use that label. If you see that label, you can be assured that at least 95 percent of the ingredients are organic.

There are other labels that can be helpful. Not all manufacturers can afford to go through the USDA Organic certification process. Think about a small farmer, for instance, who can't afford to do that.

One of the other good labels is "Food Alliance Certified." It's meant for smaller food manufacturers who meet certain standards so they can get a certification as well.

Another reliable label is "Nationally Certified Grown" which many of the smaller food manufacturers use.

Toni: Shopping at a local co-op can also be helpful. And once you do your homework and read the labels, then you can stick with the same products to save time.

Tip number 10 is buying gently used products so we're not always buying new. This tip not only helps the earth, but also saves us money, right?

Micaela: Yes. It's a great way to save money as well as reduce your consumption in general. When making a purchasing decision, I try hard to think: "Could I buy this used? Is that a good option?"

For me, the biggest category is probably children's clothes. I buy a lot of my kids' clothes at the thrift store. I have two boys and they tend to burn through clothes quickly. So, I figure why spend a lot of money on new clothes? And I also feel better about buying something used and giving it a new life.

Toni: I have a friend who is a master at this. For Christmas, she bought friends used books from the used book store and they were in great shape. She paid half price or less. And she just got a refrigerator for 80 bucks that she got off an Internet site. Her kids have worn vintage clothes for years.

One of her daughters used to get teased because she didn't have designer clothes. She'd pull together really creative outfits with her vintage clothes, though. And guess what? A month later, the same girls who had ridiculed her were copying some of her fashion choices. She's now studying fashion design in college.

Micaela, do you recommend craigslist to find used products?

Micaela: Absolutely. Craigslist is a great place to find used things, mainly because you can search for exactly what you need and find options that are located near you.

EBay is good, too, although you will pay a bit for shipping and wait a little longer.

You can also shop at a traditional thrift store or consignment shop. And swap sites where you swap products with other people are another option. There are swap sites for baby clothing and lots of other items. You might sell something of your own, but instead of getting money, you get a certain amount of points that you can bank.

Toni: What about the FreeCycle site?

Micaela: FreeCycle is another great site where everything is free. And craigslist also has a free option. You can post something in the free section and people can just come by and pick it up. As they say, one person's trash is another person's treasure.

Toni: A friend of mine started a non-profit called Kidz Klozet in a church in north Minneapolis where you can donate your gently used kids' clothes, and then families that need clothes can stop by and shop for free. I love it when people take it to the next step and ask, "How can I help those that don't have enough?"

One thing we haven't talked about yet is deodorant. Are there any safe, yet effective, deodorants that are free of toxins?

Micaela: There are a couple of key ingredients that you want to avoid when buying a deodorant. Aluminum is one of them – because there's a link to some neurological diseases like Alzheimer's. Most antiperspirants contain aluminum, so look for something that's aluminum free.

Another ingredient to avoid that's often in deodorant is triclosan, which is used to kill odors. It's an ingredient that can cause drug resistance in bacteria, and it's also used in a lot of anti-bacterial hand soaps.

You also want to avoid aerosol deodorants.

As far as finding a deodorant that's effective, it really depends on the person. I've heard that a lot of people really like the deodorant crystals – crystal rock that's made from mineral salts. It may seem a little odd to rub rock crystals under your arm, but a lot of people swear by them for odor control.

Toni: Thank you, Micaela, for sharing all this valuable information.

Contact information:

Micaela Preston

Mailing address: 312 Harriet Avenue S., Minneapolis, MN 55408

Phone: 612-823-8962

Email address: mindfulmomma@yahoo.com

Website: *www.mindfulmomma.com*

Resources:

Book: *Practically Green: Your Guide to Ecofriendly Decision-Making* by Micaela Preston

Blog: *www.mindfulmomma.com/*

Recipes:

Tub and Tile Cleaner:

www.mindfulmomma.com/2009/09/homemade-tub-tile-cleaning-reme-dies.html

Simple Sink Scrub: *www.mindfulmomma.com/2007/10/homemade-cleani.html*

"Dirty Dozen" Fruits and Veggies: *www.ewg.org/foodnews/summary.php*

To determine the safety of beauty products: *www.ewg.org/skindeep/* and *www.organicdivas.com*

Great Ways to Connect as a Couple

Meet the Experts:

Dan Devey, father of four, from Canton, Michigan, is the owner and developer of Coolestdates.com, a premier website for dating ideas. Coolestdates.com was developed in 2002 and has been featured in the Wall Street Journal (November 18, 2002 – "The Best Way to Keep Romance Alive"). The site has close to 1000 different ideas in 29 different categories, and it attracts 40,000 visitors monthly.

Kevin Anderson, Ph.D., is a poet, writer, psychologist, humorist, storyteller, and dynamic public speaker. Kevin has a private practice in psychology, working with couples, families and individuals on a variety of life problems. In 2003, Kevin's book *Divinity in Disguise: Nested Meditations to Delight the Mind and Awaken the Soul* was named one of the best books of the year by Spirituality and Health magazine. His second book, *The 7 Spiritual Practices of Marriage*, has led to many international, national and local speaking engagements for married couples. He and his wife of 28 years, Claudia, live in the Toledo, Ohio area.

Meet the Parent Guest:

Ann Searles is a mother of three, and she and her husband, Mike, have done a great job of making a weekly commitment to their relationship for nearly 20 years.

******

Toni: Dan, you have a great story about how you set up strategic dates when you were looking for a spouse. You wanted 10 to 12 different attributes in a spouse so you chose dates that would help you find a woman with those attributes. Can you share that story with us?

Dan: Sure. I viewed dating as something that you did to find out what attributes were important to you, so when I was 18, I sat down and put together a list of attributes that I was looking for in my future spouse. Then I listed things that I would need to do to attract that kind of person.

I think I listed 13 attributes for a future wife. I listed things like someone who's loving, who would be a good mother, and who would be creative and enthusiastic, intelligent and thoughtful. Those were all things that were important to me.

I also listed the attributes that I would need to develop to attract that kind of person and I set goals to help me achieve those attributes. Then I used dating as a strategic way of filtering and finding qualities that were important to me and that would ultimately help me find the person that would help me achieve those goals.

Toni: That's an incredible story, and you found your spouse and are happily married.

Dan: Yes.

Toni: It's so difficult for married couples to find the time to devote to each other, and I think babysitting is a big stumbling block for many parents. So let's share a few ideas. If you can't afford to go out or you don't have a babysitter, what are some dates that you can have at home without the cost of babysitting?

Dan: Well, there are some simple things you can do.

I like the idea of making homemade bread. You can knead the dough together and then relax with a good book or watch a video while the dough rises and bakes. Then let it cool just enough and enjoy hot bread with butter and honey.

I also like ideas where you're providing a service to others. Maybe you could put together thank you cards to send out to servicemen overseas.

Another idea might be to design your own dream house. Start by sketching floor plans and then build miniature furniture and rooms from cardboard boxes. Then incorporate way-out ideas, like a spiral slippery slide to get from one floor to another. The point is to be creative and to think outside the box.

Toni: Oh, isn't that fun? Or you can plan your next vacation. Or sample different wines and cheeses. Or cook together. The point is to find something relaxing to do together.

Another barrier for many couples is the *cost* of going out. Let's say that you're able to find a babysitter but you don't want to spend a lot of cash for the date. What are some low budget ideas that you can share?

Dan: One thing you might do is go to a free concert in a mall or school or church or civic center. The entertainment section in your local newspaper will list those types of things that are going on.

You can make a couple of pans of brownies and then drive to friends' houses or to the elderly in your neighborhood and deliver a small plate of brownies. You can visit your friends for a while, and when it gets a little late you can go home and finish off the brownies.

Toni: Excellent! I live in the Twin Cities and there are some museums that have free Tuesday nights or first Saturdays of the month. So it can be helpful to use the Internet and local newspaper as sources for finding low-budget ideas.

Dan: You don't have to spend a lot of money to find something good to do.

You can find a friend to visit at the hospital or you can make get well cards together. You can put together poems or funny verses and encouragements. You can view dating as something that you do to have fun, but also to reach out to others and make their days better. It'll enrich your marriage if you do.

Toni: I love your idea of adding service to dating. I don't think many people think about service when they plan dates together.

Next, please share some romantic date ideas. I know you have lots.

Dan: Here's a creative way of coming up with three different romantic ideas. Put together three envelopes, each with a different date. Then have your spouse choose one of those three envelopes. She can either choose to accept that date or trade it in for one of the remaining two envelopes. Then you go and do that immediately.

And here's an idea to get started. I really enjoyed putting together a treasure hunt, where you write clues on note cards telling your spouse where to go and you put the clues in places around the community. You have a friend or relative give her the first clue and ultimately the final clue leads your spouse to a restaurant where you're waiting at a table with flowers.

Toni: You *are* creative!

Dan: Your spouse will be thrilled to the gills.

Another idea is to plan a weekend trip somewhere close, even if it's only an hour or two away. You can call ahead to the hotel and have your dinner waiting in the room, along with flowers and dessert.

Toni: I think mystery adds an element of romance to a date. Do you agree?

Dan: For sure! Here's one of the dates that I really enjoyed recently. I made reservations at a gourmet restaurant. I packed a travel bag for my wife and I made up some chocolate-covered strawberries. Then I called her from work and told her that we were going out, that I'd arranged for the babysitter, and that I'd be picking her up.

There was an element of mystery. Then after dinner we went to a dinner theater to watch an Irish step-dancing show and stayed at a hotel near the theater with a hot tub in the room. The next morning we went to a local museum and it was a really memorable day.

Toni: All the women are thinking, "I want a guy like Dan. Clone him! I want a guy who likes to be romantic."

Dan: Another thing you can do is put together a message inviting your spouse to a romantic getaway and cut the invitation up into pieces. You can send a few pieces at a time during the week. Or you can put those pieces into balloons and cover her floor with the balloons. Then you can pack up the bags and get someone to watch the kids so you can go away for at least two nights. A little bit of intrigue and romance goes a long way.

Toni: Absolutely. What's your all-time favorite date, Dan?

Dan: My all-time favorite dates are simply the ones where I get to spend time alone with my wife. It can be spending a little money or a lot of money.

I've enjoyed going on a cruise with my spouse for a full week and leaving our children with their grandparents. I think the key is just making sure that you have time for each other.

Toni: Let's talk about babysitting. We don't have relatives close by so we have set up a trade with another family. For instance, we'll have a 24-hour getaway and our friends will watch our children; and then six months later, they'll have a couple's getaway and we'll watch their children.

Do you have other ideas for babysitting?

Dan: I think trades are a great idea. My church group often sets up a night out for adults. Couples can drop off their young children and the older youth provide babysitting to all the younger kids. It gives us a chance to go and do something and our kids are close by being taken care of.

Toni: Our church started that once a month after a colleague and I gave a presentation called "Parents, Reclaim Your Couple Time" at church. It's such a great service to provide couples the opportunity for free child care.

I was also in a Mom's Club and they started a babysitting co-op. So, if you volunteer for two hours, you then get two hours of babysitting in return. I think if we're really creative about babysitting, we can find ways to reduce the cost.

Dan: Another way might be to invite three or four couples over to your house and hire two babysitters to take care of all the kids in the basement.

Toni: Fun!

Dan, you've been fabulous! Parents, be sure to check out *www.coolestdates. com*. It's an amazing website.

******

My next guest is **Kevin Anderson.** Kevin is a writer, psychologist, poet, public speaker and the author of *The 7 Spiritual Practices of Marriage*, which is available on Amazon. Kevin also organized a date night for parents in the Toledo area, where he lives with his wife Claudia and their five children.

Toni: Kevin, you have so many great things to share with us today. We know that sex and money are two issues that can cause trouble in a marriage, but you say there's a third topic that's just as important for us to focus on. What's the third of the big three, Kevin?

Kevin: If you look in any marriage therapy textbook, sex and money are the big two, but for some time I've been saying it's really the big three, and the third one is *time*. People are struggling tremendously with their time as a couple.

Toni: I couldn't agree more. Are you recommending time alone with your spouse when you say time together?

Kevin: I think there are a multitude of things we need to look at concerning time for a couple: time to connect emotionally; time for affection; time for dates; time for sex; time to plan bigger adventures; time for financial planning and college planning; and time to plan their life together.

Toni: Has it been your experience that many couples let their marriage slide to the bottom of the priority list? Have kids taken center stage these days?

Kevin: Right, there's no doubt. I see that in my practice and many experts are saying that many marriages are child-centered. But a really healthy family has a strong marriage at the center. Children are awesome; nobody can question that, but you don't kill off the goose – the marriage that produced them. I think some of the running around caused by too many activities begins to starve the goose of what it needs to really thrive.

Toni: Why do so many of us think that our marriage can be put on autopilot?

Kevin: I think the model that we have for true love in our culture is that the relationship is perfect in the beginning. If we were an artist, we'd think we had the perfect masterpiece at the beginning rather than just a blank canvas that we're going to need to work on for our whole life together.

So this model where we think we have perfection already, and all we need is an occasional bit of connection or time to keep it tuned up, is very different than what marriage really is. Marriage is challenging, and it needs daily time and daily connection. If we don't do that, we're not going to continue building it. So I think we actually need a whole new paradigm of what true love is and what marriage is.

Toni: Tell us what paradigm is more realistic and would serve us better....

Kevin: I've been reviewing research on young people and what they say they want in a partner. Ninety-four percent of young people say they're looking for their soul mate. Yet, a tremendous number of young people are skeptical about marriage, and often they've grown up in some sort of difficult circumstances. I think the soul mate language is misleading because it implies perfection. The expectation is that I'm going to find the perfect person for me and it's just going to be great from then on.

I prefer a different twist: soul companion – somebody that I can walk through life with during the good times and the difficult times; somebody I will stay in touch with every day; somebody who I can plan with and we can walk through it together. That doesn't imply perfection and so it's actually more doable, more achievable, and deeper than the expectation of perfection from the beginning.

Toni: We've all heard about building "attachment" and how vital it is to our children so they feel loved and are emotionally healthy and produc tive; but you take that concept and apply it to marriage too. Tell us more about that.

Kevin: This is a very hot topic in marriage research. Sue Johnson is writing the most about the topic. She has a book called *Hold Me Tight*, which is the lay person's introduction to this. A securely attached child feels that their parent will be there for them when needed and yet feels secure enough to explore the world and not be too needy. The breakthrough that we're now realizing is that we replay these energies as adults in marriage. We turn to each other and hope to find the other person there for comfort and for communication. If we don't find them there, we can replay some of the energies from childhood, which are: I don't feel secure; I don't feel connected.

Yet we have a culture that's all about independence. We're all striving to be independent. But in marriage, Johnson says, "There are only two options: secure dependency or insecure dependency." So, it's a fascinating theory and I think that couples that want to go a bit deeper could take a look at her work.

Toni: You have a book *The 7 Spiritual Practices of Marriage*. Can you share some of the practices that you strongly believe in?

Kevin: I can quickly go through them.

1. Create a shared vision is really to make sure you're building the same marriage together. It involves some regular meetings to discuss what you are building and how it's going.

2. Make connection the norm is one that we'll be talking about in more detail later.

3. How to **bring honor to conflict** is a huge area.

4. Another is to **give up the search for the perfect lover**, which is all about accepting the person you're with.

5. **Work on the "I" in marriage**, which means if you want something to get better, take a look at yourself.

6. **Make love a gift** is about a spiritual model of sexuality.

7. **Walk the sacred path** is about having a deep heart and awareness of sacredness in the deeper part of life and in your marriage.

Toni: Working on the "I" seems very important. Are people quick to blame the other person and try to change them?

Kevin: It's the most natural thing in the world. When I teach classes, I bring in a giant candle snuffer that I made out of a 10-foot-long piece of PVC pipe and a big lampshade. I go around in the audience and I say, "You know, if you were my wife, there's just that one little thing I'd like to get rid of. Let's just snuff that out right now and we could be perfectly happy."

People laugh uproariously because we all know the tendency. One woman in the crowd elbowed her husband and said, "You're a snuffer. I knew you were a snuffer."

Toni: That's a great story.

Kevin: Many parents have kids on teams, and the coach is always saying, "There's no 'I' in team." It's the most common thing you hear. One of my daughters said, "Yeah, but did you hear the 'me' in team?"

But, at any rate, there's an "I" in marriage and we all need to be taking a look at that. How can *I* be a better spouse, a better soul companion?

Toni: Next, we're going to talk about practical ideas for gaining time together as a couple so we can "make connection the norm." You have a three-second idea. What is that?

Kevin: The first objection people have is, "Connection sounds great, but I don't have time every day to do that."

So I say, "Do you have three seconds?"

For eight years, my wife Claudia and I started every day with a bow to each other in the morning. We put our hands over our chest, in a prayerful position, and gave a nod of the head. To us, it means: "I honor you and I will try to honor you today." For those that are more spiritually minded, it might be "I see God in you," but in any case it's different than just stumbling past somebody to get to the bathroom as the first energy of the day.

Toni: So couples can find a ritual that feels comfortable to them and make that a habit. That's the idea, isn't it?

Kevin: I spoke to a group of ministers and one of them said, "Have you got anything else, because there's no way I'm doing that bow with my wife."

My own daughter saw a picture of my wife and I doing this in the local paper and she fell on the floor saying, "That's the stupidest thing I've ever seen," and I said, "Get used to it, that's the way we start our day."

Toni: How can we connect if we just have 30 seconds?

Kevin: I've had couples come up to me years after I've made a presentation and say, "We've never forgotten the 30-second hug."

I ask couples to stop and embrace each other for 30 seconds. It's always a good laugh because after 15 seconds I say, "You've made it half way," and people think it's been two minutes by then.

I tell couples it's only .03 percent of your day, and if you can invest that 30 seconds daily, you're most likely not going to show up in my office for marriage therapy, because you have to be doing pretty well with somebody to be able to hold them for 30 seconds.

Toni: What great advice!

I attended a psychology conference on mindfulness. One of the exercises they had us do was to stare into the eyes of the person that was sitting next to us. We had to stare for one minute without looking away. I can't tell you how powerful that exercise was.

It could be a great exercise for couples too. I felt this flood of compassion for the guy who happened to be sitting next to me and he must have felt this flood of compassion for me because he gave me a book he had written and wrote a beautiful inscription in it. We had never met before. It was really powerful.

Kevin: When we slow down and get on that slow wavelength to just look for a minute, as you did, the energy that's there can be marvelous. Sometimes we're in high gear and feel there's no time for it, but that's an illusion; we can always take time.

Toni: What if we have 15 minutes, Kevin?

Kevin: Bill Doherty at the University of Minnesota talks about couples developing a ritual of 15 minutes of having coffee together each day just to talk. I use the word "ritual" because it's something that we repeat over and over. It's something that has deep meaning.

In our home, I like to be a little more structured. I like to sit down and have a "gratitude ritual," which is just a simple question: "What are you grateful for today?" It's an interesting entry point into a conversation instead of "How was your day?"

A lot of times, one member of a couple doesn't really want to hear too much about how the other's day was: "Do I have to listen to a half hour of stress again?"

Sometimes my wife and I will do a high/low: "Tell me a high from your day and a low from your day." One woman said that she tried it with her children and used the language, "Tell me a 'grateful' and tell me a 'grumble.'"

It touches a little deeper than "How was your day?"

Toni: I love your suggestions. There's a lot of research on gratitude and how it can help us to be happier individuals by just acknowledging those things that we're grateful for each day.

What can we do on a weekly basis?

Kevin: Dan covered the importance of dating. Yet a recent Gallup survey of couples found that 17 weeks was the average time since the couples went on a date.

So, the idea that couples might be going on a date once a week is getting lost. Every two weeks might be more realistic.

I stress not only dating, but also couples committing to meeting with each other in their own home once a week, just for an hour or so. They should set a regular time to sit down and talk.

The meeting should have at least two parts. One part is business. What's going on this week? Let's coordinate things. The other part is longer range: "Where are we going with this whole marriage and family thing? How are we doing? What are some fun things coming up? What are some challenges we need to look at?"

If you do this, you start acting like people that own the marriage together and you work to move it forward.

Toni: I don't know any couples that do that, Kevin. It makes so much sense to me when you say it, but honestly until you said it, I don't think

I would have thought about it…. "Let's look at our marriage long-term and try to plan to keep it together."

Kevin: This started in my own marriage when my dad died and I was really struggling with that. My wife came to me and said, "We've been meeting once a week, but how about meeting once a day with me? I just want to see how you're doing."

So we started that eight years ago and we meet five days a week at 7 a.m. We start every day with a meeting and put our relationship first.

Toni: You are walking the walk! I bet people are thinking, "How do I find the time? My kids are involved in so many activities. I work. I've got laundry to do. How the heck am I going to fit all this in?" How do you find that time, Kevin?

Kevin: Well, the first thing is to let go of the illusion that there isn't time. The way that we spend our time is a statement about our values. So the first thing to say is: "It's not just finding the time, it's reserving the time in advance."

I'm a writer and I learned a valuable lesson from a writer's program. One of the guests said, "A lot of writers talk about writer's block where they just sit around and can't write because their muse or their inspiration hasn't shown up."

The leader said, "You know what? You have to show up yourself at the same time every day in your writing place and then the muse will show up and meet you. But if you don't show up, the muse or the inspiration is going to jump over your house and go into the next one where somebody's shown up."

So that's the way it is with marriage meetings. Pick a time to meet and then the only question is: Am I going to show up or not?

Toni: You have five kids, Kevin. Do you set limits on the number of activities your kids can be involved in?

Kevin: We have done that, but not in a systematic way. We assess as we go along. I don't think we've ever had a child in more than one sport at a time, though; then they can focus on that one sport.

This will be hard for some parents, but we've said "no" to all of the traveling sports. I'm not trying to turn my son, who's into every sport that comes along, into a professional athlete. He may have the talent to do that or he may not, but we're not centering our whole family life on that kind of goal. It may sound kind of harsh, but wow, it's amazing when couples come in and say, "We never have any time. I spend a weekend in Cleveland and she spends the weekend in Cincinnati at different sports events."

Toni: Parents really have to set boundaries and be firm if they want to find some balance. We need to put our marriage first in a sacred place.

You have given us so many great ideas, Kevin. Everyone has three seconds, everyone has 30 seconds, everyone has 15 minutes, and everyone can make a once-a-week commitment.

I give you a lot of credit, Kevin, for meeting parents where they're at and giving them a variety of options for deepening their relationship. Thank you so much!

******

Ann Searles will now join us. Ann and her husband Mike have been married for nearly 20 years and they have three daughters. Ann and Mike have done a great job of making a weekly commitment to their relationship. They lead busy lives, but somehow they've made a habit of having a weekly date. Ann, how do you do it?

Ann: Mike and I were married for about six years before we had children. We started from the very beginning of our marriage to have weekly dates. We found our life was crazy with careers and social commitments, but we always set aside Thursday nights as our night.

When we had children our schedule was crazy – I'm sure other parents can relate. We were exhausted. There was no way that we could think about having a date night like we had done prior to having children.

But after a year, we realized we really needed to set time aside to connect as a couple. After we had our first child, we would just have date nights at home. When our youngest went off to kindergarten, we moved our date to lunch on Thursday afternoons.

Toni: You've been flexible on the amount of time together and the location, but you've maintained the commitment to time together.

Ann: Absolutely. I think that's what has made it fun. Our dates before children were completely different than what we're doing now. We would go to movies; we'd go out to dinner. Each of us would take a turn picking the date activity.

We'd surprise each other and it actually deepened our relationship because there would be times when my husband would pick something like visiting the Minnesota History Center, even if that wasn't my favorite. It made me realize that this is something that's important to him and vice versa. I would pick a round of golf, and even though it wasn't his priority, he knew that it was important to me. So we created even more respect for each other.

Toni: I think it's so important to switch up who's planning the dates. Do you take turns each week now?

Ann: We try to do that. There are those Thursdays where we're just exhausted and we only have a half an hour, but we still make that commitment, even if we just sit there and read books together.

Toni: I know a married couple who will read the same book out loud to each other and then they'll have discussions about it. They'll pick a really great, juicy book that they want to read together and they lounge in their bedroom and read. It sounds romantic to me.

Ann: People may chuckle and think, "Oh, boy. What kind of date is that, reading books?" But there is a connection that's made because you're committing to each other and you're doing something that you both enjoy.

Toni: What difference do you think it's made in your marriage to make a weekly commitment to each other?

Ann: It's kept our marriage very strong. People say, "How can you do it with all of your children's activities?" We would be remiss if we didn't take time for each other. We're doing it for our marriage and it's important.

Toni: I think that people forget that we're modeling for our kids how a relationship should work. They shouldn't grow up thinking that a marriage can keep going on autopilot.

Ann: Absolutely. My husband and I often talk about how the respect he shows me will impact the choice of future spouses for our girls. If you have a solid marriage with good communication and dedication, then you can tackle problems. The time we spend together on Thursday carries me throughout the week.

Toni: I have a friend who's been married about 25 years. She and her husband had date nights every Friday. When their kids were little, they would put the kids to bed and then start their date at 9:30 p.m., until one in the morning.

She said that it helped keep the "lovey-dovey" feelings going throughout the week. She said we really have to take the time to open the door to the possibility of love; it isn't going to magically happen on its own.

Ann: Absolutely not. We'll have times where we'll pick out our favorite bottle of wine and just look into each other's eyes. When you're so busy making lunches and driving around to different activities, you really don't have that eye connection. It really deepens the relationship.

Toni: Do you two ever take weekend getaways?

Ann: We have grandparents who will take the girls for the weekend. Once a month we also make a commitment to go out to dinner. We have a rule that if we're in the car we'll talk about the children, but then once we get to the restaurant we don't talk about the children. It's our time.

Toni: I love it. That's a great rule.

<u>**Contact Information:**</u>

Dan Devey

Website: *www.coolestdates.com*

Kevin Anderson, Ph.D.

Mailing Address: P.O. Box 74, Monclova, OH 43542

Phone: (419) 861-2269

Email Address: *kevinanderson@divinityindisguise.com*

Website: *www.divinityindisguise.com*

<u>Resources</u>:

Kevin Anderson, Ph.D.

The 7 Spiritual Practices of Marriage: Your Guide to Creating a Deep and Lasting Love (available through Amazon)

Counseling or speaking engagements arranged by calling (419) 861-2269 or by emailing *kevinanderson@divinityindisguise.com*

New Year's Resolutions to Make Your Family Stronger

Meet the Expert:

Barbara Z. Carlson is the President and co-founder of the Putting Family First – Making Time for Family initiative. She is also co-author with Dr. William Doherty of the book on family balance titled, *Putting Family First: Successful Strategies for Reclaiming Family Life in a Hurry-Up World*.

Barbara received her degree in elementary education from Gustavus Adolphus College. She has been a teacher, service-learning coordinator and the executive director of a community-wide initiative to build healthy communities and healthy youth. Barbara is the mother of four children, who have provided her with over 100 years of accumulated parenting experience!

Barbara gives frequent presentations on building assets for children, facilitating workshops on helping families find balance in their lives, and challenging families and communities to build nurturing environments for all.

Meet the Parent:

Anne Naumann is a mother of two – an 11-year-old son and a 12-year-old daughter – and she also works as a teacher. The Naumanns have made a strong commitment to putting family first.

✶✶✶✶✶✶

Toni: We're talking today about New Year's resolutions for building a stronger family. I love the New Year because it gives me a chance to step back and say, "How can I improve and do better than last year?"

When talking about New Year's resolutions for stronger families, I can't think of a better organization than the Putting Family First: Making Time for Family initiative because that's what Barbara and Bill are all about.

Many people make New Year's resolutions to exercise more or to lose weight. In your opinion, Barbara, how many people do you think sit down and say, "Let's make a New Year's resolution to make our family stronger"?

Barbara: I think that's a really great question, Toni. If you ask any parent what their priority is in life, they'll say it's their family. But, if you look at how they spend their time, you might really wonder. Families today are too often incredibly busy.

Toni: I think many parents think they're spending lots of time with their kids, but what does the research tell us?

Barbara: Some great research has been done by Dr. David Walsh and the Institute on Media and the Family. He talks about quality time and meaningful conversations, not the time we spend with our kids saying, "Hurry up. Get in the car. We're late." or "Feed the dog."

His research has shown some bad news. The average school-age child spends half an hour a week alone with their dad. Moms do a little better with two and a half hours a week.

Then we look at things like non-school reading. It's only half an hour a week. Computer time, for fun, is seven hours a week. Nine hours a week playing video games. Thirty-five hours a week watching television.

So if you add up the screen time, kids are spending about 44 hours a week on screen time, which is more than the normal work week, and only half an hour, or two and a half hours, with their parents. So, it's not great news.

Toni: Parents also spend a significant amount of time in the car taking kids to their various activities.

Barbara: Absolutely. Families today spend an enormous amount of time in their cars. Does car time count? Absolutely, it can count if you're having meaningful conversations, if mom isn't on her cell, if dad isn't on his iPhone, and if the kids aren't all plugged into a DVD.

You see lots of families riding together, but they're certainly not interacting together. So we need to be intentional about making that time in the car really count as family time too.

Toni: So part of it is we have to unplug our kids.

Barbara: Exactly. Some families will have a conversation starter book in the car that has intriguing questions that the kids can take turns answering. Or they play games where the family is actually interacting with each other.

Toni: Your business partner, Bill Doherty, from the University of Minnesota, is well known for the research he's done on families. Bill says the number one protective factor in keeping kids drug and alcohol free, preventing pregnancies, and staying in school is the time spent with their family. He says that we've got this all turned around.

Barbara: Yes. We know a very basic foundation of healthy child and youth development is close family relationships. We know that children spell love t-i-m-e. If you spend time with me, you show me that you love me, that you care about me, that you like me, that you *want* to spend time with me. So it's really important that we have that time together with our kids.

When I talk with parents, I always ask them to practice TLC. We all know that children need tender loving care, but I use other words for TLC. The "T" stands for Talk. I ask parents to really sit down and talk to each other, to talk about what they want to see happen in their family. They need to decide what is so sacred in their family that nothing is going to interfere with it.

Sacred time could be family meals, visits to grandparents, family vacations, or worshipping together, or whatever you decide. What is so sacred in our family that it's not negotiable – even if it means missing a hockey game or a practice?

On our website, we've heard from families who were ostracized because a daughter went to a sister's wedding, or whose little girl was told she was not a good team member because she went to her grandmother's funeral.

The "L" stands for Listen. I ask parents to truly listen to their children. Are the children doing what they really want to be doing?

I was talking to a reporter from the Washington Post, and she said that her friend's son was a jock in high school and college, and her friend was so proud of his boy that was playing football. She asked the boy, "Do you like playing football?" and the father was horrified when the boy said, "Not really." It had never occurred to the father that his son was playing for him.

So, we really need to listen to our kids and look for warning signs like they're not eating well or they're not sleeping well. Is there a reason? Are they just so busy that they feel like they can't do anything well?

The "C" stands for Connect. We need to connect with our kids every day – often and in many different ways. What times during the day will become that sacred, connecting family time?

Toni: I think listening is so critical. It's pretty rare when we sit down, face-to-face, eye-to-eye, and just have a conversation with our kids, and not when we're multi-tasking.

Barbara: That's so true. I remember a little girl who was so frustrated. She was trying to tell her daddy something and she finally grabbed his face between her chubby little hands and said, "Listen to my face." She wanted eye contact, and even though he may have been listening behind the newspaper, she couldn't tell that.

So we need to sit down at their level, look them in the eye, react – and if we truly want to show them we love them, we'll turn off our iPhone and our Blackberry.

Toni: I love the idea of sitting down to determine your family's priorities. Some of you may be familiar with the research that the Search Institute has done. They developed *40 developmental assets* essential for children to become healthy, caring and responsible adults (*www.search-institute. org/developmental-assets/lists*). Barbara, please share your top three assets with us.

Barbara: All 40 assets are wonderful things that each kid should have in their life. The first time I heard Peter Benson talk about them, I ran home, put our kids to bed, sat my husband down and said, "Which of these do our kids have, and if they don't have them, how can we get them?"

But I find when I talk to very busy young families and I say, "All you need to do is put these 40 things in your kids' lives," their eyes kind of glaze over. So, I talk about the *three* that I think are really at the top of the list.

The first one is ***having caring adults in each child's life***. Research actually says that each child needs at least five adults that truly care about them, that think they're everything in the world, and that they could go to if they had a problem, even if they couldn't talk to their parents.

The second developmental asset is **having boundaries and expectations for our kids**. I can promise that part of a child's job is to push the envelope, but if they don't know where the line is, then they'll go much farther. We need to tell our children many times what the values are in our family.

One of our biggest jobs as parents is to teach our kids values. If we believe sixth graders shouldn't be drinking, we need to make sure that our kids know that's one of our values. If we believe that it's unhealthy for a teen to be sexually active, we need to tell them that and not just expect that they're going to know it.

Boundaries are really comforting to children, and family boundaries let them know how far they can go. It makes them feel safe. And as much as they might object, it shows that we do care about them.

I want to make it really clear that when we talk about having expectations – and high expectations – for our kids, I don't mean that we expect perfection from them. I think that we have too many children today who are suffering from feelings of failure because they got a B+ instead of an A.

Here's the third asset. I think it is so important that **we encourage our children to volunteer in the community and teach our kids about giving back**. They're part of a family, part of a neighborhood, and part of the global family, and we need to help them understand how great it feels to do something for somebody else.

Toni: I agree. Volunteering is a win/win for everyone. It can be simple things like helping out an elderly neighbor by shoveling snow, or making a meal for someone who just had a baby.

Or you can volunteer out in the community at a food shelf or help the homeless. There are hundreds of opportunities for volunteering.

Let's get back to your earlier point about spending more time together as a family. Family meals are an important building block when we're talking about family time together. Barbara, give us the bullet points of the benefits of eating meals together as a family.

Barbara: Wonderful research has come out of CASA, which is The National Center on Addiction and Substance Abuse at Columbia University. They've shown clearly that families who eat meals together have kids who do better academically in school and who get along better socially where kids gather, like the playground and the cafeteria. Kids are better adjusted psychologically; they feel better in their own skin. They have less involvement in high-risk behaviors such as drug abuse, alcohol use, smoking, and early sexual behaviors. According to dieticians, they eat less fat and a more nutritionally-balanced diet. Kids also feel more connected to the world. If they spend time with their family, they are part of a bigger whole; they aren't a single little entity by themselves. So those are all great things that can come from just having family meals.

Toni: Parents work long hours and kids are involved in lots of activities. Do you have some strategies for helping families to actually have the family meal together?

Barbara: The first thing that families need to work at is finding the time together for meals. Our kids grew up with a dad who's a physician and who didn't get home until late, but we thought it was so important that we all eat together. So the kids would have a good snack after school and get their homework done. Then we would often eat dinner at 7:30 or 8:00 at night, but it was important that we all be together because that was the time when we could talk, we could debate, we could discuss, we could talk about the highs and lows of our day.

I grew up in a family where my father was a landscape designer. He had very seasonal work and summers were incredibly busy. But he would always take a break, come home and have dinner, and then go back to work – because eating together was that important.

We know that some families cannot eat dinner together because the parents work night shifts but families can also eat breakfast together.

Toni: I'm glad that you clarified that meals can be breakfast, lunch or dinner because that opens the door to more connecting time for families.

Barbara: CASA tells us that in order to get all those benefits that we just talked about we need to eat together at least five times a week. So, out of 21 meals, we should be able to find five times that we can be together.

Toni: Sometimes you can be really creative. If you're going to the soccer field, get there 30 minutes early, bring a picnic basket and eat dinner there. As long as you're together, it's a family meal and the kids will think it's fun.

Barbara: Absolutely. I know one family that does that.

I know another family that couldn't eat meals together but they spent every night before bed in the hot tub together and that was their time to connect. The dad said, "I think my boys actually liked it because it was dark and we didn't have to have eye contact when we were talking about certain subjects."

It's just important to find that connecting time every day.

Toni: I agree. We need to make a concerted effort to find that time, whether it's chit-chat time at bedtime, mealtime, or hot tub time.

And Barbara, how can we carve out time for family *events* when we're all together?

Barbara: Well, that would be another resolution. A great New Year's resolution would be to make a family game night or family fun night together once a week. Companies are now promoting family game night and we can learn so much by playing games together.

Here's another idea: for the last four years at Putting Family First, we've created a Putting Family First Challenge.

We ask parents to find 21 minutes a day for 21 days to connect across the table as a family. And we chose 21 days because behaviorists tell us it takes three weeks to form a new habit. We've had people writing back to us saying, "Thank you so much for reminding us how important this is. Our kids won't let us give it up now."

Toni: I think it's important to put family time on the calendar. I love the accountability that a calendar brings.

I think we're teaching kids lots of things if we decide to take that challenge. The most important lesson is that family time is important and that we make a commitment to spending time together. And since many kids spend 40 hours a week on screen time, getting rid of chunks of screen time would be a great way to open up space for family time.

Barbara: Absolutely. And parents will say, "I just don't have any time," but if they keep track of what they're doing each day, they're amazed at how much time there really is.

Toni: Let's also talk about couple time, because if anything seems to slide off the map in our child-centered culture these days, it seems to be couple time. What can we do to get back on track with connecting as a couple?

Barbara: Toni, that's so important, and that could be a New Year's resolution too. It's been said that the greatest gift a man can give his children is to love their mother – and of course it's also true that the greatest gift a woman can give her children is to love their father. We need to be connected to our spouses to do our very best job raising our kids. In our family, we had a regular date night; the sitter would just show up and there were times we were so busy we forgot that she was coming. But it reminded us that we needed time together.

Before we could afford to have a sitter, my sister and I took turns. She would take my kids one week and I'd take her kids another week.

The dates don't even have to cost anything. It could be going out and walking around the lake. It could be having a cup of coffee together. It's just tuning in to each other and spending time together that's important.

The Office for National Statistics finds that, on average, couples spend two to two-and-a-half hours a day together, including weekends. One third of that time is just watching TV together, which isn't great connecting time.

We're seeing too many families today that devote everything to their kids. Then, once the kids are off to college or move out, we see an alarming rise in divorce among 50- and 60-year-olds because they don't know each other anymore. It's so important that we keep that connection going.

Toni: I agree. I did a show on couple time, so if this topic interests you, look at Chapter 14 in my book because the guests shared great ideas.

One statistic that I shared was that married couples spend, on average, just four minutes a day in meaningful conversation.

Barbara: Isn't that amazing?

Toni: It is amazing, and the number one activity that couples did together was watch television, so we really have to unplug.

I just want to mention a resource. There's a conversation starter book called, *Keep Talking: Daily Conversation Starter for the Family Meal.* We tried it at dinner and we all really enjoyed it.

Barbara: We have some ideas on our website too. *www.puttingfamilyfirst. org/family-connections/mealtime*

Toni: On another topic, many kids these days are overscheduled. We also need to make sure that our kids have downtime to relax. Do you have some recommended guidelines to follow?

Barbara: Toni, I think that's such an important point. The American Academy of Pediatrics actually came out with a statement that kids need time to just be kids. They need time to relax, to daydream, to play whatever they want to play.

Some people say that we're ruining leadership opportunities for kids. If you tell a group of young children today to go out and have a pick-up game, they have no idea how to do it, because they've always been told where to go, what time to be there, what color socks to wear, and how to play the game. Everything has been done for them. So, we're really taking away leadership opportunities from kids and the ability to use their imaginations.

A few years ago, I was dumbfounded when a parent said to me, "I'm scheduling a play date." And I said, "What's a play date?" When we were growing up, we just ran out and played, and it was the same with our children. Now, it apparently has to be scheduled.

Toni: When our oldest daughter was 12, she didn't like to be in a lot of activities. On Friday nights she'd have to call 12 or 13 girls to find one girl that could come over and hang out. A lot of her friends were in traveling sports so they were busy Friday, Saturday and sometimes Sunday. I put a positive spin on it by saying, "At least you have that many friends to call," but my heart just broke for her because no one was available.

Barbara: It's a sad statement that 12-year-olds are that busy, but we've had other families say the same thing: that their children can't find someone in the neighborhood to play with. There are children that live there but they're off doing their activities. So we really need to make sure that our kids have time to just be kids.

Toni: Absolutely. Research also tells us about the positive benefits that come from being outside, walking in the woods and communing with nature. It helps kids lower their stress level. And connecting with nature helps them to become better recyclers.

Research also tells us that brain development occurs when kids have unstructured downtime. I have a free article called, "Surprising Secrets to a Successful Summer" here: *www.getparentinghelpnow.com/myfree-bookresources.*

Barbara: This may be the first generation of children that doesn't live as long as their parents because of so much screen time and inactivity. We have rising obesity among our children, and rising diabetes too, which used to be an adult disease. So it's becoming a crisis. We really need to be intentional about getting our kids up and moving.

Toni: Absolutely.

Earlier we talked about volunteerism. What are some good ways for families to find volunteer opportunities?

Barbara: There are opportunities all around us and, as you mentioned, even very young children can help clear the sidewalks for an elderly neighbor, or bake cookies to take to a shut-in. Nursing homes love to have children come and visit or sing songs to the people living there.

You can contact a faith community for ideas. You can also call your local food shelf or local clothes closet and ask them for ideas on what you could do to help. And children who belong to Boy Scouts, Girl Scouts, or Camp Fire Girls are encouraged to volunteer as part of their creed.

Our newspaper in Minnesota lists volunteer opportunities every week. When children are old enough to receive an allowance, it's important to teach them about the balance between saving, spending and sharing. It's a great way to help kids understand about volunteering, giving back, and giving to others.

Toni: Another great New Year's resolution would be to volunteer as a family at least once a month. I find it's helpful to find a place where we like to volunteer and then return to that place so I know the dates and times they're open. I can just put it on the calendar and we're more likely to follow through.

I read that most people break their New Year's resolutions within three weeks. Any tips for meeting the goals that we set?

Barbara: This is such a great question, Toni. I think one of the best ways is to involve the children from the very beginning. Let them help you decide on what the resolutions are and how often an event is going to happen, such as family meals or game night or whatever you choose to do. I find that children are very good at keeping us honest and keeping us on task.

Stephen Covey is a well known time expert, and he says that the key is not to prioritize what's on the schedule, but to schedule your priorities.

Toni: I love that.

Barbara: Yes, isn't that great? You can have a family meeting and ask, "What do we want to do this year to make our family even better?" and let the kids be part of it.

Toni: Covey also has a book, *The Seven Habits of Highly Effective Families,* that has helpful information.

Covey suggests that families develop a family mission statement. He asks, "Would you get in a plane with a pilot who didn't have a flight plan to follow?" Of course not. So why should we let our family life proceed on autopilot without a plan?

A family meeting is a great place to start the process for developing the mission statement. I have an article here to help parents start using family meetings and another article to develop a mission statement: *www.get-parentinghelpnow.com/myfreebookresources.*

Barbara: Write down the family meetings on a calendar. They're just as important as a doctor's appointment or going to a birthday party.

Toni: I like rotating the leadership responsibilities for the meetings so everyone has a turn leading the meeting. Everyone can also take turns picking the family events.

******

I'm going to talk next with **Anne Naumann**, a parent of two who has been not only talking the talk but also walking the walk on putting family first.

Right from the get-go, you and your husband decided that family time was going to be a priority. What are some of the strategies that you two are using to connect your family on a daily basis?

Anne: As a couple, Tim and I created a list of things we enjoyed doing and then started doing them. We then realized we could also do those activities as a family.

We go for walks, ride bikes, ice skate, or ski together. We ask the kids what they like to do and then incorporate that into family time.

A lot of our activities are extremely simple. We have a ping pong table in our basement and we'll play ping pong together. We see how long we can keep a rally going.

My daughter loves to sing and dance. So we'll just turn on music and dance around. It doesn't have to be a huge thing that we plan; sometimes it's spur of the moment. And those tend to be the best times and the favorite times.

Toni: You also set up times so that you're connecting each day.

Anne: We look at our schedule for the week and figure out when we're all going to be able to connect. It could be early in the morning before everybody heads off to school. Sometimes it's much later, like 8:00 at night. Most often, it revolves around a meal, although not always.

And we read a book out loud as a family almost every night.

Toni: You also try to have the kids get their homework done early so when you come home from an activity you can still spend 20 minutes playing ping pong together.

Anne: Yes. Or maybe we'll pop popcorn and play a game or talk about what the kids have done.

Toni: I think it's very important for parents to realize it doesn't have to cost a lot of money, and it doesn't have to take a lot of planning, because we're all on overload anyway. You've had success with spontaneous activities.

My guess is that you have to say "no" to quite a few things to make time for your family time. Am I right?

Anne: Yes. We do have to say "no" to quite a few things.

There's a lot of pressure on parents and kids to keep up with everybody else. We've used a family planner for a long time and we've found that helpful. For example, if you're thinking of incorporating an activity into your life, it can help to look at things like time spent in the car to and from the activity, how much it's going to cost, time spent in the activity, and time that the kids who aren't in the activity spend watching – because that's all crucial time that you could be doing something else.

We've also decided that the kids will pick an outside activity that they really like and that's their focus. In other words, they have one sport that they get to do at any given time. It's also helped them to understand that you don't get everything you want all the time, right away. I think we tend to live in an immediate gratification society.

Toni: Exactly. When we talk about overindulgence, the obvious thing we think of is buying kids too much stuff, but we can also commit too much time to kids' activities.

Traveling sports, in particular, sap time from a family. We're not saying, "Don't do sports," but it's important to look at the impact on the whole family.

I'm curious. What kind of benefits have you seen for your kids by making family time a priority and limiting some of the activities that they're involved in?

Anne: Many times people tell us our kids are calm. They aren't whiners. They don't beg for things because we don't ever say, "No, you can't have it." We tell them, "Not now; let's put it on a list."

If we have something planned and we're rushing to get there and I start to feel frenzied, I'll see if the kids really want to do it, and if they don't, then we don't do it.

We just did that the other night, and everyone calmed down, and we felt so much better because we truly enjoyed our meal versus feeling like we had to rush through it to get to the next activity.

The kids tend to be more grounded, if that's an appropriate term. They know what's important and we talk together a lot. I really value their opinions on things.

Toni: Is it hard bucking the trend?

Anne: Sometimes it is. People sometimes look at us as if they're thinking "very strange." But these are values that my husband and I set up. When we plan events to do as a family, nothing can change that. It goes down in ink and that's what we're going to do. No friends can come. I think if you value family time, then the kids start to value it, and they really look forward to a lot of the things we do.

Toni: Thank you Anne, and thanks to Barbara Carlson for all the great tips on keeping our families strong.

Contact Information:

Barbara Z. Carlson

Mailing Address: 5270 Yvette St. Loretto, MN 55357

Phone: 763-443-6200

Email Address: bzcputtingfamilyfirst@msn.com

Website: *www.puttingfamilyfirst.org*

<u>Resources</u>:

You can get a copy of the Search Institute's 40 Developmental Assets here: *www.search-institute.org/developmental-assets/lists*

Best Back to School Tips

Meet the Experts:

Lynda Binius Enright is a registered dietitian and received her Master of Science degree in nutrition from the University of Minnesota.

Lynda works in private practice where she provides individual nutrition counseling for weight loss, healthy eating for individuals and families, disease prevention and disease treatment. In today's environment, feeding a family well is challenging. Lynda has a passion for helping individuals and families take control of their health with good eating habits that fit into their lives. Learn more about Lynda's services at *www.bewellconsulting.com.*

Audrey Thomas, owner of Organized Audrey, LLC, has the philosophy of "Why not transform your life as well as your space?" As a productivity expert, she helps others understand their disorganization before teaching them the skills they need to get and stay organized.

Thomas is a national speaker and is the author of *The Road Called Chaos; 50 Ways to Leave Your Clutter;* and *What's For Dinner?* – a home study course on the topic of menu planning.

Audrey is the Past-president of the Minnesota chapter of the National Speakers Association and is also a member of the American Society of Training and Development.

******

Toni: Lynda, we need to make sure that our kids eat properly so they have the brain power and energy to be able to have a successful school day. We've all heard about the importance of feeding kids breakfast in the morning, but can you remind us why it's important?

Lynda: Breakfast is so important because it's the time where we're putting back the energy that has been depleted overnight. We've gone a long time without eating, so we need to fill our tank back up to start our day with the energy that our body needs to move and that our brain needs to function well.

It's interesting when you look at research on kids and the benefits of breakfast. The research is solid. It shows that kids who eat breakfast tend to have higher grades. They're better able to pay attention in class. They're more likely to participate in class discussions than the kids who skip breakfast. So that's solid enough information for me to confirm that eating breakfast is important.

Toni: And for me too! I know we need a balanced meal in the morning, but are there some nutrients that really pack the brain power for our kids?

Lynda: It really is about that balance. It's making sure we're getting good healthy carbohydrates, good protein and healthy fats. Let me tell you why each of these is so equally important.

The complex carbohydrates are what our brain uses for energy. So, when we eat something that is a good healthy carbohydrate, which might be a fruit, a vegetable, whole grains or dairy products, they give our brain a steady supply of energy.

When we eat a sugary breakfast that's really refined, our blood sugar goes up and we get some quick energy to our brain, but it doesn't last very long. Our blood sugar drops and we get an erratic supply of energy to the brain, which can make behavior erratic. It can make learning more difficult for kids. So feed your kids complex, healthy carbohydrates instead.

Toni: Great.

Lynda: The second part is healthy proteins. Proteins are made up of amino acids, and those amino acids are building blocks for the messengers that carry information and signals throughout our brain.

So if we're not nourishing and building those signals, we don't have a brain that's functioning as efficiently as one that's nourished well. Sources of healthy proteins are whole grains, dairy products, eggs, lean meats, and beans.

The third component is healthy fats. I recently read a research article that compared the brain to a stick of butter, basically made up mostly of fat. If we're not nourishing it with the right kinds of fat, our brain just can't function as well.

Americans have plenty of fat in their diet, but we're not getting the right kinds of fats. Our diet is made up of a lot of omega 6 fats. This is the sole kind of fat in all sorts of processed, packaged foods. Corn oil and soybean oil are good sources of omega 6 fats. However, what we're really lacking is the omega 3 fats. Eggs, healthy fish like salmon and tuna, walnuts, flaxseeds and canola oil are all good sources of omega 3 fats.

So these three components are all equally crucial to get our kids started in the morning.

Toni: I know there are moms and dads out there saying, "That's all well and good, but I have 10 minutes in the morning to throw something together for my kids. It needs to be quick and it needs to be easy.

Lynda, you've been kind enough to put together some back-to-school breakfast and lunch ideas that are available on my website: *www.getparentinghelpnow.com/myfreebookresources*

Please share some of those quick, easy breakfast ideas with us.

Lynda: Cereal is a basic American breakfast and certainly can be a fine way to start the day. Just make sure you're focusing on whole grains. The first ingredient on the label should say "whole wheat" or "whole oats."

Then look at and compare the grams of fiber to the grams of sugar on the nutrition facts label. Make sure you're getting as much fiber as sugar, or more.

Look at the ingredients to see what else is added. Are there artificial colors and sweeteners? For some kids, these can really affect their behavior negatively.

What can you do to add more nutrition? Get a good whole grain cereal and then add some nuts, yogurt and/or a piece of fruit to the cereal. Then you'll get all the components of carbohydrates, protein and fat.

Cheerios is a fine option, but choose plain Cheerios, not the sweetened variety because this has a lot of extra sugar. Cascadia Farms and Barbara's Bakery brands are great, and Kashi is one of my favorite brands.

People typically think of breakfast as cereal or eggs. It doesn't have to be like that. If your kids like chicken for breakfast, or a turkey sandwich, or leftover pizza, that's fine. Leftover rice is great. You can add some nuts and dried fruit and heat it up. It's kind of a substitute for oatmeal. You can make simple things that don't take a tremendous amount of time.

Toni: I love your idea of thinking outside the box. If your child loves rice, can it be white rice or does it have to be whole grain rice?

Lynda: White rice certainly has good nutrition, but it's great to squeeze in whole grains wherever you can. So, if you can switch to a brown rice, or wild rice, which is a great whole grain also, you're just going to be giving them an extra boost of nutrition and healthy proteins.

Toni: An egg tortilla is one of the fun recipes you provided. I noticed that you said you can scramble an egg in a microwave. How the heck do we do that?

Lynda: It's very simple. All you do is whisk together an egg and some milk in a bowl. You can add some cheese and vegetables to make an omelet. Put it in the microwave and just heat it until it's cooked through. It will probably take a minute or two, and about half way through, mix it up a little bit better.

It's such an easy, quick way to make eggs. You don't even have to dirty a pan.

Toni: I'm going to try that!

I know you're not a big fan of school lunches, but some schools are striving to make meals more nutritious.

Lynda: For school lunches, I think the key is to educate our kids on the best choices they can make. My kids were talking about the fruit that's served at their school. They said it's always canned fruit with whipped cream on the top. They didn't understand why there was whipped cream on fruit.

I said, "Are there any other choices?"

And they said, "There are apples and bananas." So I told them they can choose an apple or banana instead of the highly sweetened option.

Educating them about what their choices are for school lunches can be really helpful.

But, I still prefer to pack my kids' lunches. I can make sure they get a good healthy balance of foods, and that it's something they like and will look forward to eating – so they don't trade it with the kid next to them at the table.

You don't have to just make a sandwich. You can send whole grain crackers, tortillas, pitas or whole wheat pasta, so they get good complex whole grain carbohydrates.

Add fruits and vegetables wherever you can. They're good finger foods that they can easily grab. Chop them in interesting shapes for younger kids, so it's fun for them.

Add some healthy protein like chopped up chicken, or cheese, or nut butters like peanut butter or almond butter. Just make it something fun that's easy for kids to grab in the 15 minutes they have to eat lunch.

Toni: I love your idea of sending finger foods. It makes it seem more like a snack or a party. Give us a few ideas on healthy snacks we can send to school with our kids.

Lynda: Snacks don't have to be packaged, processed food. They can be a piece of fruit, trail mix, string cheese and some whole grain crackers. Or if you like to cook, you can make muffins or cookies that can be packed with nutrition, like healthy whole grains, nuts and seeds.

Toni: Thank you, Lynda, for all your great tips. I know that many parents will find your suggestions inspiring.

******

Toni: Next, **Audrey Thomas** is going to help us get through the mound of paperwork that comes home with our kids.

Audrey is a certified professional organizer who owns the business Organized Audrey. You can look her up at *www.organizedaudrey.com.* Audrey's philosophy is, "Why not transform your life as well as your space?"

Audrey is a national speaker and author. Her books include: *Skills and Responsibilities for Tots to Teens; 50 Ways to Leave Your Clutter;* and *What's for Dinner?* These products and others are available on her website.

Let's start with organizational tips that can get us out the door on time. We all know that we're supposed to lay out the clothes the night before, but what else can we do?

Audrey: I have two children, and when my son was young, everything had to be a game. When he laid out his clothes the night before, I had him lay them out on the floor in the shape of a human body. When he got up in the morning, he could easily slip into his body, so to speak, and it was fun for him.

Toni: Oh, that's such a cute idea. You also have some ideas for accessories for girls.

Audrey: Girls tend to take a long time to figure out what they want to wear, so I encourage them to look at all their accessories: jewelry; how they're going to do their hair; ribbons and barrettes; belts, purses and scarves. I have them choose all that the night before. It saves a lot of time, a lot of hassle, and maybe a few arguments in the morning.

Toni: I like to have my kids check the weather the night before so they can dress appropriately for the weather.

Audrey: We really like using *www.weather.com*. Even a five-year-old can go online and check the weather.

We would have our kids check the weather forecast because it gives them some responsibility. Then they can lay out their raincoat, hat and boots, and they've got everything they need; so they're not running out the door to the bus and you're yelling, "Hey you forgot your hat."

Toni: You're a big believer in checklists. What kind of a checklist might be appropriate for a younger child?

Audrey: Before our kids learned to read, we used pictures. We had a checklist that the kids went over the evening before school and a checklist to use in the morning.

The evening checklist might be: Is your homework done? Is your backpack set out by the back door? Are your clothes laid out? Is your lunch part-way made?

As our kids got older, they had more chores and responsibilities to do around home so the checklist was longer. Did you walk the dog? Did you take care of the kitty litter box? Did you empty the dishwasher?

The other checklists that were very helpful as our kids got older were sports checklists and activity checklists so they remembered to take everything with them for football practice after school.

I remember the time that my son was in fourth grade and I had to bring him a very embarrassing piece of equipment that young boys wear. He wasn't allowed on the field until he had it. He was so embarrassed. It only took one time, and then it was added to the checklist and it never happened again.

I would help them create the checklist, but they had to take the responsibility to review the checklist and gather everything: If I'm going to my clarinet lesson right after school, do I have my music? My theory book? My clarinet? Everything they needed for that particular activity.

Toni: I like making lists because it gets the information out of my head and onto a piece of paper, so then I don't have all that clutter still in my head. I love the idea of giving them more responsibility too.

Audrey: Planning ahead teaches them a great skill.

Toni: I feel snowed under from all of the paperwork that comes home from school. I'd love some tips.

Audrey: Ever wonder if your elementary school or preschool owns stock in forestry?

One of the things that we like to implement for families that we consult with is a "kitchen command center." Think of the shape of a milk crate. You can buy open file boxes that are designed to hold a hanging file, but they're in the shape of a milk crate.

The box is 12 to 14 inches deep and it sits right at the end of your counter or wherever you tend to empty backpacks and bring in the mail. You can set up files there that really manage your family's schedules, your activities and your kids' activities. Then the papers don't have to stack up on the kitchen counter.

Toni: Do you have a file for each child, and sub-files for each of the activities they're involved in?

Audrey: I create a hanging file for each person in the family that goes in the very front. Then I list other files alphabetically.

I have a file for each child's school. You might have a child in elementary school and a child in middle school, so each of those schools has a folder because you'll get a directory and other things like that from each school. Then I have a file folder for each child's activity and/or part-time job so they can put their schedule in that file.

If they've got papers that they're bringing home, I have a file folder that says, "Forms for Mom and Dad to sign."

I taught my children at a young age that when their teacher gave them a form that had to be signed and brought back to school, it was their job to get it home. I provided the hanging file at home, but they had to take the form out and put it in that file folder.

That part was *their* responsibility. It was then our responsibility to check that folder by the end of the evening, write out any checks, fill out the form, and then put it back in the child's backpack. That was *our* job.

We each had defined roles so we avoided a lot of last-minute problems.

Toni: Sounds great. I'm going to do that.

You also recommend setting up a "homework central" station for your kids. What's important in setting that up?

Audrey: Well, this came about because I had a child who had a hard time sitting still, concentrating and getting his work done. What was taking an hour probably could have been done in a half hour.

He would sit down to do his work and then he'd say, "Oh, I need to go get a Kleenex." Then he'd come back and say, "I need to go get a red marker." Then he'd go get a compass.

So we took a cardboard box (but it could also be a clear tub) and decorated it – and we put all the supplies in the box. Everything you can imagine went into that tub: a dictionary, a thesaurus, a ruler, markers, crayons, index cards, a calculator and batteries for the calculator. That way when he sat down to do his homework, everything was there.

Our kids did homework at the dining room table because it wasn't near a television, it was out of the path of the kitchen, and there wasn't a phone nearby. So, that's where they did their homework Monday through Friday. They had everything they needed to concentrate and get their homework finished.

Our son quickly learned that he could get outside a lot quicker to play with his buddies if he would sit down and concentrate.

Toni: I agree. I've done that for years. We call it a homework basket and those supplies are used exclusively for homework. If you need a marker to make a birthday card, you don't get it out of your homework basket.

It sounds like the dining room table worked great for your family. It can also be helpful to ask children where they think a good spot would be to do homework and then they have some ownership.

Still, some kids get off task, so what organizational strategies can help them stay on track?

Audrey: We've worked with families who have kids with special needs, such as attention deficit disorder. The child may be disorganized and not know what to do about it. The child may be too embarrassed to ask the teacher for help, and mom and dad normally aren't looking at their lockers, so we help them set up their backpack and their locker. Every quarter, I ask to see their locker.

Toni: That's a great idea. As parents, we don't necessarily think about our kids' lockers, but for older kids, they're an important part of their life.

Next, Audrey and Lynda are going to each give us a zinger – the best tip that they can throw out. So, Audrey, hit us with your zinger.

Audrey: The product is called "Clocky" and it's a rolling alarm clock. This is great when you're trying to teach kids the responsibility of getting up on their own – maybe fifth or sixth graders.

Once you hit the snooze button it literally rolls off your dresser and starts rolling all around the floor making noises, so you *have* to get out of bed to shut it off.

It's about $50.00, and it can be purchased at *www.nandahome.com*.

Oh, that's so fun! Lynda, let me hear your zinger.

Lynda: What I'd like to leave parents with is the idea of getting back to eating *real* food. We've gotten so far from eating real food in our diets.

We're eating highly processed packaged foods that have artificial sweeteners and yellow dye number 5 and red dye number 5, which are not nourishing our body or our brains.

So take the time to educate yourself about the foods you eat, look at labels and read ingredient lists. I know it's overwhelming when you go to the store and there are thousands of choices, but take a bit of time to figure it out. Once you get the hang of it, then you'll know which brands to buy and what chemicals to avoid. It becomes much easier. You simplify your life a lot, once you do the research ahead of time.

Toni: I agree. I've done that with granola bars. I've spent 10 or 15 minutes looking at the nutrition label of all the granola bars and found maybe one or two that I consider good for us to eat. It's worth the investment in time because it makes it easier to shop the next time.

I want to share something that the kids and I did. We put together seven different nutritious breakfast menus and then we assigned a day to eat each of them. For example, on Monday, we'll have yogurt parfaits with nuts on top. It's been so great for my husband and me in the morning, just to know that today is yogurt parfait day – nutritious and easy. And the next day is whole wheat pancakes with sausages.

The kids enjoyed putting the menus together. We can switch it up if they get bored, but it has really streamlined our mornings.

Audrey, I know you had a couple of other products to talk about…

Audrey: Yes. One is called a Math Noodler Game, and it's made by Edupress. They have one for grades two to three and one for grades four to five. When my kids were young, they learned a lot via games. The link is *www.edushop.edu4kids.com.*

The other product is a family wall calendar. It's called, "A Family Tracker Wall Calendar" and is available at *www.TimeToo.com.* It's large and you can put it up on the wall and keep track of everybody's schedules. You know where everybody's going to be, and it's all contained in one place.

Toni: I have a huge dry erase calendar I bought at Staples. We color-code activities for different people. Is that something that you recommend?

Audrey: I definitely advocate that. Assign one color per person so that at a glance you can see which child is going to which activity. Then also use a separate color for carpools. So, if you're driving the carpool that day, or picking up, then that's noted too.

On Sunday nights we'd gather around the calendar and we'd review the activities for the next week.

Toni: I love it.

Audrey: There were no surprises in the schedule either the night before or on the day of an event. We knew ahead of time who was driving where.

Toni: I love family meetings and being able to look ahead at the week. You can also review the calendar each morning to remind the kids about their activities and who is being picked up. We keep our calendar right by the kitchen table for that purpose.

Lynda, one other thing: please give us a quick summary of what enriched flour is….

Lynda: When you look at the food label, you want the first ingredient to say "whole." Whole wheat or whole oats. Enriched simply means that the grain has been refined. The outer layers have been removed, which is, unfortunately, where all the nutrition is. All the vitamins, minerals, fiber and healthy fats have been taken out and the grain has been enriched with specific nutrients like B vitamins. We need those added nutrients to prevent deficiencies, but we're still losing a lot of nutrition when the grains are refined and then enriched.

Toni: Thank you for that great information.

Contact Information:

Lynda Enright

Phone: 612-581-4668

Email Address: *lynda@bewellconsulting.com*

Website: *www.bewellconsulting.com*

Audrey Thomas

Phone: 1-866-767-0455

Email Address: *info@OrganizedAudrey.com*

Website: *www.OrganizedAudrey.com*

Resources:

Lynda Enright

For tip sheets and podcasts on healthy meals and snacks for you and your family, go to *www.bewellconsulting.com/pages/resources.html*

Audrey Thomas

What's for Dinner? – DVD and Menu Planning Workbook *www.organizedaudrey.com/products/what-s-for-dinner*

50 Ways to Leave Your Clutter – *www.organizedaudrey.com/products/office-business-products/organizing-books*

The Road Called Chaos – *www.organizedaudrey.com/products/office-business-products/organizing-books*

Frosting, Bows and Bags Under My Eyes – Holiday Organizing –*www.organizedaudrey.com/products/frosting-bows-and-bags-under-my-eyes*

Family Fun Nights:
Have a Blast with Your Kids at Home

Meet the Expert:

Debra Immergut is a senior editor at FamilyFun magazine, where it's her job to dream up unique ideas for activities and crafts that parents and kids can enjoy together. She lives with her family in western Massachusetts.

******

Toni: I've been a subscriber to FamilyFun magazine for about 12 years and it's a fabulous magazine with so many fun ideas every month. It's truly my favorite parenting magazine. So congratulations, Debra, for the great job you do.

Debra: Thank you so much.

Toni: We're talking about fun things that you can do with your kids at home that don't cost a lot of money. Debra, you've put together so many great ideas for us today and we're going to start out with some ideas using kitchen science. You have a great idea for creating crystal trees at home.

Debra: This is a really terrific project because it has a unique combination of instant gratification, which makes it so fun for kids, but it also keeps them occupied over a series of days. It's a great idea for a winter break or a long weekend when you're stuck inside.

You just need some very basic materials to get started. You take a table-spoon of table salt, a tablespoon of regular household ammonia, and a tablespoon of the old-fashioned laundry ingredient called "blue ink."

Blue ink is an ingredient that was commonly used by our grandmothers to make whites whiter, and its non-toxic. It's just a little jar of blue ink that's very inexpensive. It's been around for a long time and it's available in a lot of supermarkets. If you can't find it, there's a brand called "Mrs. Stewart's Bluing" and if you look it up online, there's lots of information about it, including all the places where it's sold in each state.

Put a tablespoon of the blue ink in with the salt and ammonia in a little bowl or saucer. Then have your kids cut a little tree shape out of some thin cardboard, like shirt cardboard. Set that little cardboard tree in the saucer with the solution.

In as quickly as an hour you'll start to see salt crystals creeping and forming up the cardboard. It's really incredible. They can run back and check it every half an hour and they'll see it changing. It continues to grow even after three or four days and it becomes this beautiful object. It's very fun for winter because it looks like a snow-covered tree by the time it's finished.

I did that with my son recently and we just loved it. It lasted for about a week. When the crystals start to fall back into the saucer, just toss it in the trash.

Toni: I'm going to try that! Here's a link to the recipe and others that we'll talk about: *www.getparentinghelpnow.com/myfreebookresources.*

I'm sure you could use different cardboard shapes for different seasons too.

Debra: Yes, you can create any shape you want to. You can also put a little food coloring on the cardboard and the crystals will soak up the color. You can make a fall-colored tree or a green tree and that's a lot of fun too.

Toni: Next you're going to tell us about how to make cornstarch clay creatures.

Debra: Cornstarch clay is another one of those classic ideas. It's very low cost and just a ton of fun.

You take 2/3 cup of salt, 1/3 cup of baking soda and a 1/2 cup of cornstarch, and you mix it up in a pot. You heat it a little bit until it becomes a sort of gluey, gooey solution, which is a lot of fun for kids. Then you let it cool and it becomes a very malleable, fun clay that they can sculpt into any shape they like.

We love to raid the junk drawer for things like buttons, nuts, bolts, sequins or other odds and ends and stick them in the clay. The kids go crazy dreaming up creations. The cornstarch clay gets very hard as it dries so they can keep their creations indefinitely.

Toni: Everyone has a junk drawer and you never know what to do with that stuff, so I love taking the idea of taking all the different objects and letting kids create something new.

I'd like to try that recipe. Even my teenager still likes squishing clay and Play-Doh sometimes.

Debra: It also makes adorable snowmen because it's so white, so if you happen to live in an area where you're not going to get snow this winter, that might be a nice substitute. They'll be small, but they'll be very cute.

Toni: And you could make holiday decorations that you could put out from year to year.

Now, let's talk about eruption in a bottle. Kids love things that explode, so I can't wait to hear how to create this one.

Debra: If you have a mad scientist in your family, this one is definitely sure to please, and it will not destroy your kitchen, so it's a nice middle road to take.

You need a plastic water bottle. Fill it 3/4 full with warm water, add a couple of drops of food coloring and 1/4 cup of vinegar. White vinegar will work just fine. Then take a little kitchen funnel, stick it in the bottle and add a heaping teaspoon of baking soda through the funnel. That mixture's going to fizz up immediately and overflow. It's pretty exciting and of course the food coloring makes it blue or green or whatever color you've added.

Here's a tip. You might want to do it in your sink or in a baking pan. Put the bottle in there before you add the baking soda so you can catch the lava as it starts flowing out.

Toni: I'm a psychologist by training and I used to use something similar to this with kids in therapy sessions.

We used to use film canisters, which of course, people don't use much anymore. But I would put down a plastic table cloth and then we'd mix up the ingredients you mentioned inside the film canister but I'd quickly put the lid on the canister. It would then blow off and the volcano would erupt.

The point of the experiment was to show them that if you keep your anger all stuffed inside, you can get those explosions, but if you let it out when it's just "little anger" – by talking to someone – then your anger won't explode in that way. Kids loved it!

Next, let's talk about indoor games that we can play at home. You have an idea called "beat the clock."

Debra: Beat the clock is a surprising and exciting game that you can play inside. It involves picking up pretend time bombs.

First, collect old alarm clocks or kitchen timers. The best ones have a little tick sound to them. Set them to go off every 10 or 15 minutes, depending on the age of the kids.

For younger kids, give them more time. For older kids, challenge them with a shorter time.

Then you take these alarm clocks or "time bombs" that you've set and hide them around the house in laundry hampers, in a dresser drawer, or at the back of a closet. Obviously the kids are sequestered so they don't see you hiding the clocks. Then you set them loose and their goal is to find all the clocks and deactivate the alarms before they go off.

Hilarity ensues!

Toni: What fun! We're going to have a pile of kids over for Thanksgiving, so that would be a great activity to set up.

Debra, you also have a hula hoop game that sounds like fun.

Debra: It's a fun game that's great for those times when you're hosting a crowd in your home or you just happen to have a big group of kids over.

All you need is a hula hoop. You stand all your players in a big circle and then slip the hula hoop onto one person's arm. Have all your players join hands and then the players have to find a way to move the hoop all the way around the circle without letting go of each others' hands.

It becomes a cooperative game and people get into incredible contortions to try and shrug this hoop along the line. It's a really fun activity.

My kids tell me it gets really interesting when there are people who are different heights. So, if you're doing it as a family with adults and kids, my guess is you're going to have even more giggles because it gets even harder.

It's a great ice breaker. You can use it to build up an appetite before a big meal or to wake everyone up afterwards.

Toni: Absolutely! Give us a quick summary of indoor wax paper skates.

Debra: This is the perfect quick idea. A reader told us about it.

Here's what you do. Move all of the furniture in your living room to the walls. Then cut squares of wax paper big enough for people to stand on and fold one piece up above each ankle, using a rubber band to secure the wax paper around the ankle. So then everyone has ice skates and they can slide all around the living room floor. The mom said they would put on some music, dance or pretend to skate in a circle, and have a great time.

Toni: That sounds like a blast!

Next we're going to talk about some big ideas that take a little bit of work to set up, but you get a big bang for your buck.

First of all, how can our kids get some exercise in the house this winter?

Debra: One idea that I love is the all-ages gym. Oftentimes, parents have a treadmill or elliptical trainer tucked in a corner somewhere, but one way to encourage your whole family to spend more time getting fit indoors is to create a workout area that's inviting for *everybody*.

So, along with your treadmill, put a few other pieces of equipment out.

We heard from a reader in Washington who added some simple things like an exercise ball and a mini trampoline next to her treadmill in the spare bedroom. She put in a TV for exercise videos and a music player for some fun tunes. She found that the family actually loved spending time in there together and everybody got some exercise. What could be better in the middle of winter than that?

Toni: I've talked about getting a mini-tramp for years. I think I'm going to buy one.

Debra: I've always wanted one too. They look like fun.

Toni: I think the kids would love it! Your next idea is called "the basement sports center."

Debra: A reader told us about this too. The basement sports center really makes the most of an indoor space in the winter. This mom put some artificial turf carpeting in the basement, covered the window wells with netting, and put a bit of padding on the corners of the walls. And presto, an indoor soccer arena! They set up two mini soccer goals and they just let the kids go to town down there. They even set up a video camera on a tripod to record their games.

Toni: Live action cam!

Debra: You could do field hockey, football, gymnastics, or baseball with a whiffle ball.

Toni: I have a friend with a big long basement. She made a bowling alley out of it.

If you're the creative type you can also set up some "let's pretend" areas.

Debra: If you have kids who love to play dress up, here's an idea. A reader in Michigan told us about a pretend boutique that she and her daughters made. Instead of trying to stuff all the dress up clothes in a closet or a basket, she set up portable clothes racks and hung everything on hangers.

She set up some shelves for their shoes and handbags, and some hooks on the wall to hang up the feather boas, and a nice full length mirror.

Their two daughters got hours of enjoyment pretending that this was a boutique where they could come in, select their outfits, and try them on. And it was a fantastic way to showcase their costume collection.

Toni: We have something similar in our basement, and my husband built a stage that we keep next to the costumes. You can hang a spot light and put up a curtain so that you actually have a performance stage in your basement.

Debra: We had a reader tell us about setting up a stage and recording studio. They started with the curtain, some Christmas lights and some spotlights, which were initially just big flashlights. One of the kids would be on lights, one kid would be performing, and another would video tape the show. This whole entertainment center was there in their basement.

Toni: Fun and creative!

Speaking of recording, I know you have a twist on this too, and you call it "stop motion animation."

Debra: Well, I'm sure that some of you remember Gumby, or maybe you've seen the Wallace and Gromit film?

These are films that are made with a technique called "stop motion animation" where they create little clay characters by moving them, snapping individual frames, and then stringing the frames of film together so they create movement.

It was a very labor-intensive process in the days of Gumby, but now it's all been digitized. You can actually download free or very inexpensive software and do this with your digital camera or digital video camera.

You can take anything your kids can sculpt, like clay creatures, but one of our editors just used some lollipops and pretzel sticks. By laying them out and then moving them slightly, they created animation. So, the lollipops became the branches of a tree and then the tree leaves fell off by taking the lollipop wrappers away.

Each time they moved something, they would press a key on the keyboard. The camera was connected to the computer, so it would snap a frame. Then the software strings it all together in a very professional-looking video.

The kids were fascinated by it. It took them about an hour to make a 10-second movie, but that 10-second movie they watched over and over and over again.

Toni: That would be an awesome project to do over a holiday break from school. The kids could do a little bit each day and wind up with a minute-long cartoon.

Debra: Exactly. If you factor in the time it takes to come up with your story line, create your characters, and figure out what your props are going to be, this could be a wonderful multi-day project.

Toni: That sounds really fun and so creative! I've never heard of that, so thank you for sharing that.

And here's another idea: A parent named Chris wrote in and said they have a family picnic every Sunday night. Isn't that fun? They put the table-cloth on the floor, eat dinner and watch a movie. She said they've done it for five years and they just love that night together. Sometimes she packs a brown bag meal for each person and then it's like they're unwrapping a present with a surprise dinner inside. What a wonderful idea!

And Tammy wrote in with this idea. She lets her kids use shaving cream or washable finger paint in the tub. She said it makes tub time so much more fun.

Debra, you have an idea for at-home newscasts. What's that?

Debra: This is another idea that we got from one of our incredibly creative readers. One day the family was at home and they were a little bored and not knowing what to do, so she set up her video camera and a little desk with a map of the United States on a wall behind it; and they created their own newscast.

The mom and her kids took turns being the camera man, the news anchor announcing the news, and the weather man giving a weather report. When dad came home, they had a whole newscast ready to show him.

Toni: Fantastic! You have another idea called "restaurant at home" and I've tried it out. One day when I was working at home, I asked my daughter and her friend to play restaurant and make me lunch.

They had such fun doing it that whenever I see her friend, she asks, "When can we come over and make lunch for you again?"

Not only is it fun, but they gain skills learning to plan a meal, prepare it and then clean up.

Debra: Yes, it's fun and educational. It helps kids learn their way around the kitchen so they can help you out a bit too.

Toni: Another parent, Amy, also sent in an idea. She saves some of her kids' Halloween candy and uses it when they make their gingerbread house. Isn't that a fabulous idea?

Debra: That's very smart.

Toni: Debra, you have more great ideas and they're on my website: www.*getparentinghelpnow.com/myfreebookresources*

There's one called "Critters that Keep Out the Cold," and you also have one for making a welcome banner for the holidays.

Thank you so much! You have been an incredible guest!

Contact Information:

Debra Immergut

Website: *www.familyfunmag.com*

Resources:

Fun Family Activity Ideas: *www.getparentinghelpnow.com/myfreebookresources*

Stress-Free Holidays

Meet the Experts:

Elizabeth Scott, M.S., has spent years counseling, coaching and educating families on effective strategies to manage stress, maintain healthy relationships and live a balanced lifestyle. She's been interviewed on national television and radio shows, and in national publications like USA Today and Woman's Day as well as CNN.com. She's written hundreds of articles on various aspects of stress management for About.com, which can be found at: *www.stress.about.com.*

Beth Tabak is a Business and Life Coach, writer, speaker, and owner of Starting Now. She coaches individuals to experience the vastness of their abilities, whether it be in their personal or professional life, by taking new actions that achieve new results.

Kathy Franzen, owner of Project Partners Organizing, has five children, three step-children and several grandchildren. Kathy has been a teen mom, a single parent, and a step-parent. She has over 30 years of household and family management skills, and she's developed practical organizational tools to keep families moving forward.

******

Toni: With the holidays coming, I thought it would be a fabulous time for us to do some pre-planning and bypass some of the stress that inevitably comes with the holidays. Holidays are supposed to be fun, right?

I've invited three professionals: a stress management expert, a life coach, and a professional organizer, who together are going to help us sift through our priorities, simplify our lives, cope with difficult relatives, and use organizational tools.

I want to first welcome Elizabeth Scott. Elizabeth, there are a lot of reasons that we experience stress over the holidays. We all do too much. We may have difficulty with some of our relatives. We may spend too much money and regret it later. And we have such high expectations.

So let's start with high expectations. How can we make our expectations more manageable in order to reduce some of the stress we normally experience?

Elizabeth: That's a really good question because so many people have unrealistic views of the holidays. We remember our childhood holidays through those childhood glasses where everything is perfect. Then we see the messages on the media, with all the beautiful pictures of perfect food, perfect houses, perfect parties, and we try to recreate that in real life. But that's not always possible because there are only so many hours in a day and we all have busy schedules already. So trying to pile on so many added activities during the holiday season can cause a lot of stress.

The first step is to realize that it might not be realistic to visit every relative, attend every party, and make or buy every gift that you'd like to. Something has to give somewhere. So first look at all the things you're planning on doing and see if your plans are realistic. You can write everything in your day planner and see what fits into the time allotted.

Four weeks between the major holidays sounds like a lot of time, but once we see that it's mostly weekends and nights that are available, because we already have tight schedules, we realize there isn't much extra time.

So one thing we can do is to start taking shortcuts, which is really okay. You can shop online and get holiday cards that already have your pictures printed on them and all you have to do is sign them. It's better than doing it the perfectionist way, which is what a lot of people do, and then they don't even get their cards sent out or they're still scrambling to buy gifts the night before the big day. If you allow yourself to take some shortcuts and relax those insane standards, it can go a long way toward providing stress relief.

Toni: It sounds like we have to get to get rid of our perfectionism. So if you send out holiday cards, you have to lower your expectations by streamlining the production of the cards and say to yourself, "At least I sent out cards."

Elizabeth: Absolutely. Even putting together a nice email with your picture and a little update and sending it to your whole list is better than not sending a greeting at all.

The holidays are a prime trap for perfectionists. What people don't realize about perfectionists is that they actually are big procrastinators because they build up these huge expectations in their mind. Then they don't get anything started until they have time to do it justice so they often end up getting only halfway done and just scrapping the whole thing.

I think we all know people who have had experiences with that. But this holiday season just try getting it done without being a perfectionist. If people get something from you, they'll appreciate it more than getting nothing.

And children will appreciate store-bought or pre-packaged holiday cookies just as much as they'll appreciate cookies made from scratch.

The holidays need to be more about fun than about high expectations. If we relax, we can have more fun and the people around us can have more fun because they'll see that we're relaxed. We set the tone for our families.

Toni: If you have perfectionistic standards, it's going to take a lot of time, and that freaks you out because you think, "Where am I going to find eight hours to do this?" Then you procrastinate because it feels overwhelming. Whereas, if you pick the simple route like emailing a holiday card, you can accomplish a lot more with less stress.

Elizabeth: Absolutely. Or if you send a pre-printed card, you can print out the address labels and stick on stamps in a couple of hours and people will appreciate that just as much as a big handwritten note. Maybe you can email a longer letter when you have more time.

What our families remember, and appreciate, is just having fun with us.

Mothers, in particular, end up becoming so stressed that we don't even enjoy the holidays. Any other time of the year, if we have parties to go to, we're excited; but during the holiday season we might say, "Oh no, I have another party to go to tonight," and it starts to feel like work.

But if we can take some shortcuts on this other stuff, we have more time and energy to do the things that can really be fun.

Toni: Let's look at another huge category that causes us stress, especially in the current climate of double-digit unemployment: we spend too much. How can we rein in costs?

Elizabeth: There are several strategies. First of all, remember that the thought counts more than the money spent. That's a huge one because we've been programmed to believe that more money means more caring. Our kids are great at helping us believe this too.

Our children will make a list of things that they would like, and we'll want to give gifts to our extended family, but if we remember that it's really more about the thought than the gift and find ways to convey that to the people that we care about, we can spend a lot less and still feel like we gave some great gifts.

One way to do that is by personalizing gifts. I love giving gift baskets with smaller items. I've given my brother-in-law, who loves going out, a gift basket with fun things for a date with my sister. It can be really thoughtful to give "a date in a basket."

Or you can make handmade holiday gifts if that's something you enjoy, and you can start long before the holidays. You can crochet a scarf for about $2.00 and the recipients don't have to know that it was that inexpensive to make. It's the thought that counts when making handmade crafts. If it's something you enjoy and you're not too busy to do it, this can help to relieve financial stress. Knitting or crocheting can put some people in a kind of meditative state, so it can actually help relieve holiday stress.

Toni: But if that sounds stressful or overwhelming, then don't even go there.

Elizabeth: Exactly. Don't try to make yourself be something that you're not. Don't try to make yourself enjoy things that you really don't enjoy. If it feels like work, skip it because there are other options. In fact, this is a perfect time to talk to your friends and extended family about getting together and finding ways to help everybody save money.

Early in November, some of my friends and I decided to do a cookie exchange instead of buying each other specific gifts. And who doesn't enjoy cookies? It combines a holiday get-together and holiday gifts, and it's fun and inexpensive.

Toni: Ornament exchanges are also great to do with friends, and having a white elephant gift exchange can also be a riot.

Let's talk next about relatives – another potential stressor for the holidays.

Elizabeth: We talk about this in family therapy. Something very interesting happens when the extended family gets back together. Even though you're a productive adult, and you've moved on and have a new family of your own, you revert back to the role that you played when you were a kid and this can be stressful.

A spouse may look at you and say, "Who are you?"

Maybe you tease your siblings when you get together or they tease you. Dealing with everybody's different personality characteristics can be difficult because you're not used to dealing with them. It's important to remember that people don't have to be perfect for us to love them.

If you can think ahead about pitfalls that may occur, or little things that can be frustrating, so you're not surprised, and perhaps even make some contingency plans, it will make things easier.

For instance, if you're still single, and your grandmother always asks, "When are you going to get married?" prepare a response ahead of time, or try to avoid the topic, or change the subject, or just accept that she's going to ask, get it over with and move on.

Toni: What else can we do to cope with relatives over the holidays?

Elizabeth: To take the stress out of the situation, imagine that a difficult relative is just a quirky, fun book character and don't take it personally. If you pay attention to how they act, they're going to act that way no matter what you do. So don't take it personally and don't take it as an attack or let yourself get engaged.

You can also mentally count up the number of times you get frustrated by your parents and then just let it go. Have some stress relief techniques in mind that you can use. Breathing exercises are perfect for when you're in difficult situations with people because you can use your technique while stressors are happening and people don't even have to know.

Practice deep breathing from the diaphragm and then just let your frustration go.

The biggest thing to remember is to focus on what you love about these people; focus on why you appreciate them and don't focus on the little things that can be frustrating and stressful. And don't let yourself get negatively engaged.

Toni: I think using positive self-talk can be helpful too. You can tell yourself, "It'll be okay. It's only one hour of my life." Framing it that way can put some perspective on it.

You can also try to shield yourself from people that you know are going to bother you. If Aunt Martha really irritates you, then try not to sit next to her at Thanksgiving dinner.

If someone asks you an irritating question, you can always redirect the conversation back to them. People love talking about themselves. So you don't even have to take the bait that's being set for you. Pretend it's a chess game and make a defensive move to save your bishop.

Elizabeth: I've used those strategies too, and they work!

Toni: We'd be remiss if we didn't mention seasonal affective disorder. Tell us briefly what it is and where people can get help if they need to.

Elizabeth: Seasonal affective disorder, or SAD, is basically the winter blues. A lot of people experience this and it can be officially diagnosed.

Basically, when there's less light, they tend to experience depression, and they can be sleeping more, or having trouble sleeping, or waking up in the night and not being able to get back to sleep. Those are the big hallmarks of SAD.

It can start in the fall and go all the way through winter. If you, or somebody that you live with, seems to be going downhill emotionally at that time of year, there are a few things you can do if it's not too serious.

Make sure that you're taking care of yourself, that you're eating right, that you're sleeping enough, and that you're getting some exercise, like taking a walk in the morning to get as much sunshine as you can. Even just focusing on gratitude has been shown to work with depression.

But, if you feel that you need more help, don't be afraid to talk to your doctor because light therapy, medication and psychotherapy may be helpful.

Toni: So if you suffer from a mild case of the "winter blues," try some of these suggestions for a couple of weeks, but if they don't seem to be helping, your physician may be able to help you find an effective treatment. If symptoms are more severe, see your doctor immediately.

******

Beth Tabak is joining us now.

I found Beth by doing an Internet search on stress-free holidays. Beth wrote an article called *10 Tips to a Stress-free Holiday. www.selfgrowth. com/articles/Tabak2.html*

There are several tips that really stood out in your article, Beth. One was to reminisce about last year with your family and ask, "What did we like about last year's holiday celebration?" Then you have a phrase: "not that again!" Tell us what that means because I love the sound of that.

Beth: Well, that came up when my husband and I first divorced. We used to have Christmases where the kids could just tear open the gifts and it was fun and exciting. Then after the divorce, we had a holiday at his home, and he and his new wife wanted to do it more formally where everybody opens one gift at a time. It was a disaster. So for years after that we used the phrase "not that again!" because my kids did not want to do that.

So the first step is to reminisce about previous holidays so we can learn from the past. You can set up two columns on a sheet of paper. On one side put "what works" and on the other side put "not that again!"

List the activities that really bring you joy and that come naturally. I liked when Elizabeth mentioned doing a craft that brings you joy, because you're going to reduce your stress when you're doing activities that are authentic to who you are. Do anything that comes naturally, that clicks into place, so you can leverage your strengths and passions and values.

Then, in the "not that again!" list, write down your challenges and past catastrophes. Add anything that drains your energy or puts you in a funk. By doing this, you can really set boundaries to protect yourself.

Toni: And you also have to be able to say "No."

I loved another idea from your article: choosing a theme for the holidays that you can get excited about. For instance, if you picked a theme like giving to others, then you can define how you will use your time during those four weekends before the holiday. You can pick activities that support that theme.

Beth: Absolutely. The theme for the holidays is really about maintaining your focus but in a fun, creative way because you have a theme that everyone has chosen together.

I know some people have a very tight budget this year, so one way to relieve some stress would be to pick a theme like "simply sensational" that's happy and uplifting. It says: "I'm going to make this a wonderful holiday even if I have to watch my dollars."

Another idea would be "home for the holidays" if you're always running around; or "faith and family first" to honor your spirituality.

I love the quote "Be the change you wish to see in the world" by Mahatma Gandhi. If you're service-oriented, that's a great quote to use as a theme. Or you can use any quote that gets you excited and motivated to aim for stress-free holidays.

Toni: I think "giving to others" is what holidays are supposed to be about anyway, so by doing volunteer projects you're going to get so much more back than you would from shopping.

You recommend that people set three priorities and make decisions based on their theme. What might that look like?

Beth: You can select between one and four priorities; you'll be scattered and overwhelmed if you pick any more than that. When you know what your priorities are, you can then set your boundaries and you'll know what to say "yes" to and what to say "no" to.

For example, if your top priority is to be service-oriented this holiday season, and somebody asks you to help prepare a neighborhood party, take 24 hours to think about that. Ask yourself, "Do I really want to spend a lot of time on the neighborhood party when I really want our family involved in service-oriented projects?"

Toni: When you prioritize, it does make it easier to say "no." And we all should heed your advice about waiting 24 hours; I think that's a wise idea.

Beth, you created a tool called "Create a Map." Tell us about that.

Beth: We all have different lifestyles, so you can create a personal map that works for you. First set up four columns on your computer. Then, at the top of the page, write down your theme and list your four priorities underneath it.

In the four columns, put your personal to do's, your business to do's, your holiday to do's, and miscellaneous to do's. I put everything on that one map and then flip it over and put my holiday budget on the back side. I carry that with me the whole month of December and then check things off as I go.

I encourage people to make their list as soon as possible. Write everything down to get it out of your head and onto your map today so you can get started taking action.

Not taking action is really what causes anxiety. Having a theme and the map will help get you started, and as you make progress and check things off, it will relieve the stress.

Toni: Absolutely.

There's a website that I really like for holiday planning called *www.christmas.organizedhome.com.*

Cynthia, the owner of the website, suggests using a six-week organization plan. She breaks the tasks down into big categories, like getting organized week, gift and giving week, get cooking week, decorating week, and celebration week. Then, each week you focus on completing those specific tasks. I like the idea of chunking the tasks together so you can feel a sense of accomplishment when that category is done.

Beth: Yes, that's called blocking your time, and when you block your time, you can get clearly focused, store the time for that task, get it done, and get it behind you.

Toni: Then you feel so good because now the house is decorated, or all of the presents are bought.

Beth: Before you know it, you have your feet propped up and you're sipping your nice little holiday drink and you're enjoying your family.

Toni: Wouldn't that be incredible?

Beth, you're a single parent and so many families are blended families. You and your ex-husband have some ideas on how to help reduce holiday stress with your kids. Can you share a few of those ideas, please?

Beth: Every divorced family is different, but it really breaks my heart to see all the stress during the holidays. My suggestion is to maintain love in your heart when you're dealing with your ex, no matter how you feel, and try to compartmentalize any of the difficult feelings that you may have from the past.

Instead of breaking up our family when we divorced, we said we were "restructuring" it. It's more like he's a brother who you still may fight with, but you can get along too. And instead of trying to one-up each other with gifts for the kids, we said they were from mom and dad or from the family.

Also, it's important to set boundaries around what you can handle and what you can't handle.

Toni: Exactly. You may not want to spend the holidays with the ex-wife so you can just say, "I feel uncomfortable with that."

Beth: Communicating differently and becoming a better listener is also really important. With the kids we just aim to make it fun. We actually spend Christmas Eve and Christmas morning together and then we do things separately. It gives our kids a sense of family support. They understand that mom and dad aren't getting back together, but they love having that support system there.

Toni: Thank you, Beth, for providing so many great ideas.

******

Kathy Franzen, a professional organizer and owner of Project Partners Organizing is now joining us.

Toni: You were a teen mom and a single mom and now you're a step-mom, so please weigh in on how you coordinated holiday activities.

Kathy: It can be very confusing. Our kids are grown now and they have their own families and their own in-laws, so occasionally we'll have our holiday on a day that's not the actual holiday. We also involve the grandchildren as much as we possibly can – in decorating, gift making and sending greeting cards.

Toni: Then children feel they have a purpose during the holidays, and they feel important.

It might be helpful to think ahead and ask, "What are some of the roles that kids can have?"

I like to have a holiday craft set up on a table, one that kids can do independently. Or kids can make the place cards or a centerpiece while the adults are preparing the meal.

Kathy: Right. They could make placemats or window decorations. My son is serving overseas so this year I'm going to have the grandchildren each create a drawing and send it to him because I know he'd love to receive pictures that all the children have made.

Toni: Even if you don't know someone personally who's serving in the military, that would be a great idea!

I'm entertaining for Thanksgiving this year and I'm a little nervous, Kathy. Help me get organized!

Kathy: First, identify what you want the day to look like; make sure your expectations of the day are realistic. Next, pick your guest list. Then identify what kind of things need to happen for the day. Decorating is one task, although some people don't do much decorating for Thanksgiving; but regardless, you have to clean and organize your home.

I would buy the food a week ahead of time; you want to stay out of the grocery stores the closer you get to Thanksgiving. But make a list of last-minute items that need to be fresh, so you can go to the store and quickly get what you need.

Then prepare as much food ahead of time as you can. What kind of things can you freeze ahead of time such as an appetizer or a cheese dish? Put together spice packets with dry ingredients for the dishes you're going to be preparing and set them aside or freeze them. Also, a lot of desserts can be made ahead of time and frozen.

Toni: What else can we do to make meal planning easier?

Kathy: Most important of all is to delegate as many of the food items as possible. There's nothing wrong with having somebody else bring something. Oftentimes I'll make the main meal and then delegate appetizers, desserts and beverages.

Toni: Sometimes we'll have an appetizer "dinner" where everyone brings their favorite appetizers and we just graze on appetizers. Another idea that we love is a fondue dinner. We cut up all sorts of meats, seafood and vegetables and make yummy sauces for dipping. Then, of course, there has to be chocolate fondue for dessert!

Kathy, let's talk about gifts. What time-saving or money-saving tips can you give us?

Kathy: Some people love to shop and I say, "Go for it, if that's what you love to do."

If you are going to shop in stores, make a list of everyone you're going to purchase something for and write down some ideas for each person so you're not just wandering around the store. Then shop during a time when there's likely to be fewer people. I like to have my Christmas shopping done by Thanksgiving.

You can also give gifts of experiences rather than stuff. As a professional organizer I go into homes, and I see so much stuff that people don't really need. They get things as gifts and they don't know what to do with them.

You can give a gift of event tickets, or a membership, or a gift certificate for foot massage or back massage.

Toni: Or babysitting, so a couple or a single parent can have an evening alone!

Kathy: I think trading gifts you've already received can be fun too, and then you're not spending money. You're also getting rid of things that you don't need.

Toni: I read about using a gift idea planner and listing the person's name, clothing sizes, favorite colors and hobbies. You can write down your gift ideas and what the price is, so you can keep track of your expenses.

You can also use a master shopping list, so if a meeting runs short and you suddenly have 30 minutes, you can use that time efficiently and buy something from your master shopping list.

Kathy: You can also keep that list and use it for anniversaries, birthdays and other times when you want to buy gifts for people on your list.

Toni: Another question: Is it more time efficient to wrap gifts all at once?

Kathy: I like to wrap gifts as I get them and then I don't have to worry about hiding them or the kids getting into them. But other people might want to have a big marathon wrapping time and involve the kids. It's a matter of deciding what you want out of that experience.

Toni: Help us out with decorating. Should we do it all at once? What's the best way to get our homes looking beautiful for the holidays?

Kathy: To get the decorating done, do whatever works best for your schedule and your life.

One of the things I do recommend is weeding out the broken items and things you haven't put out in a few years. Then make a list of things that you want to replace or buy, and get them on sale after the holidays.

Toni: Yes, that's a great idea.

Thanks to everyone for the great tips!

Contact information:

Elizabeth Scott

Email Address: *escott@elizabethscott.info*

Website: *www.stress.about.com* or *www.ElizabethScott.info*

Beth Tabak

Mailing Address: 1818 American Elm Ct, Sugar Land, TX 77479

Phone: 281-343-1691

Email Address: businesslifecoach@comcast.net

Website: *www.StartingNowCoaching.com*

Kathy Franzen

Mailing Address: 1691 W. White Ash Drive, Balsam Lake, WI 54810

Phone: 651-592-6870

Email Address: kathy@ProjectPartnerServices.com

Website: *www.ProjectPartnerServices.com*

Resources:

Elizabeth Scott

8 Keys to Stress Management

Stress Management Articles: *www.stress.about.com*

Workshops and Coaching: *www.ElizabethScott.info*

Facebook Group About Stress Management: *www.facebook.com/about-stressmanagement*

Beth Tabak

Complimentary Coaching Session: *www.startingnowcoaching.com/life-coachingservices.html*

Bonus Gift: "25 Parent Tips to Help Kids Avoid Sabotaging Actions and Experience their Full Abilities" *www.startingnowcoaching.com/id72.html*

Lose the Mommy Guilt for a Happier You

Meet the Experts:

Aviva Pflock and **Devra Renner** are two of the authors of *Mommy Guilt: Learn to Worry Less, Focus on What Matters Most, and Raise Happier Kids.*

Aviva is a certified parent educator. She's a child development specialist with a focus on early childhood and adolescent behaviors and she has three children.

Devra is a clinical social worker. She's a consultant for Zero to Three, a national, nonprofit organization that provides parents and professionals with knowledge about early development. She works with children and families in a variety of settings in her work and she has two children.

Julie Bort is the third author of *Mommy Guilt* but was unable to join the interview.

Toni: I love my radio show but I have to tell you that I felt mommy guilt almost every day this summer. When I was working, I felt like I should be with my kids being the fun mommy over the summer. And when I was with the kids, I was thinking, "I have a pile of work to do!"

You did a survey for your book and you found out that an astounding 96 percent of moms feel guilt about their parenting. So, what's up with mommy guilt? Where does all the guilt come from, Aviva?

Aviva: Guilt comes from a few areas, but first I want to say that, although there's a lot of guilt out there, by and large, moms are happy. Moms aren't out there feeling guilty and miserable. We're generally happy, but when you're responsible for the life of another person, you're going to second guess yourself every once in a while and sometimes that's okay. Guilt can be a great check and balance.

There are internal and external reasons for feeling guilty. The internal reasons may include guilt about your decision making and your responsibilities. The external factors may include the keeping up with the Joneses' mentality and feeling like you're being judged by other people.

Toni: So you can be guilty but happy?

Aviva: Absolutely.

Toni: Well, that's good to know. Devra, please share your definition of guilt with us.

Devra: We're not talking about a criminal type of guilt. It's nothing that you're going to be arrested for. We like to say that guilt is a catch-all phrase for all of the negative emotions of parenting that you might be experiencing.

It's far easier to bring up a conversation with other parents or co-workers regarding any negative feelings about parenting by saying you feel a little guilty about something. If you were to take all of those negative emotions about motherhood or parenting and put them in a salad bowl, guilt would be the vinaigrette that covers the whole salad.

Maybe you second-guess yourself or think you could've done something better. That's the internal area that Aviva mentioned. It's different from shame, which is more humiliation-driven.

Toni: Do dads feel guilty about their parenting?

Aviva: Fortunately, we're seeing a lot more dads involved with parenting now. Dads don't use the term "guilt" though.

Dads name more specific emotions that feed into guilt. Maybe they're angry. Maybe they're frustrated. Maybe they're unsure about what to do in a situation.

As Devra said, it seems like women toss all these feelings together and call them "guilt."

If you ask a father if he's feeling guilty about something, as we did in the survey, he'll give you this funny look, like it doesn't even make any sense to him. Guilt is not what he associates with it. So the same emotions are there, but moms and dads label them differently.

Toni: So, a woman is less likely to say, "I'm frustrated" or "angry" about parenting because it's socially unacceptable for her to express anger, but it's socially acceptable for her to feel guilt.

Aviva: Exactly.

Devra: It's not as socially acceptable to say I feel like I've been "neglectful" or "angry." Those words seem to bring out a different type of conversation and reaction from whomever we're speaking to.

Toni: Right. They might bring out child protection!

Devra: Exactly. But is anyone going to call child protection because you decided that the dishes in your sink weren't as important as singing with your baby?

Toni: Saying, "I've neglected my child" would probably be the worst thing a mom would want to admit to.

In your book you state that there's "good guilt" and "bad guilt." Devra, what do you mean by that?

Devra: What we mean is that guilt is a normal emotion. Most folks feel guilt about something. It may not be about parenting. It may be about something else.

We talk about good guilt and bad guilt sort of like a radio station. It's something you can tune into and turn off. Or sometimes it's just white noise in the background.

Good guilt can mean that you realize you're not taking any time for yourself when you look at your calendar. If you color code your calendar with your activities and your kids' activities, you may notice that the calendar is full of their activities. Maybe you're doing too much and you need to scale back.

Bad guilt could be when you leave your child with a babysitter for an hour and you can't enjoy your hour away because you're consumed with getting back home or calling home and finding out if everything is okay. Bad guilt may impair your social functioning, and that's not good for you.

Toni: We do color code our calendar and I have to say the kids have far more colors than my husband and I have. I always feel so happy when I have a mom's night out or a date with my husband and see my color on the calendar.

You found five or six top guilt producers. Aviva, please share those with us and then we'll dive in with very specific, practical tips on relieving some of the mommy guilt.

Aviva: Yelling at your child is constantly in the top three – and often number one, with the exception of parents who have very young infants.

I found this extremely interesting because your tone of voice is one thing that you have sole control over.

So many other things that people can feel guilty about – like time with yourself, time with your kids, cleaning your home, working outside the home, the right schools or the right food choices – you may not have as much control over.

Other causes of guilt that came up repeatedly were having enough time to spend with your spouse, having enough time to spend with each of your children, and keeping your house clean.

Toni: You also found that as children get older moms feel more guilt.

Aviva: The guilt doesn't go away as kids get older, unfortunately. It just changes. There are different issues that you have to deal with as your family changes.

The other really fascinating thing is that there were no differences between a stay-at-home mom and one who worked out of the home. Moms were all feeling equal levels of guilt, just about different things.

Toni: We have a caller named Juliann who has a question for you.

Juliann: We have two working parents and one child who's four in our household. We'd like your perspective on how moms and dads feel about sharing responsibilities for making doctor appointments and scheduling after-school activities.

What kinds of changes have you seen between our generation and our parents' generation where the mother was solely responsible for those types of activities?

Aviva: First, I want to say that more dads than moms do morning drop-off at our elementary school, which I think is great.

And we are seeing dads more involved in day-to-day things with their kids.

I hope parents make it less of a gender issue than looking at who can make it work in their schedules. No mom should feel like they have to be at every doctor's appointment. Dads are certainly capable and really enjoy being able to be involved in all those things. If you can work it out that you can both go, even better.

Juliann: That's great. That's what we try to do at our house and it does work out pretty well.

Toni: I've seen research on this subject, and it shows that dads now are far more involved than our fathers were. It's not only good role modeling, but it also increases a child's self-esteem, whether it's a boy or girl.

Moms get more help and dads benefit by feeling closer to their kids. So it's a win-win for everyone.

We're going to talk about solutions now. Yelling is the number one issue that parents across the ages feel guilty about. So, give us some strategies around yelling less so we feel less guilt.

Devra: Change your tone of voice. Instead of yelling what you want, whisper what you want. It will still get your child's attention.

As our kids are getting older, we have a habit of yelling from room to room when we want something. Stop yelling.

Require your child to come find you if they need something. You go and find them when you need something.

With older kids, you can establish a code word. When you feel that you're getting out of control, or if the kids can see that mom or dad is about to lose it, use the code word. Use this instead of having a yelling match.

Keep in mind that yelling is scary to kids, particularly if they're little and you're taller than them. Just the fact that you're bigger than they are is imposing enough. Raising your voice raises the stakes.

If you come from a family of yellers, hopefully you're going to want to not pass it down from generation to generation. Allow yourself the freedom to say, "I'm not going to be a yeller." It's first making a decision to communicate differently, then making the effort to change. If you slip, simply say, "I just yelled. I'm sorry. Let's try that again."

Toni: Those are great tips, Devra.

Spending time with your spouse is another thing that moms feel guilty about. Why the heck do we feel guilty spending time with our spouse? Our relationship is the cement that holds the family together, and without it the whole family can fall apart. It doesn't make sense to me that we'd feel guilt about this.

Aviva: Yes, if it weren't for your spouse, the kids wouldn't be there, right? So you want to keep that relationship healthy and intact.

I think the way it was worded on the survey, the guilt comes from *not having enough time with your spouse* – yet when you're with your spouse you feel guilty that you should be including your kids.

It's really necessary to do things as a couple, because your kids will grow up and move out and you need to have something in common to do and to talk about.

Be creative. Move the baby monitor into the garage, hop in the back seat of your minivan, and enjoy some time alone with your spouse. Pretend you're young again.

Know that time with your spouse is important in your life. As you say, it's the cement that holds the family together. It's okay to let the kids know that there's time for the two of you.

Toni: Kevin Anderson, one of my guests, had fabulous ideas on how to make connections even if you only have three seconds, 30 seconds, 15 minutes, or an hour. It doesn't have to be an official "date" where you get a babysitter, go out and spend money. It can just be making an effort to connect in little ways every day. (*See Chapter 14: Great Ways to Connect as a Couple.*)

Now let's return to one of the top guilt producers … food. Once in a while we're going to let our kids have junk food. In fact, I totally forgot about dinner last night; I had nothing prepared.

What can we do about guilt that results when we feed our kids some junk food or forget, like I did last night, to make dinner at all?

Aviva: We have an entire chapter in our book *Mommy Guilt* about "the guilty gourmet." Parents are concerned and worried about what they feed their kids.

We like to say it's important to "legalize and regulate," which means that you don't have a complete ban on junk food in your house.

It's also important for kids to learn portion control. Kids have a really good sense of what their body needs when they're little. As they get older, we interfere with that sometimes.

So it really helps if you learn exactly what the nutritional requirements are for your child at their developmental age.

Let's say you have a toddler. It will shock you how little a toddler needs. Some days they can survive on half a bagel and other days they go through your entire refrigerator like the very hungry caterpillar.

As far as feeding kids the right foods, I don't think there's any universal right that you need to worry about. Just provide nutritional options and set whatever limits on junk food that you're comfortable with.

Toni: Forcing kids to eat and saying, "You can't leave the table until your food is gone" backfires. Ellyn Satter, the author of *Secrets of Feeding a Healthy Family* has great advice on this subject. *(See Chapter 12.)*

How can we get rid of guilt when we take time for ourselves?

Devra: This comes up a lot. When moms do have some time alone, they think, "Maybe I should run to Target and see if they have sneakers for my son." As opposed to thinking, "I have some time alone; maybe I should watch a TV program that I recorded."

It's important to have some time alone to reenergize yourself. It's okay to feel good about taking care of yourself. You need that time.

Toni: I think it's critical to take time for yourself.

As we're talking about this topic, I'm imagining being on a plane during an emergency. You're supposed to put on your own oxygen mask first, but I'm picturing moms putting on their kids' masks first because they panic about their kids rather than doing what makes sense.

Is that the kind of reaction you get from moms when you talk about time alone?

Aviva: Moms seem to think that if they're taking time for themselves, they're taking attention away from their child or denying their child something.

I don't think it's taking away from your child. I think it actually contributes more to their life. You can each do your own thing and then come back and share what your experience was like. Kids want to hear those things from you.

They need to know that there's an adult world out there and that they will grow up and be able to participate in it. If you're not doing any of those things, then you're really not showing them what that world is like. So, it does benefit your child when you take some time for yourself.

It's not difficult to create time for yourself. Find something that you used to enjoy and haven't done in a while. Or look up something that you haven't ever done and try it.

My son is taking Spanish right now. It's a language that I've always wanted to learn and I thought maybe I'd take a class.

Toni: If a mom takes time for herself, her child will, in fact, be healthier. Right now too many parents are leading child-centered lives. The world shouldn't revolve around kids and it's so important that they know that. We need to role model that every person has needs and lead by example. Parenting shouldn't be this selfless activity where we're stripped bone dry of energy.

Aviva: It's also not servitude.

Toni: So many of the suggestions for time alone that you've given today are restorative. Time alone also ties back to the number one source of guilt – yelling. Moms, you will yell less if you get a break! Then you'll have less guilt.

Everyone will benefit if you give yourself time to do as you wish. Have a little fun! Lighten up!

Let's talk next about guilt and a messy house.

Devra: I think you leave it that way until your kids leave for college!

If your house doesn't have bacteria growing in it and no one's coming to your refrigerator asking for penicillin, then I think you're probably okay.

Your house is going to look lived in, and you get to decide what your standard of living is going to be. But the other thing is, don't think that the responsibility of keeping a home clean is just yours.

Toni: I couldn't agree more.

Devra: Our spouses and kids can help us. Everyone can do it together. In our house, we call it household responsibilities. We don't even call it chores because it's everyone's responsibility.

Toni: That's a nice re-frame. I like that.

Aviva, you have seven principles in *Mommy Guilt* that you believe can help relieve some mommy guilt. Please share those tips.

Aviva: I'll preface this by saying that you don't have to do them in order and you don't have to do them *at all*. These are just suggestions that we think may help you.

First, you must be willing to let some things go.

Prioritizing is a huge issue for everyone. The main thing is: don't feel like one thing always has to be your top priority. Keep in mind that your priorities are going to change day-to-day, and sometimes minute-to-minute.

If you're at work completely absorbed in something and the phone rings and the school nurse says your kid just broke their arm, then guess what? Your priorities get to change. You can shift so that your kids are at the top of the list for a little while until you get that dealt with. So, keep your priorities fluid as you go through life.

The second one is: parenting is not a competitive sport. Don't have an attitude of keeping up with the Joneses. Don't feel like your child has to be doing everything that your neighbor's kid is doing at the same age.

We may want our kids to all walk at the same time and we may give in to peer pressure about that, yet we don't want our kids to give in to peer pressure later, so we need to be good role models. We have to keep that in mind.

The other part is that we don't all parent the same. If you want your spouse's help, then stop correcting him if he doesn't do things your way when he's helping, because then he won't want to help anymore. Everyone has their own style of parenting, so be open to that.

The third one is to look towards the future and see the big picture. Don't get overly hung up on the here and now.

Do you really want your child to eat all of their green beans on the plate or do you want your child to develop good healthy eating habits throughout life? Keep the big picture in mind and don't worry so much about the little details.

The fourth one sounds like the opposite, but it's a good complement. Learn when and how to live in the moment. Instead of a two-minute walk to the mailbox with your child, let it be a half-hour adventure as they look at every bug and turn over every rock. Enjoy every moment that they're living in.

Kids are great at doing that. If we can follow their lead, we may get a great adventure that we wouldn't have had if we had rushed through it.

Number five: get used to saying "yes" more often and being able to defend your "no." This is my favorite one. "No" is an easy knee-jerk response. Your kids want to paint. "No, it'll be a mess."

Instead, teach them how to prepare the area to prevent a mess and then let them have some fun painting. Maybe you'll get a half hour to sit and read a book while they do it. Teach them the whole process. You'll control the environment; you'll be able to clean up afterwards and it may actually, in the end, be easier than the knee jerk "no" because they may keep battling with you to say "yes."

The sixth one is: laugh a lot, especially with your children. Humor is a great parenting tool and an often overlooked one. Remember, it's okay to laugh with your kids, even during a disciplining moment.

My girls were arguing all day one day. I finally sat them both down on the couch. I was lecturing them. My son, who was about two at the time, came in and he started mimicking everything I was saying. We all just started laughing and it relieved the tension. It got us through that moment.

Toni: It's usually kind of scary to hear your kids repeat what you're saying to them.

Aviva: Oh, yeah. The little live mirrors.

The last one, number seven, is: make sure you set aside specific time to have fun as a family. That doesn't mean you need to add a 25th hour to your day. It means try to find those family moments within your day.

When you're getting dinner ready, turn that into some fun family time. Turn the music on. Pull out some drinks to have. No alcohol for the kids, but pull out some juice and pull out some snacks. You have appetizers when you're waiting at a restaurant. Why not have a kiddie cocktail hour you can all enjoy as dinner's being prepared? Release that tension and have some fun together during a time that's normally not fun at all.

Toni: Great principles! Now I want to talk about humor; I want to talk about laughing. I want more ideas about having fun!

Devra: Aviva and I always say that humor is the most underused parenting tool and one of the most effective.

When my son was an infant and he was crying, I'd go through the list of whether he was wet, hungry, or tired, and sometimes I still wouldn't know what was bothering him.

So, I'd sing a song to myself. I'm a big Rolling Stones fan and it would be "You Can't Always Get What You Want." It reminded me that even if I couldn't figure out what was going on, he had his needs met.

Well, when my kids got older and they'd whine or cry for something, and I knew that they had what they needed, I'd sing the song to them.

It wasn't to taunt them; I'd just start singing and dancing and they'd start dancing and singing too. As they got older I'd just say, "You know what Mick says?"

Well, one time in a grocery store, my son, who was about three, wanted something. I told him it wasn't on our list and he threw himself down in the middle of the aisle and started to have a tantrum.

So I said, "Hey, what does Mick say?" and he kind of paused for a minute. Then he got up and grabbed my hand and we started to walk down the aisle.

A man turned to me and he said, "I'm sorry, I was eavesdropping. Can you please tell me who Mick is and why he has such power over your child? That was amazing."

I said, "It's Mick Jagger from the Rolling Stones."

My son started to sing the song to this man. So believe me, humor is something that will stick with your kid.

Humor sticks with them far more than yelling or a spanking. Years later, my son and I were watching the Super Bowl when Mick Jagger and the Rolling Stones performed at half-time.

I turned to my son and I said, "Hey, look who's on the Super Bowl. It's Mick Jagger."

My son stood up and said, "I'm not watching this. I don't like Mick Jagger. He doesn't let kids get what they want."

Toni: That's a great story.

I should mention I also have some additional tips on reducing Mommy Guilt here: *www.getparentinghelpnow.com/myfreebookresources*

Next, I'll be talking with Char Wadell, a mom who – believe it or not – has no mommy guilt!

Char, you're a mom of two. You're a beautician, a florist, and you compete with your girls as an equestrian. You're one of those rare people in the world, just four percent of moms, who don't feel mommy guilt. Char, how the heck do you do this?

Char: I think it was evolution. When the girls were small, I did have guilt and I'd compare myself or my kids to others. But as time went on, I picked myself up by the bootstraps and told myself, "I'm a good mom. I just need to move forward and do what I need to do. I'm trying the hardest I can and doing the best that I know how. I should give myself credit for that."

My dad was a testimony to that. He said, "No one wrote the book for you. You just have to do the best you can."

Toni: I love that phrase, "I'm doing the best that I can." I find that it calms me down when I start to get upset.

When your kids were little and you took Early Childhood Family Education classes, were there more opportunities for comparing your kids? Parents might say, "My child started walking or talking at this age."

Char: Absolutely. Because I was a stay-at-home mom, I was involved in a lot of mothers' groups with children and toddlers; and that's what we sat around and did, unfortunately. I look back on it now and see that we were too busy worrying about what we *weren't* doing instead of giving each other credit for what we were accomplishing.

Toni: Isn't that the truth?

I was at a New Year's Eve party and I was chatting with another mom. I asked, "What are your kids up to?"

She answered that her girls were in traveling sports. They competed in elite programs and they were traveling to Chicago and California for events. Then she asked, "So what does your daughter do?"

To my daughter's credit, as a seventh grader she tried out for three new sports. As a teenager, it took a lot of courage on her part. But I had to do this mental check and tell myself, "It's okay, Toni. Your child doesn't have to be an elite anything at 12 or 13 years old."

Is that how you think about it, too, Char?

Char: I really do. I've given my girls all kinds of options. I encourage them to try all kinds of stuff.

I've been a fortunate mother of two daughters who have excelled in showing horses, which is a sport I absolutely love. So that was a gift in itself, but now they're changing and they want to try other things too.

You have to grow with your children and accept the changes. Try not to get hung up on what you wish they would do. Just think, "We have a new adventure. We have to close that chapter and move on to another one."

Toni: I think you have to keep your identity separate from your child's, and not live through them and what their accomplishments are.

You've also been really honest with your girls and told them, "Hey, mom's not perfect."

Char: I've been honest with my girls almost to a fault even when they were little. Sometimes they'd drive me crazy. I was a stay-at-home mom and I'd lock myself in the bedroom and say, "Mom's not the best mom right now. I have to stand here for a while for a time out." And I'd give myself a time out.

Toni: I admire you for doing that. More parents need to have the guts to do that.

Char: I said, "If I have to come out and call your dad, we're all in trouble. So leave me alone."

As the girls got older, sometimes I would cross emotional barriers and sit down and just cry with them and say, "You understand this is really hard for me?" I wanted to show them that parenting is hard sometimes.

Sometimes I really don't know what to do but I want to listen to them. Sometimes I get mad and sometimes I yell. We don't yell all the time, but we're one of the louder families on the block. They know that there's always equal time for everyone, though. As teenagers they're like, "It's my turn now."

Toni: Let's be honest. Everyone on the planet will yell at their kids at some point. It would be impossible not to. I agree with Devra and Aviva that we need to do our best to keep a lid on it, though.

I've always thought we can't be perfect, so let's not even put that expectation out there.

You've also done a great thing. You've found a passion in floral design. What brought you to the point when you pursued a passion of your own?

Char: I went through high risk pregnancies with both my daughters and I ended up being a stay-at-home-mom, which is a gift in itself, but it just zapped my identity. It zapped who I thought I was.

It was really hard for me to come from a professional world and then all of a sudden be a stay-at-home mom. I really had to do a lot of searching. I'm a creative person. I like working with my hands.

I ended up going back and taking short courses, like a night course or a weekend course. And I ended up getting certified in floral design. I started trying new things for myself, just like I encouraged my kids to do. I got really excited and looked forward to the next new thing I was going to try.

Toni: And you're a happier mom as a result.

Char: Oh, absolutely! I have a whole new network of friends in each little thing I dabbled in and it's wonderful.

Toni: Char, thank you for your honesty. It was great to have you and Aviva Pflock and Devra Renner as my guests today.

Contact Information:

Aviva Pflock and Devra Renner

Email: *aviva@parentopia.net* and *devra@parentopia.net*.

Website: *www.parentopia.com*

Are You Accidentally Raising a Wimp?

Meet the Expert:

Hara Estroff Marano is the editor-at-large and a writer for Psychology Today, and she's an award winning author who wrote *Nation of Wimps: The High Cost of Invasive Parenting*.

Meet the Parent:

Laurie Vinyon, a mother of three, is a high school teacher who strives to find balance for her family.

******

Toni: Hara, I have to tell you I love your book.

I think it's an important book because it illuminates a silent epidemic looming on college campuses and in the workforce. To start with, tell us what "invasive" parenting is.

Hara: Well, invasive parenting is sometimes known as helicopter parenting. It's parenting that crosses the boundary into doing things that children should be doing for themselves. It erases the boundary between parent and child, with the parent taking the responsibilities that children need to be gradually allowed to take on, in order to develop and grow and to become responsible adults.

What parents seem to have forgotten is that the goal of raising children is to raise independent, autonomous human beings. We've got to let them go. We've got to make sure they're able to function on their own.

What I mean by wimps – a term I use a little bit facetiously – is psychologically fragile.

When parents take over tasks for kids, the assumption is that they're too fragile. Kids internalize that message. There's lots of evidence that kids are breaking down psychologically in record numbers and that's where my book started, actually.

Toni: What is the epidemic that's occurring on college campuses?

Hara: Well, that's precisely where the book started. Ten years ago, I got wind of the fact that there were extraordinarily large numbers of kids with depression on college campuses. I made the assumption, which actually turned out to be wrong, that this was a phenomenon of eastern elite schools. I live in New York City and I thought, "This is the pressure to get into Harvard and Yale."

I called the head of the health center at Harvard University and I received a list of all the directors of campus counseling centers in the U.S. In very short order, I learned that this was a phenomenon around the country, at all kinds of schools. Before the end of the day, I was in touch with over 400 campus counseling centers around North America, and I discovered that record numbers of kids were breaking down psychologically.

Major depression, anxiety disorders, panic attacks, eating disorders – which are really disorders of perfectionism, huge problems with self-mutilation especially among girls, and binge drinking were all prevalent on college campuses.

The binge drinking is not the kind of binge drinking we did in school, but a much darker, much more purpose-driven way of drinking. It's a determination to get drunk to get around the fact that kids increasingly lack social skills and they need some kind of experience that is all their own. So getting falling down drunk and blacking out becomes a kind of experience you can own.

So these kinds of things are going on and the numbers just keep increasing.

Toni: What percentage of college students are we talking about?

Hara: Well, it's very interesting; there are all kinds of surveys. The American College Health Survey is probably the best known and perhaps the most reliable. The numbers are astonishing. We're talking about 25 percent of students experiencing serious depression and that is the ones who will own up to it. And that's only depression; we're not talking about the other disorders.

There are all kinds of things that we haven't had before, at least not in such numbers. For example, stalking is a huge problem on college campuses. Stalking is a phenomenon where people cannot accept rejection. Someone dates and then their date breaks up with them, and this is kind of par for the course, right? No one adores being rejected, but you don't fall apart.

But some people literally cannot accept it. They're much more psychologically fragile nowadays. They're also narcissistic and they really believe they shouldn't be rejected, so they stalk and pursue their prey. This is a real problem and there are actual murders on campus as a result of stalking. Whoever heard of this when we went to college? It just didn't exist.

Toni: I think it's a quiet epidemic that isn't well known outside of college campuses.

Hara: Colleges are very engaged in trying to find ways to solve the problem. The big problem for them is that the donors that give money to universities don't give money to student health services; they give money for football fields. So the student health services are under enormous pressure to treat so many people, but with diminishing resources.

Toni: I really hate to blame parents, because so many people have guilt around their parenting; but your research found that there are concrete things that parents are doing that can gradually lead to the type of mental health breakdown some kids are experiencing in college. What are we doing wrong?

Hara: Well, that's the question I began asking. In 2002, I reported on this crisis on campus and it made headlines all around the country. In 2004, I went back to my sources and asked them again what was happening. It turns out that things were much worse. There were more kids with more serious problems.

Then I really began asking, "Why is this happening?" It turns out that parents are doing things for their kids and the kids end up with no coping skills. So, lacking coping skills, they hit a minor speed bump, like being rejected or getting a C in history, and they can't cope with it. And then they fall apart psychologically.

Toni: Specifically what are parents doing?

Hara: If a kid forgets a book or a paper at home, the parent doesn't allow the kid to experience the discomfort of that; the parent runs it over to school. Parents write term papers for their kids. When the kid gets a grade that disappoints the parent, they don't turn to the kid and say, "What do you need to do to correct this?" Instead, they call the teacher to get the grade changed.

They manage their kids' time. They have life plans for their kids. They choose their kids' college courses. They go on job interviews with their kids. They're not giving kids independence. They're even scheduling for their college kids. College students should be making their own schedules.

Toni: Every parent wants the best for their child, so they think they're helping their child when unknowingly they're really harming the child.

Hara: Right. This is the incredible irony. There is such a thing as doing too much and not giving your kids increasing latitude to do the things they need to do to gain coping skills. That's what these kids are missing.

So, why is it that those who mean only the best for their children wind up bringing out the worst in them? When you do too much for them, it cripples them. It gives them a sense that they're not able to cope, and it literally deprives them of the opportunity to gain coping skills.

Toni: One of the points in your book that really hit home for me was overprotecting your kids. I'll be the first to admit that I was one of those parents and I truly started making changes after reading your book.

One of the things that caused me to change my behavior was when you laid out the facts about the very small percentage of kids that actually get abducted, and in most of those cases it's done by someone they know. Really we should be focusing our attention on keeping our marriage strong, since the emotional damage that kids experience as a result of divorce is far more prevalent than abduction.

Tell me more about this overprotectiveness.

Hara: The overprotection of kids really stems from two separate beliefs about kids. One is that the world is very dangerous. There are all these child molesters hanging around out there and all these people who want to kidnap my child, and it's much more dangerous than it's ever been. That's one stream of thought and it's totally wrong. This is not just a matter of my opinion; it comes from Department of Justice data over the past 16 years. Over the years, hysteria has increased, but child victimization has remained very low. Most victimization of children occurs by people who are known to the children such as grandparents or a disaffected ex-spouse who steals the kids. It's not from the stranger that people are imagining.

But, the fact that parents are imagining it is a sign of the anxiety that parents feel, which I think they are feeling for other reasons. It's kind of a free-floating anxiety.

The other reason parents are overprotecting their kids is that parents are really worried about the future *success* of their kids and so they over-manage their lives. They plan everything out for their kids; and play has to be taken out of the equation because parents think that play is not on the fast track to success. But play is actually good for kids' brains and I spend time talking about that in my book.

So, you have two separate reasons why parents are overprotecting their kids. One is to assure their success in a world that's increasingly uncertain, and the other is to try and safeguard their children from all these imaginary, overblown predators and child victimizers.

Toni: I see this every day in my life. Things have gone haywire when I see seven-year-olds playing sports or Little League baseball five or six days a week. Don't get me wrong, I think sports are very important for kids, but I don't think that family life should revolve around a sport.

Hara: It becomes professionalized and it's no longer run by the needs of the children, but by the demands of the adults.

Toni: The scary thing is that parents are not stepping up to the plate, literally or figuratively, to say "enough" to the people who are organizing the leagues. I think parents fear that if they speak up, their child won't make the team or won't get as much playing time, or they'll be seen as a whiner.

Hara: Or I'll be seen as a parent who doesn't love her child enough; I'll be seen as a bad parent. That's one of the fears driving parents these days. Parents are extremely judgmental. Parents are judging each other as "bad moms" or "good moms," and a lot of parents really fear that they'll be thought of as the bad parent.

So now the new standard of being a good parent is not just going to all your kids' soccer games, but showing up for all the practices too, which is just ludicrous. It's just an insane demand, but you see parents everywhere thinking that if they don't do it, they're going to be thought of as a bad parent and they don't want that stigma attached to their child.

Toni: Absolutely. Hara, we have a question from a caller named Stephanie.

Stephanie: I'm curious what you would have done in my situation…. I dropped my two oldest children off at camp this week, about three hours north of where I live, so it was a long drive.

About half an hour later, as I was driving home, I got a phone call from my 10-year-old daughter. She'd forgotten her swimsuit. The counselor had told her she could always swim in her tank top and shorts, but I could hear the trepidation in her voice.

I'm not one for rescuing my children, which is probably why my daughter was crying – she figured I was going to say she had to suck it up.

So I would like to hear from you: where is the balance in bailing out your children versus letting them suffer the natural consequences and maybe a little bit of grief?

Hara: Partly it depends on how long the camp was, but if it was for a week I probably would have said, does she have enough tank tops and shorts that she could use? I can understand her disappointment, but I would have said, "Gee, it's a short enough time. I think you could make do." I'm sure everything would have been fine after some initial disappointment.

Even mailing the swimsuit using an overnight delivery doesn't sound like a horrible overstepping of boundaries. If you drove the swimsuit three hours up to camp, I would think, "Hmm, there's a boundary being crossed here." What did you wind up doing?

Stephanie: Since I was only about 30 minutes from the camp I went to Target and bought a bathing suit and drove it back up. It added about an hour to my trip. But, I'm taking money out of her allowance for the extra gas it took me to do that and for my time and energy.

Hara: Or maybe have a checklist the next time she goes off to camp so that everything goes along with her.

Stephanie: Yes, definitely!

Toni: Stephanie, what a great question because many of us are faced with situations where we wonder whether we should rescue our kids or not.

Hara, I want to give parents more strategies for preventing their kids from becoming "wimps." One of the things that you suggest is to teach kids problem-solving skills. I've put a problem-solving form on my website, *www.getparentinghelpnow.com/myfreebookresources*, that parents can use, but tell us why it's important for kids to learn problem-solving skills.

Hara: Because life is uncertain, and it doesn't always go as planned, and there are always obstacles, big and little – everybody needs to know that they can surmount them. One of the great times to build problem-solving skills in kids is during the course of any activity. For instance, if you're in a mall, ask your kids, "What would happen if you got separated from Mommy? What would you do?"

You would encourage your child to know that if he or she ever got separated from you, you would stay exactly where you were, and your kid should come back to where you were. Or the child can go to the nearest store and ask for an announcement to be made over the mall's public address system.

What you're doing is teaching children to be level-headed in situations where they can think their way through to a solution – so that a child can go to the nearest adult and say, "Can you help me? I got separated from my mom."

Toni: Yes. And it's also important that your child knows your cell phone number.

Hara: What if you're out hiking and you lose the trail? Pick any kind of situation and ask "what if" questions so the child learns that there are ways to handle the kinds of common problems that arise; and the child can be level-headed and think through how to handle the situation and make a good choice.

Toni: Another suggestion you make is that we learn how to criticize our kids.

Hara: Oh, it's so important.

Toni: With the whole self-esteem movement in the '70s, we were told that "everyone's a winner" and that we should praise kids. Criticism got flushed away, and so this is a skill I don't think many of us used. Tell us why we need to criticize our kids…

Hara: Because nobody's perfect. And nobody should be perfect, because failure is a wonderful teacher. Kids should be given room to make mistakes. The danger in criticism is that parents deliver criticism in a way that gives children the mistaken notion that they need to be perfect. Criticism implying that affection or approval is conditional on good performance, which is the message that kids get, is lethal to them.

That makes love all too conditional. Sometimes parents don't even have to say a word. Suppose a child brings home a report card that's got four A's and one B and a parent looks at the report card and frowns and raises his or her eyebrows. That delivers a message to a child. What's destructive is the actual or threatened withdrawal of affection or approval, or the expression of anger when the child disappoints.

So, if a kid doesn't do well at something, the best thing to do is turn to the kid and ask, "What do you think you need to do to complete this as well as you would like to?" That way, the kid comes up with their own solutions to their own problems. They own the problem and they begin to acquire skills, and then they develop this magical quality of self-esteem. Or a parent could ask a child, "What would you do differently next time?"

It's important to offer kids support, verbally and non-verbally. If your kid has trouble with math, you could empathize with your kid – "Gee this stuff is hard, isn't it?" – but don't give the answers and don't take over for them. Allow them to develop the solution to their problems.

Capitalize on the child's own disappointment instead of letting your disappointment run the show.

Toni: Exactly. In our family, we've started talking about mistakes at the dinner table. I'll say, "Gosh, I really made a big mistake today. I got the time of the soccer game wrong. The game was at seven but I thought it was six. What could I have done differently?" So I get them problem-solving about my blooper.

Hara: Right, that's great.

Toni: I'm modeling that mom makes mistakes – actually lots of them – and that in our family, we talk about mistakes. And I want them to be good problem-solvers so I sometimes ask them to help me solve a problem.

I'll also ask them, "What was a mistake you made today or something that you wish you would have done differently?" Then we talk about it. It brings to light that life is about learning from our mistakes and not treating them as failures.

Hara: There are parents who think that by admitting a mistake it diminishes their authority over the child, when in fact, what it really does is let children know that you can make a mistake and still do well in life. You can be not perfect and still be fine in life. Kids idealize their parents. It's very important for them to know that mommy or daddy isn't perfect and wasn't perfect growing up, and they still turned out to be okay.

Toni: Hara, when you said that love becomes conditional upon a child's achievement, it just hit me in the gut and I felt such sadness.

Hara: Well, that's lethal. It's what turns kids into perfectionists, which is a one-way ticket to misery for a lifetime, as a matter of fact. It's almost a guarantee of depression; kids feel like they can never do well *enough*. At best, such kids will never be good problem-solvers; they'll never be innovators. At best, they'll be conformists throughout life. It doesn't do anything good socially and it doesn't do anything good individually for a child.

Toni: And if we're perfectionists, it's not only damaging to us; it's dangerous to our kids.

Hara: Especially to our kids.

Toni: Exactly. Next, we'll be joined by Laurie Vinyon, a mother of three and also a high school teacher. I've observed Laurie for a number of years since her daughter was in my Girl Scout troop and Laurie's doing things a little differently. Laurie, you're not over-scheduling your kids and that's why I invited you to be a guest. I want to see how you're bucking the trend of over-scheduling….

Laurie: I have to tell you that it's a constant challenge, because there are so many opportunities for all three of my kids. So it's a hard thing to do. I just get the calendar out and say, "You guys get to have a few choices, but we can't do it all."

Toni: Do you say "no" more than you say "yes" to activities, Laurie?

Laurie: I say, "Here are your choices, kids. What's the most important thing to do? Let's see if we can work that into our family schedule."

Hara: It's really important that you're giving kids some responsibility for setting their own schedule. That's good.

Toni: I like the fact that you're prioritizing, because the reality is you have three kids and you're married and you work and there has to be some balance.

I just want to point out that I have an assessment on my website called, "Are Your Kids Over-scheduled?" that may be helpful for parents: *www. getparentinghelpnow.com/myfreebookresources.*

Laurie, you live in an affluent area. Do you feel a lot of pressure for your kids to get on the treadmill and go faster and faster?

Laurie: I'm blessed to have kids who like to do a variety of different things, and so they haven't honed in on one super-passion that they're driven to do every single day. The challenge is deciding between traveling sports versus community rec programs.

I'm not ready to have one child's sport dominate our entire family's schedule over the weekend, for example. Going to a tournament three hours away and staying overnight two nights for basketball for a nine-year-old sounds kind of crazy to me. So, I have been saying "no" to those types of things. But, I do have a question for Hara regarding support.

Sometimes it feels like I'm alone. I don't think any of us has malicious intent. Everyone's trying to do the best they can. Do you have any suggestions for how to get support from other adults for the choices that you're making, if you're not doing the traveling teams or if you're trying not to over-schedule your kids?

Hara: Well, first of all, different attitudes very commonly exist between spouses on the level of independence that kids can have. I believe that that's an important marital issue that needs to be settled by the parents and they need to have a united front. It needs to be discussed backstage, away from the kids.

The other problem is that other parents are very, very judgmental these days about what you do and how much you show your love to your kids by showing up at every soccer practice or getting on the traveling team and wrapping family life totally around a child's schedule, which is such a bad idea for so many reasons.

It really does require some self-confidence, and I don't think it helps to put down what the other parents are doing; but it does help to explain some of the advantages of what you're doing to other parents.

Toni: Laurie, a helpful resource is *www.puttingfamilyfirst.org*. Two researchers put this organization together to fight back by telling sports organizations and others that we don't want to live our lives like this.

It's a whole movement based on the work of Dr. Bill Doherty and Barbara Carlson.

Hara, Laurie's leaving some time in her kids' day for play by not over-scheduling them. Why is that important?

Hara: The traveling sports thing is really bad for kids because it really grows out of adults' needs. They're organizing it. They tell the kids where to stand, where to play, and what the schedule is. It's not growing organically from the needs of the kids.

Free play where kids come together, set their own rules, decide how to play the game, and move in and out of different positions, actually builds the brain. It stimulates growth in the parts of the brain where kids learn to pay attention and learn to get control over their behavior.

Even though play by definition is not goal-directed, it winds up giving kids the mental machinery for being goal-directed in the future. It's vitally important for growth.

Traveling sports teams are goal-directed. Their goal is to win, but it's the adults leading the game so children don't make those gains.

Toni: I have an article called, "Surprising Secrets to a Successful Summer" that summarizes the importance of play, if you'd like more details on that: *www.getparentinghelpnow.com/myfreebookresources.*

Laurie, the other reason I invited you was because you're a high school teacher. Have you seen the effects of some of the things that Hara's been talking about with students at your school?

Laurie: Absolutely. I really see a need for kids to learn coping skills. As Hara mentioned earlier, they can fall apart at the littlest things. I see so much anxiety and depression with teenagers and it seems like such high stakes for them. Now, part of that certainly is developmental, but part of it is learned behavior too. We should probably have a class in high schools on stress and leisure management.

Toni: Great idea. Thanks, Laurie and Hara, for a great discussion.

Contact information:

Hara Estroff Marano

Email: *hmarano@psychologytoday.com*

Connect With Me

Hi! I'm Toni Schutta, the author of this book, and I've been helping families for 19 years as a Parent Coach and Licensed Psychologist. On a daily basis I help parents, like you, find solutions that work to everyday challenges that you're facing so your family can be happier and more peaceful.

I can help you get your kids to listen the *first* time you tell them to do something, reduce back talk to zero, reduce yelling to once a week or less, create a positive discipline plan that works, get your kids to bed on time and complete homework and chores without a lot of hassle!

I've helped thousands of parents get results like these through my group programs and one-on-one private parent coaching. I can help you solve your parenting challenges, too, so your family can be happier and you can have more fun with your kids.

To get started, sign up now for my free Quick Start Report, "3 Essential Strategies to Get Your Kids to Listen the First Time," that's available here: www.getparentinghelpnow.com.

I'd like to invite you to join my Raise Great Kids Community too. Together, I'll help you implement one key strategy per month for raising great kids so you can have the support you need for making positive changes. www.raisegreatkidscommunity.com

If you'd like an opportunity for a complimentary "Happier Family for You Planning Session" so I can learn more about the challenges that you're facing and help you develop a next-step action plan to create a happier family you can apply here: www.getparentinghelpnow.com/planning-session

Hope to connect soon! toni@getparentinghelpnow.com